The New Century of the Metropolis

In this century the majority of the world's population lives in metropolitan regions, which are often seen as problematic because of their size, density, and environmental problems. What if the underlying problems are economic inequalities, climate change, capitalism, and the sharp divisions between urban and rural areas?

Tom Angotti is fundamentally optimistic about the future of the metropolis, but questions urban planning's inability to integrate urban and rural systems, its contribution to the growth of inequality, and increasing enclave development throughout the world. Using the concept of "urban orientalism" as a theoretical underpinning of modern urban planning grounded in global inequalities, Angotti confronts this traditional model with new, progressive approaches to community and metropolis.

Written in clear, precise terms by an award-winning author, *The New Century of the Metropolis* argues that only when the city is understood as a necessary and beneficial accompaniment to social progress can a progressive, humane approach to urban planning be developed.

Tom Angotti directs the Hunter College Center for Community Planning and Development in New York City and teaches at the Graduate Center and Hunter College, City University of New York. He co-edits *Progressive Planning* magazine and is a Participating Editor for *Latin American Perspectives* and *Local Environment*. He is the author of *Metropolis 2000* and *New York for Sale*.

The New Century of the Metropolis

Urban Enclaves and Orientalism

Tom Angotti

Routledge
Taylor & Francis Group

NEW YORK AND LONDON

First published 2013
by Routledge
711 Third Avenue, New York, NY 10017

Simultaneously published in the UK
by Routledge
2 Park Square, Milton Park, Abingdon, Oxon OX14 4RN

Routledge is an imprint of the Taylor & Francis Group, an informa business

Library of Congress Cataloging in Publication Data
Angotti, Tom.
The new century of the metropolis : urban enclaves and orientalism / by Tom Angotti.
p. cm.
Includes bibliographical references and index.
1. City planning. 2. Urbanization. 3. Economic development—Social aspects. I. Title.
HT166.A358 2011
307.1'216—dc23

ISBN: 978-0-415-61509-9 (hbk)
ISBN: 978-0-415-61510-5 (pbk)
ISBN: 978-0-203-11419-3 (ebk)

Typeset in Sabon
by Cenveo Publisher Services
Printed and bound in Great Britain by
TJ International Ltd, Padstow, Cornwall

Dedicated to Occupy Wall Street

Contents

List of Illustrations   *ix*
Preface   *x*
Acknowledgements   *xii*

PART I
Urban Fallacies   I

1 The Metropolis in the Twenty-First Century: Problem or Solution?   3

2 Urban Orientalism, Planning and the Metropolis of "The Others"   26

3 Urban and Rural Dependencies and Divides   41

PART II
Enclaves and Orientalisms   **57**

4 Last Chance for the Urban Village? The Urban–Rural Divide
   and Food Sovereignty in India   59

5 Orientalist Roots: Palestine and the Israeli Metropolis   75

6 Lessons from Twentieth Century Socialism:
   The USSR and China   94
   TOM ANGOTTI AND SAMUEL STEIN

7 The Free-Market Metropolis and Enclave Urbanism   113

8 Latin America: Enclaves, Orientalism and Alternatives   132

PART III
Looking Ahead   **153**

9   New Century, New Ways of Planning   155

    Notes   *164*
    Selected Bibliography   *187*
    Index   *190*

Illustrations

Figures

2.1	New Urban Enclave in Hanoi, Vietnam	28
2.2	Post-Colonial Philanthropy in India	30
2.3	Store in Tokyo	31
3.1	Modern Tokyo and Rural Relic	49
4.1	Village Market in Kerala, India	60
4.2	Street Life in Dahanu, Maharashtra, India	61
4.3	Orientalist Order and Chaos	62
4.4	Disneyland in Kozhikode, Kerala, India	68
5.1	Dubai: Duplicates of New York City's Chrysler Building in the Desert	76
5.2	The Israeli Wall	78
5.3	Jaffa Today	83
5.4	Israeli Settlement in Galilee	85
5.5	Israeli Settlement in East Jerusalem	88
5.6	Bedouin Village in the Negev	90
6.1	Building Marked for Demolition, Kunming, 2005	107
7.1	Public Works Support Private Land Development: The U.S. Interstate Highway Network	119
7.2	New York, New York in Las Vegas	123
8.1	Caracas, Venezuela	133
8.2	Gated Community in Dominican Republic	135
8.3	A Barrio in Caracas, Venezuela	138
8.4	Organic Farm in Alamar, Havana	149
9.1	The Multigenerational Olive Tree	162

Figure 6.1 by Will Rhodes, with permission.
Figure 7.1 from the Metropolitan Design Center Image Bank, with permission.
All other photographs by Tom Angotti.

Tables

1.1	Metropolitan Population (cities over 750,000) in 2000 and 2010 (in '000s)	9
1.2	Largest Metropolitan Regions in the World, 2010	10

Preface

One of the main themes of my book *Metropolis 2000*, published by Routledge in 1993, was that the modern metropolis was a revolutionary new form of human settlement marking a major step forward in human development. I argued that the metropolis was "here to stay" and criticized the doomsday views that cities are problematic because they are too big or dense, not properly planned, produce poverty, and are irredeemably mired in narrow local politics. The subtitle, *Planning, Poverty and Politics*, hinted at my argument against the prevailing anti-urban biases.

I originally planned to update and revise *Metropolis 2000* but when I started to do so I was quickly convinced by reviewers that a mere updating was not enough. First, enormous changes occurred in the last two decades that fundamentally altered the global urban scene going into the twenty-first century. By the end of the first decade of this century the majority of the world's population lived in metropolitan regions and cities. China, Brazil, and many formerly rural nations in south Asia and the Middle East had rapidly urbanized in the last two decades. The context for "planning, poverty and politics" shifted with the emergence of a scientific consensus on global climate change, the development of the internet and cell phones, the breakup of the Soviet Union and the socialist camp, and the growing hegemony of global finance capital and real estate in urban development all over the world. At the same time, the principles and practices that have governed modern city planning since Victorian England became universally accepted guideposts for urban development even though this seemed to only magnify, for me, their failure.

As I thought about updating *Metropolis 2000* I also became more aware of the problems in my original work. I had categorized the diverse types of metropolitan regions and broad regimes of planning, not as static ideal-types but dynamic categories that overlap and intersect. As the urban world has become larger and much more complex, however, these regimes made less sense and looked more and more like static ideal-types. In this new volume, I have employed a different set of concepts and categories instead of trying to define the many urban regimes—an encyclopedic and impossible task in any case. Instead of outlining types I try to better explain major global trends. The notion of *dependent urbanization* also needed further explanation in this current environment of increasing global interdependence and the ubiquitous role of finance capital and real estate. I introduce the concepts of *urban orientalism* and *enclave urbanism* in this book and show how they work together with dependent urbanization, particularly in the chapters on India, Israel/Palestine, the United States and Latin America. There are now only remnants in the world of "the Soviet metropolis" which was the subject of a chapter in *Metropolis 2000*. This is replaced by a new chapter that tries to understand the lessons to be learned from the history of twentieth century socialism, including a look at Russia and China today. Here and throughout the book I place greater emphasis on the huge divide between urban and rural areas (barely discussed in *Metropolis 2000*), the central role of capitalism, growing inequalities and the environmental challenge posed by global climate change. In several chapters I look at new efforts to construct alternative paradigms for urban development based on changing the relationship between urban and rural and promoting social justice and the right to the city. All of the case studies and examples are highly synthesized, necessarily omit many details, and risk being overly schematic. Each of them was chosen for its ability to illustrate the main themes; many others could have been included, but that will have to be left for future study.

By focusing on the big questions, this narrative is somewhat daring and speaks to the prospects and problems of the urbanized world in the new century. My goal is to describe the process of urbanization as it is unfolding; however, this is not mainly a work of description and there are many reports by international agencies, cited in our documentation, that do a much more thorough job of it. Nor is my goal to analyze in detail the enormous diversity of urbanization experiences around the world; this would be impossible in one volume and a highly presumptive enterprise for a single individual to undertake. I realize that this expands the risk of oversimplifying and falling into the orientalist trap that this entire enterprise seeks to reject. My purpose here, however, is to neither fixate on nor fix orientalist urban planning, only to point the way towards alternatives. Indeed, the purpose for this entire excursion into the twenty-first century metropolis is to understand how it relates to the much larger questions of global change, sustainability, resilience, and survival.

This book is written by an urban planner for urban planners, and unlike much of abstract social science its ultimate objective is to inform practice. However, throughout the book I define urban planning in the broadest way as the application of human consciousness to the urban environment. In the new century of the metropolis most of us in the world will be urban and most of us can and must be planners, architects and designers. The resilience and sustainability of life on earth will depend on individually and collectively reestablishing an intimate relationship with land, water and other species.

Acknowledgements

I am especially indebted to Samuel Stein, Hunter College graduate urban planning student who provided valuable help with the research and writing. Sam is truly exceptional among graduate students for his broad knowledge base, enthusiasm for ideas, attention to detail, and writing ability. He drafted portions of Chapter Six on Russia and China after socialism. I am fully responsible for the final version. Many thanks to Chester Hartman, Clara Irazábal, and Peter Marcuse for their comments on individual chapters.

Many thanks to Oren Yiftachel of Ben-Gurion University in Beer Sheva, who organized the conference, *Urban Informality: Global Trends and Israel/Palestine* in 2008; Emily Silverman at Technion University in Haifa, who put me in touch with many scholars and activists; Schmuel Grog of Bimkom; Carol Upadya and the National Institute for Advanced Studies in Bangalore which hosted me as a Fulbright Specialist in 2009 and brought me in touch with many scholars and activists; Professor Fukuo Akimoto and his assistant Yoshitaka Kujita of Kyushu University, who arranged for many presentations and meetings with civic and professional groups in Japan; and Mario Coyula in Cuba.

I appreciate the serious discussion and criticisms of draft chapters by students in my Urban Orientalism class at the CUNY Graduate Center, and by students in the Environmental and Urban Studies Program at Bard College.

Part I

Urban Fallacies

Chapter 1

The Metropolis in the Twenty-First Century

Problem or Solution?

This is already the century of the metropolis. More than half the world's population now lives in metropolitan regions.[1] If current rates of growth continue, by the end of this century almost all people in the world will live in large cities. Everything will be urban and "rural" areas will be giant empty spaces—unpopulated enclaves of industrial agriculture, mining and forestry. Urban planning, which in the twentieth century sought to solve urban problems, will be indistinguishable from all other professions seeking to improve the quality of human life. Every place will be "urban" and everyone wishing to improve the human condition will be an "urban planner."

Should we mourn or celebrate this urbanization of the world? Are cities a problem or a solution to our problems? Are cities just giant wells of despair, inequality and environmental degradation or beacons of human hope, progress and healthier environments? Will they exacerbate climate change or prevent it?

Everyone interested in making a better world in the twenty-first century—the urban planners of the world—should first recognize that these are the wrong questions. We will see in this chapter how cities are neither the problem nor the solution. They are places where both problems and solutions are located, and much more. We ask the wrong questions because too often we have a distorted view of the metropolis and the world, one that is bound by the histories of colonial and imperial relations and our own limited experiences. We are looking only on the surface and not paying enough attention to the growing segregation and inequalities within and among urban areas—that is, in the entire world. Especially during this period of global economic crisis, we also fail to make the connections between global capitalism, climate change, the abandonment of rural areas and urbanization. To focus on the metropolis in the century of the metropolis is to undertake the incredibly difficult and complicated task of understanding the multiple dimensions of everything going on in the human world.

The modern metropolis was born in the last century and is still relatively young. In the more than two millennia since the first human settlements appeared on the earth, most people lived in rural areas, small towns and cities. There were never more than a few giant cities with a population of over a million people—for example, imperial Rome and Beijing. By the year 2000, however, there were some 500 metropolitan areas, most of which formed in the twentieth century. The metropolis flourished in every region of the world, rich and poor, north and south, east and west. The twentieth century brought on an urban revolution and its product was the modern metropolis.[2]

The majority of urban dwellers today live in Africa, Asia and Latin America, in metropolitan regions that are not well understood in the "developed" world, where most of the theories about urbanization and the practices of urban planning come from. These theories and practices are based on giant myths describing the "underdeveloped" metropolis as a giant, homogenous landscape of chaotic, unsanitary, and dangerous "slums." The myths treat the people who live and work in these cities—that is, most of the urban dwellers in the world—as a single undifferentiated mass of poor people. The poor "slum" dwellers are a vaguely defined "other." This mythology leads to real world policies that blame the other for urban problems and effectively make things worse for them. As we show throughout this chapter and book, the problem is not the city or its population but the capitalist economic and social relations that are its foundation. To address urban and environmental problems we must first understand and change these relations.

In the twenty-first century, if metropolitan regions continue to expand at the current pace (although that is by no means a certainty) by the end of this century almost all of the world's population could reside in large cities. This would culminate in the historic transformation of the world from a rural to urban one. However, this great transformation coincides with other unprecedented trends in human history: global climate change, sea level rise, deforestation, the accelerated extinction of species, food insecurity, and the alienation of human society from the natural world. These environmental challenges raise serious questions about the capacity of humans to sustain themselves beyond this century on the earth, which after all has been around for billions of years, most of them without humans. In *Collapse*, Jared Diamond alerted us to the historic precedents of societal collapse which occurred when people were unaware how their relationship to the local environment was eroding their resilience.[3] While the environmental and public health problems of this century might be mitigated by new technologies and practices, the most powerful economic regimes in the world, and the military machines that protect them, may make it impossible to move beyond mitigation to survival. Indeed, underlying the environmental crises is an even greater crisis—the global meltdown of finance capital, particularly since the latest crash in 2008. This deep cyclical downturn has opened our eyes to the interconnections between urbanization, climate change and the global commodification of land, water, and all that can be commodified, deepening the stark partition between urban and rural areas that originated with industrial capitalism and the modern metropolis.

To get to the heart of the urban question in the twenty-first century, therefore, we need to dig deeply into all aspects of human society and nature—economic, social, and political. As a first step, we will need to dispose of the many fallacies and prejudices that keep us from getting at the roots and developing strategies for the future. The first fallacy is the urban fallacy.

The Urban Fallacy

Aren't giant cities responsible for at least some of the planet's economic and environmental problems? After all, big cities consume more energy and goods and are responsible for most of the pollution and greenhouse gases in the world. They sap natural and human resources from rural areas. They concentrate capital, labor and power, and create enormous inequalities across physical space, between urban and rural areas and within cities. Aren't cities by definition too large, dense, and conducive to social disorder? Don't cities always breed poverty and concentrate it in huge "slums"?

This is the first part of the grand urban fallacy inherited from the twentieth century. Actually it was born at the cusp of the century, along with the moralistic Victorian notions of pathological poverty and the undeserving poor. It was given a political revival in response to the worldwide urban uprisings of 1968, with conservative voices like Edward Banfield arguing that the city created and reproduced anti-social behaviors in poor people and people of color.[4] For years after this, the rhetoric about "slums" was rejected by many as racist and reductionist, but has now been brought back into the mainstream with "soft" declarations and new versions of global philanthropy. In 1999, the United Nations launched their "Cities Without Slums" initiative.[5] In their 2003 document "The Challenge of Slums," UN-HABITAT argued that past "slum up-scaling" projects failed because of a lack of sustained commitment and resources, without challenging the fundamentally flawed vision of the root causes of urban inequalities.[6] UN declarations aside, however, the perception that cities breed poverty and social disorder is pervasive. *Forbes Magazine*, in a story on the global shift towards a majority urbanized world, declared bleakly, "the future of the city is a vast Third World slum."[7] This is the urban fallacy—and the world as seen by many in the global centers of wealth and power.

The other version of the urban fallacy says that cities are the solution, not the problem. The recent book by Edward Glaeser, *Triumph of the City*, argues that cities today are the best hope of humanity, "our greatest invention."[8] Even though most people living in cities lack decent housing and basic services, the standard of living in cities is generally better than in rural areas and cities have many more economic and cultural opportunities. Glaeser says the problem isn't the size of cities or urban density; in fact the larger and more dense cities turn out to be wealthier, healthier and greener. Greater energy efficiencies are possible in cities and in some densely developed central cities people use less power and water and produce less waste.

However, while Glaeser helps debunk the myth that high urban densities necessarily produce social and environmental problems, and acknowledges the many urban problems around the world, he also sees the metropolis from the vantage point of the most powerful and privileged urbanites in the world, which leads him to overlook many inconvenient truths. It is a rosy picture of the city as seen from the central business districts of the world and their leaders like New York City's billionaire mayor Michael Bloomberg, who are keen on saving energy, attracting more wealthy people, and branding their wealthy enclaves as attractive green destinations.[9] There is a rising chorus of urban optimists who believe that trends are moving in the right direction and we need to encourage and emulate the greening of Manhattan. They say that because the standard of living in cities tends to be higher we will all be better off when we all live in cities; high-density living saves energy and makes for a greener planet; and cities are where new technologies and smart growth policies will have the greatest impact. However, this presumes that these benefits will be distributed equally and available to everyone in large and diverse metropolitan regions.

The urban fallacy is the notion that the world's problems are caused by big cities or that they will be solved when everyone lives in big cities. This book aims to show that both versions of the urban fallacy fail to look at all the evidence and to understand cities in their broader historical and economic context. They overlook the underlying economic, social and political conditions that produce and reproduce cities. They do not probe the ways that capital and labor, and the relations between them, shape urban development and environmental and climate problems. I will argue that all urban planners in the twenty-first century should reject the urban fallacy, leave behind past idealized notions of the good and green city, and instead learn from the many grassroots alternatives offered by those who are struggling for their right to the city.[10]

These are not abstract or theoretical issues. Our understanding of the role of cities is the foundation for global and local policies that affect people who live and work there and all living species on the planet. The optimistic view of the city supports public and private investments in cities, and efforts to make them greener and denser, and the pessimistic view leads to efforts to slow urban growth and redirect resources. But only a balanced view can help find ways to address the great political dilemmas of the new metropolitan century, including global climate change, environmental damage, and gaping inequalities—all of which will now be "urban." The stakes are the highest. A failure to understand the perils and benefits of the current trajectory towards a completely urbanized world could leave us unprepared to avert the worst possible scenarios.

Before turning to a more detailed understanding of the urban fallacy in the twenty-first century, let us first look more carefully at this phenomenon of the modern metropolis and how it differs from previous forms of human settlement.

The Modern Metropolis

In his classic essay, "The Modern Metropolis," Hans Blumenfeld called attention to this revolutionary transformation:

> from its long, slow evolution the city has emerged into a revolutionary state. It has undergone a qualitative change, so that it is no longer merely a larger version of the traditional city but a new and different form of human settlement.[11]

According to Blumenfeld, the industrial revolution in the nineteenth century "dramatically reversed the distribution of population between village and city." The major force behind this was the "dual spur of specialization and cooperation of labor" which "started a great wave of migration from country to city all over the globe." This centralizing tendency, however, was soon complemented by

> an equally powerful centrifugal wave of migration from the city to the suburbs. Although ... more and more of the population is becoming urban, within urban areas there is increasing decentralization. The interaction of these two trends has produced the new form of settlement we call the metropolis. It is no longer a 'city' as that institution has been understood in the past, but on the other hand it is certainly not 'country.'[12]

Why is Blumenfeld's thesis so important? What difference does it make that the twentieth century metropolis was not only larger but a qualitatively new form of human settlement, and that it was much more complex than the company town and industrial city that preceded it? This is not an abstract question but especially critical for those who formulate strategies and undertake planning in the metropolis. A recurring thesis in this book is that the problem with planning is its reliance on traditional late nineteenth century Victorian, European and North American approaches to the much smaller industrial city.[13] Orientalist planning is unable to confront the serious problems of the twenty-first century metropolis; indeed, it serves to reproduce them.

The metropolis everywhere is a center of economic and political power, as with all previous forms of human settlement. Its ruling elites exert a central leadership role in all economic activity. The metropolitan financial centers often include industrial production, but to widely different degrees. Many have become "post-industrial cities" (a misnomer because their financial institutions retain economic control over industrial production in other cities and nations). The metropolitan elites and their corporate entities do not have to compete with the agrarian sector and actually dominate it. The metropolis is a center of both national and international finance, controlling capital investment, savings and distribution. In the twentieth century the metropolis was the center of economic and political power in centrally planned and mixed economies as well as all capitalist economies.

Blumenfeld understood that the modern metropolis is composed of a complex of developed districts and open areas and has a well-developed division of functions. The spatial division of functions corresponds with the economic division of labor. There is greater mobility within the metropolis and more opportunity for a wider variety of social and economic activities. The metropolis has a more diverse geography and economy. It is subdivided into many large districts with diverse populations, economic activities and cultural functions, and there is greater mobility, both physical and economic, among the districts.

Complexity, diversity and mobility therefore make the metropolis more resilient and able to weather economic storms; it no longer depends on a single economic activity as did the mining, factory or mill towns that vanished. Its diversity is not only in production but also in consumption, and its wide array of services and cultural activities make it a magnet for residents and visitors. Complexity and diversity make the metropolis the most stimulating and exciting place for human interaction, including personal interaction, cultural activity, and commercial exchange. After all, human interaction has been the very heart and soul of urban life since the earliest human settlements made the nomadic life of hunting and gathering obsolete.

Despite widespread doomsday predictions throughout the twentieth century that large cities were destined to fail, none have disappeared and most have grown. In the United States rhetoric predicting the demise of the city masked the uniquely North American divide between central cities and suburbs—both of which, contrary to common myths, are part of the metropolis. The presumption of "urban decline" was used as a rationale for widespread disinvestment in largely African American central cities, a reflection of institutional racism with powerful roots in slavery and legalized segregation; the suburbs in these same metropolitan regions continued to expand with the help of generous government investment. The metropolis remained intact, even in places like Detroit, Cleveland and Washington, DC, where the central cities with large African American populations were abandoned by government and lost population.

While New York City, Boston, Chicago and other older industrial cities strengthened their financial cores and became the centers of continuously growing metropolitan regions, new metropolises also arose in the southwest U.S.—the Sunbelt. Growth slowed in larger metropolitan regions but all of these metropolises have survived into the twenty-first century. Today, almost the entire population of the U.S. lives in metropolitan regions. This does not mean that metropolitan regions are destined to be eternal. They could disappear when they no longer have an economic and social foundation, or as a result of catastrophic environmental or military events; but so far the predictions of decline have been wrong.

The metropolis today is the center for economic and political power in a world that capital rules, spreading its surplus widely across the urban landscape to build business districts, upscale enclaves and the infrastructure they need to flourish. More established global financial centers such as New York, London, Tokyo, and Frankfurt now compete with places such as Hong Kong, Singapore and Mumbai. At the peripheries within and around business enclaves, however, an even greater mass of urban population has accumulated to form a huge labor pool that fuels the service sectors needed to keep the metropolis running. The mostly suburban peripheries are even larger than the financial and production centers, both in population numbers and in the amount of land they occupy. The urban peripheries are especially diverse. They are populated by migrants from rural areas that were also invaded by capital, forcing out subsistence farmers and destroying the local economies of villages, towns and small cities with giant land reclamation, irrigation, power, road and other infrastructure projects. The peripheries are defined by their social condition, not their location; they are as likely to be found in the geographic center of the metropolis as they are on the fringes. They are in the "central cities" as well as the "suburbs" and both are part and parcel of the modern metropolis.

While the metropolis is neither "city" nor "countryside," its growth has resulted in a sharp division between urban and rural places. The metropolitan revolution broke and reconstituted previous ties between the two, resulting in a radical divorce between the economies and everyday lives of those who live in urban and rural areas. Where the metropolis is most powerful, food production has been industrialized, commodified and globalized and agriculture is an activity alien to most humans; it has led to serious food-related illnesses, food insecurity, and a global food system that contributes 30 percent of all greenhouse gases to the environment.[14] Within the typical metropolis, about one-third of land is covered with asphalt and concrete and in densely developed centers residents and workers rarely see dirt and rocks (nature's prime ingredients for land). Plants, animals and other living species are put in human-controlled spaces, in zoos and on leashes, or exterminated. Urban space has become real estate, separated from its historic relationship to natural life, human reproduction, and the reproduction of all life. The separation between urban and rural is not a separation of equals; the inequalities between living conditions in rural and urban areas are greater as the metropolis soaks up ever larger proportions of surplus capital.

This is the situation at the beginning of the twenty-first century. But the prospects that the metropolis will continue to grow and evolve as it did in the twentieth century are cloudy because of the unknown consequences of global climate change and the rapidly evolving changes in energy, technology, and global capitalism. A linear progression into the future is not inevitable and increasingly unlikely. What, then, are the prospects in the twenty-first century? We shall discuss these in later chapters; for the moment let us concentrate on the immediate trends.

A New Turn for the Metropolis at the Turn of the Century?

More than 50 percent of the world's population now lives in metropolitan regions but in the more developed parts of the world—Europe and North America in particular— around three-fourths of the population lives in metropolitan areas. Latin America is at about the same level as North America. This is because, among all the regions colonized by Europeans, Latin America was the first to achieve independence, some two hundred years ago, and its national economies and elites, while economically and politically dependent on the North, over time were able to mature and secure their own centers of economic power in their own metropolises. Africa and Asia were the least urbanized, but their metropolitan populations increased most rapidly between 2000 and 2010, and that trend will surely see Asia become the largest metropolitan power in the coming decades, while Africa may very well follow suit in short order.

The majority of urban population in the world now lives in the "less developed" former colonial nations. Not coincidentally, although there are metropolitan regions in every region of the world and the most economically developed nations of the world are the most urbanized, 10 of the 15 largest metropolitan regions in the world are in former colonial nations. This contradicts the notion that a more urbanized world will necessarily lead to an urbanized world in the image of the "developed" Europe and North America. It has not.

Table 1.1 Metropolitan Population (cities over 750,000) in 2000 and 2010 (in '000s)

Region	Pop 2000	Metro Pop 2000	% Metro 2000
North America	318,654	252,154	79
Oceana	31,160	21,932	70
Latin America and Caribbean	521,228	393,420	75
Europe	726,568	514,422	71
Africa	819,462	294,602	36
Asia	3,698,296	1,360,900	37
World	6,115,367	2,837,431	46
Region	Metro Pop 2000	Metro Pop 2010	2000–2010
North America	252,154	288,803	15
Oceana	21,932	25,167	15
Latin America and Caribbean	393,420	468,757	19
Europe	514,422	533,295	4
Africa	294,602	412,990	40
Asia	1,360,900	1,757,314	29
World	2,837,431	3,486,326	23

Source: United Nations Human Settlements Programme (UN-HABITAT), *Cities and Climate Change: Global Report on Human Settlements 2011*, London: Earthscan, 2011.

Table 1.2 Largest Metropolitan Regions in the World, 2010

Metropolitan Area	Metro Pop 2010
Tokyo	36,669
Delhi	22,157
São Paulo	20,262
Mumbai	20,041
Mexico City	19,460
New York-Newark	19,425
Kolkata	15,552
Dhaka	14,648
Shanghai	13,224
Karachi	13,125
Buenos Aires	13,074
Los Angeles-Long Beach-Santa Ana	12,762
Beijing	12,385
Rio de Janeiro	11,950
Manila	11,628

Source: United Nations Human Settlements Programme (UN-HABITAT), *Cities and Climate Change: Global Report on Human Settlements 2011*, London: Earthscan, 2011.

In the latter half of the twentieth century new kinds of specialized enclaves emerged in metropolitan regions. These included giant commercial malls, mixed used satellite centers and "edge cities,"[15] hundreds of high-technology parks,[16] gated residential communities and exclusive recreational and cultural centers. However, all cities have had enclaves, and we are witnessing the strengthening of *enclave urbanism*, which increasingly defines urban places by their boundaries. They are not leading to a fundamentally distinct form of human settlement but are instead a product of new waves of suburban expansion and internal division driven by the accumulation of wealth and real estate markets. They are made possible by new supplies of surplus capital; where that capital lands is determined by the availability of vacant land and the economics of the land market. Increasingly, the marketability of urban enclaves depends on how well they are branded and packaged as separate commodities.

Metropolitan Fallacies

Do all of the serious environmental problems of the metropolis mean that the metropolis itself is the problem and metropolitan growth must be stopped in the twenty-first century? Or is the city only part of the problem? And can it be part of the solution? Even if we recognize how the urban fallacy distorts reality, we can begin to understand that, *although the metropolis is now the locus of overconsumption, pollution and unsustainable development, the metropolis itself is not the problem. The problem is with the economic and political forces that created and reproduce it. To be more specific, the problem has to do with the relations between capital and labor, not their location.*

Doomsday theories continue to decry the city, especially the very large cities, as the problem. They paint a bleak picture in which the entire earth will be blanketed with giant cities that cover the natural landscape with asphalt and concrete. But this ignores the fact that urbanization has actually concentrated human population on a much smaller footprint; even though the world population has mushroomed to around seven billion, we humans live on much less land than we would have to if we were in dispersed villages; and population growth rates tend to be lower in large cities. The problem is not concentration or dispersal but the unsustainable practices generated by a global system that relentlessly exploits land, labor and resources for profit without taking into consideration the needs of future generations—that is, our cities as presently constituted are *unsustainable*.[17]

Doomsday theories take different forms. They claim the metropolis is just too big, too dense, a magnet for migration from rural areas, a generator of overconsumption, the cause of environmental problems, and the creator of "slums." They are pillars of the urban fallacy. Many of these arguments were nurtured in the factory of ideas known as the Chicago School of Urban Sociology and continue to reproduce themselves in new and different forms.[18] Let's look at each of these arguments.

Is the Metropolis Too Big?

One of the more common versions of doomsday theory is that large cities by definition are unsustainable because of their *size*. The urban lexicon is filled with terms that suggest that size is the problem: megacity, megalopolis, hypercity and necropolis. These words are often accompanied by adjectives such as exploding, bloated, teeming, unmanageable, oversized, and chaotic. Lewis Mumford, one of the twentieth century's greatest urban theorists, talked of "megalopitan disintegration" as a characteristic of large cities from ancient Rome to modern New York, where he felt modern technology conspired with size to produce giant dystopias. He claimed that cities "...obscured for a time the human penalties of urban congestion: conditions that should have been a badge of shame became almost a mark of honor."[19]

The question of urban size is often blown out of proportion to promote the doomsday outlook. The very fact that Mexico City has a population of 20 million is considered automatic proof of the need to stop metropolitan growth. But there is no *a priori* reason why 20 million Mexican people cannot have a better quality of life living in Mexico City than if they were dispersed among the country's small towns. In fact, they generally do live better in Mexico City, despite all the drawbacks, because most rural areas in Mexico are so much worse off and have been since the Spanish conquest. The real question is whether Mexico can provide a decent standard of living to all no matter where they live. This requires economic development and planning, not necessarily a return to the countryside, although that could be part of it. However, planning and development are frustrated by Mexico's dependent and unequal role within the international division of labor. Mexican urbanization responds in large measure to the demand for cheap labor and raw materials in the developed nations of North America. Mexico's ability to plan urbanization and improve the urban environment is limited by its debt to Northern banks, reliance on oil and other exports, and increasing dependency on food and other products made in the North. These dependent relations were sealed by the North American Free Trade Agreement (NAFTA) in 1994, which had a catastrophic impact on Mexico's rural producers and forced millions to migrate north to populate the reserve army of labor in the metropolises of the U.S. and Canada. At the same time, Mexico has become an imitator of the North American model of unequal, inefficient sprawled metropolitan growth as it treats land as a commodity rather than a common good.[20]

Mumford also fed the widespread myth that large cities were invariably tied to population growth. "Even the excessive birth-rate," he stated, "may be a symptom of this deterioration."[21] This equation of urbanization with population growth feeds neo-Malthusian predictions of global overpopulation such as Paul R. Ehrlich's sensational 1968 warning about *The Population Bomb*,[22] but ignores the ample evidence that birth rates in metropolitan regions are typically lower than elsewhere and not higher. We need only look at two highly urbanized nations—Germany and Italy—where the rate of natural increase is negative, and were it not for immigration the total population would be shrinking. Also, there is no evidence that population growth, whether in urban or rural areas or rich or poor countries, itself causes environmental problems.[23] Furthermore, high rates of population growth do not cause poverty; they are a consequence of poverty. Lower rates of population growth in cities do not necessarily have anything to do with city size by itself but they are more a function of the higher standard of living and improved sanitary conditions in cities. Even though many urban dwellers are living in extremely poor conditions, their relatives in the rural areas they left are usually living in even worse conditions. Even though many people in cities may eke out an existence working long hours in poorly-paid jobs, the villages and towns they left often have no available jobs and local economies that have disintegrated, ravaged by shifting capital flows and monopoly control of agriculture. The real issue is not population size but the quality of life and social equality.

Is the Metropolis Too Dense?

Another myth is that greater *density* in large cities necessarily leads to social, health and environmental problems. In fact, density by itself has very little to do with the quality of life in cities. The notion that higher residential densities lead to crime and violence is belied by the lower violent crime rates of cities in Japan and Europe compared to the low-density sprawled metropolis of the United States; and lower violent crime in high-rise luxury housing than in low-rise.[24] The gross density of Tokyo and Osaka is about 13,000 persons per square kilometer, compared to about 9,000 in New York City and 4,000 in Los Angeles. Overall metropolitan densities vary considerably from one country to the next. For example, Dallas (Texas) has only 265 persons per square kilometer,[25] compared to 664 in Paris, 2,109 in Rome, and 5,750 in Tokyo.[26] Yet no one has yet made a case that crime and other urban problems are dramatically greater in Tokyo and Rome than in New York City, Los Angeles, Dallas and Paris.

There is no doubt that in the late nineteenth century the very high residential densities in Europe's new industrial cities contributed to epidemics such as tuberculosis and cholera. However, with the introduction of modern water treatment and sewage systems, medicine and public health measures, these problems were largely resolved in the twentieth century. These problems persist in metropolitan regions with low overall densities, not those that are compact and occupy less land. In fact, low-density urban sprawl increases pollution and energy demands and contributes to the new urban epidemics of obesity, stress and mental illness.

Density comparisons are difficult, if not impossible, in any case. Comparisons often fail to distinguish between gross density (all uses, including land under water) and net density. Net density calculations are not always comparable because they can exclude different uses. Residential densities can include open space on individual lots or only interior building space.[27] A distinction may also be made between daytime and nighttime densities. In metropolitan areas with highly developed central business districts, daytime densities in the center may be anywhere from ten to forty times the nighttime densities (yet more violent crimes tend to be committed at night; however, this does not take into account white-collar crime, which is, ironically, ignored by advocates of urban doom).

Doomsday warnings against high residential density point to overcrowded tenements and high-rise public housing projects as evidence that density causes social problems. Yet the high-rise condominiums of Manhattan's Park Avenue manage to escape scrutiny in these discussions. Certainly no one is proposing to dynamite these fortresses of wealth like the Pruit-Igoe low-income housing project in St. Louis, Missouri, which was blown up in 1972 amidst warnings against putting too many (poor) people so close to one other. The argument of density, therefore, is racially and politically charged, and in many U.S. cities has been used as a pretext by conservatives and Social Darwinists to reduce social spending for housing and other benefits reaching communities of color.

Is the Metropolis a Migration Magnet?

Cities do not stimulate migration; capital does. Push and pull factors operate to draw population from rural to urban areas. Principal among these is the pull of capital. Natural disasters and political factors, such as wars and national growth policies, have also played a role in migration at different historical junctures. For example, the U.S. invasion and occupation of Iraq sent five million Iraqis to other nations. Millions of people went to Calcutta, Karachi and other South Asian metros after they fled the wars and floods in Bangladesh. Migration due to natural disasters and wars, though significant, tends to be more transitory and is also closely related to economic and political factors that shape and constrain individual choices.

The initially high rates of population growth in metropolitan areas due to migration stabilize as the metropolis gets older. Political leaders in "developed" nations, responding to economic pressures, severely limit immigration—witness the current anti-immigrant movements in Europe and North America, for example. Even without official restrictions on immigration, population growth in metropolitan areas tends to level off and the smaller and newer metros actually grow at higher rates. Almost every major metropolitan region in the world is growing at a slower rate than the smaller and newer metropolises and cities.[28]

The U.S. and other developed capitalist countries are now restricting migration to their metropolitan areas and increasingly rely on the maintenance of labor reserves in Third World metros as they "ship jobs overseas" and to cross-border enclaves. These reserves are swelled by the continuing migration from rural areas, which, conveniently for capital, increases the reserve labor pool and drives down overall wages. The growing mobility of capital, especially since the rise of flexible accumulation and neoliberalism in the 1980s, is driving immigration even while labor's mobility is highly regulated and constrained.[29]

The Metropolis = Overconsumption?

If the metropolis is a major contributor to a bloated, inefficient consumer society, then would it not make sense to stop the growth of the metropolis as a way of reducing consumption demands? Certainly consumption levels need to be reduced in the small part of the world—North America and Europe—that consumes the largest proportion of the earth's resources and is responsible for the greatest volume of pollution. However, this would not necessarily stop capital, population and consumer society from proliferating elsewhere in the world. Again, migration and metropolitan population growth is not caused by cities but by the transfer of capital, followed by the transfer of labor and the massing of an even greater labor reserve (see Chapter Three). It is a function of the relative economic opportunities in rural areas, small towns, cities and metropolitan regions. Overconsumption—that is, growth of the wasteful consumer society—is a necessary component of monopoly capitalism and cities are basically the geographic locus. In the twenty-first century, overconsumption is evolving as a necessary feature of the metropolis.

Is the Metropolis Environmentally Unsustainable?

Big cities are not necessarily any more or less sustainable[30] than small cities or villages. The danger of environmental devastation lies not in the urbanization of the world but in the further reproduction of the inefficient regime of development that has so far dominated the highly urbanized part of the world, particularly the United States. Highly urbanized North America accounts for about 5 percent of the world population but consumes 26 percent of all energy, most of it from non-renewable fossil fuels. Africa, Asia and Latin America account for 74 percent of the world population but consume only 30 percent of all energy.[31] Per capita energy consumption is highest in North America, the former USSR and Europe, not in the rest of the world which is where the vast majority of the metropolitan population resides.

The practical political question facing the world is not how to stop metropolitan growth or depopulate metropolitan areas—both unlikely scenarios that would not necessarily lead to better outcomes—but how to stop the destruction and collapse of human societies and the rate of species extinctions; how to make the metropolis more environmentally sustainable and just and improve the quality of life for its residents and workers.

Does the Metropolis Breed "Slums"?

An often unspoken element in doomsday theories is the idea that large, dense cities are mostly giant repositories of poor people—*slums*—huge agglomerations of miserable people living in dense, unhealthy areas without jobs, adequate housing, transportation, water and sanitary services. But these notions come from elite fears that too many poor people in one place will pose a threat to the existing social and political order. For example, the exposé of urban poverty in the work of Charles Dickens fed Victorian fears that an impoverished urban working class would "contaminate" the protected world of the well-off or, even worse, join up with socialists and overthrow it. The signal foray into urban planning in late nineteenth century Europe, led by the

French monarchy under the direction of Georges-Eugène Hausmann and later copied in the Americas, was the destruction of the poor working class neighborhoods of Paris, eliminating "slums" so that the new, planned, modern city could develop. The *tabula rasa* required by modern town planning depended on the notion that the main urban problem was the *slums*.

This objectification of working class communities has become a central element in the anti-urban ideologies advocated by "urban reformers" around the world. Ever since the beginning of rapid urbanization in the nineteenth century, there has been a profound anti-urban bias in European and North American thought. From the founding of the United States, national development was equated with agrarian life and cities were perceived as breeders of disease, immorality and radical politics. Victorians in the United States and Europe preached against the evils of the modern urban age. Anti-urbanism merged with anti-immigrant prejudice as the lifestyle of immigrant workers in the slums of London, Manchester, New York and Chicago was blamed for the terrible living conditions created by industrial capital. Thus, the urban fallacy was profoundly anti-urban.

The focus on *slums* in today's metropolis, however, also flows from the growing role of real estate developers and their government allies who seek to clear urban land where poor people happen to be living so that it can be profitably redeveloped. The "slums" are sitting on potentially valuable land and they must be delegitimized so they can be obliterated. Boston's Mel King, a prominent African American community activist, once said that for him the term *slum* meant that "…somebody else defined my community in a way that allowed them to justify destruction of it."[32] *Slum clearance* was the high-minded objective of the federal urban renewal program in the U.S., the program that displaced millions of people, disproportionately poor and African American, to make way for upscale commercial and residential development. Around the world neighborhoods are defined as hopeless "slums" filled with disease, crime, and unemployment. While "slum" is used in other parts of the world without the negative connotation it carries in the U.S., such homogenizing labels continue to both obscure the underlying relations of social and political inequality and oversimplify an urban world of increasingly complex and diverse neighborhoods. Even worse, this depressing narrative about slums rationalizes the displacement of huge populations and helps destroy their communities without improving their living conditions.[33]

More benign notions of the city see "slums" not as threatening to those in power but instead as just the opposite: vast repositories of the unempowered, symptoms of unconquerable alienation and desperation. More enlightened elites as well as some progressive activists see large cities as breeding grounds for a huge mass of depoliticized people who survive at the margins of society in the "informal" economy, in the vast informal city, sharply separated from the "formal" economy and political life. The United Nations Center for Human Settlements (UN-HABITAT) has helped popularize these notions with reports such as *The Challenge of Slums*,[34] which endorses the rhetoric, advanced by The World Bank and global financial institutions, calling for "poverty reduction" and "pro-poor" policies while at the same time endorsing policies that help reproduce existing inequalities. *Planet of Slums*,[35] by popular scholar Mike Davis, rings with apocalyptic rhetoric about "overurbanization" and cities that explode like a "supernova," reinforcing widespread notions advanced by the major world powers that the majority of the world's population now living in cities is part of the problem and not part of the solution. Davis acknowledges, however, the powerful role of urban social movements, even though this seems to contradict his narrative of disempowered slum populations.

Doomsday theories of the city feed into deeper anti-urban biases that nurture nostalgic ideas of idyllic small town life free from any of the contradictions and problems of large cities. Anti-urban ideology has deep roots in the U.S., which was formed as a rural nation in the nineteenth century with a settler mentality that eliminated from its heroic national narrative the stories of brutal repression and genocide surrounding slaves and indigenous people. In the twentieth century anti-urban prejudices helped demonize new immigrant groups and African Americans who migrated to central cities.

Doomsday theories of the metropolis are manifestations of an ideological blindspot originating in Europe and North America—urban orientalism—which we now turn to for further discussion. (In the next chapter we define urban orientalism in greater detail and look at how it prevents us from understanding and planning for the metropolis of "the others.") As the world urbanizes at an unprecedented pace in the twenty-first century, the ideological and political baggage left from twentieth century urbanism increasingly confronts harsh new realities: global climate change and food insecurity, the utter failure of the theory and practice of urban planning as originally conceived in Europe and North America, and the apparent durability of urban social, economic and environmental problems.

The fundamental questions having to do with land, water, energy and human consumption—and not just urbanization—will be the determining factors in charting the world's future, urban and otherwise. New alternatives for populating and relating to the earth and other species are needed now more than ever if human settlements are to be resilient and sustainable in this century and survive into the next one.

Urban Orientalism

Both versions of the urban fallacy emanate from the privileged and powerful minority of the world that lives and works in the postcolonial centers of economic and political power. These versions exclude the voices of new immigrants from less developed nations who are living in the periphery of the wealthiest metropolitan areas; instead they reflect the views of the established elites who control the levers of economic and political power. While they are passed off as objective science, urban fallacies are highly subjective and reflect the class, racial and ethnic identities of their proponents. They are examples of what I call in this book *urban orientalism*—the tendency of experts at the center of global power to present their own subjective, culturally-biased views of the rest of the urban world as if they were fact. The concept of orientalism follows Edward Said's pathbreaking discussion of orientalism in the British Empire. He showed how British intellectuals redefined the history and culture of colonial nations as seen through the eyes of the empire. In Chapter Two, I outline in greater detail how orientalism has become an integral part of urban theory and the practice of urban planning, starting in the imperial centers of power but now an integral part of urbanism all over the world.

Edward Said used the term *orientalism* to describe an approach to the "Orient" that was born in Europe during the late eighteenth century as an integral part of its colonial empire. He showed how British intellectuals interpreted and reimagined the culture and societies of the Orient through the lens of the conquerors, in the arts, philosophy and history. Speaking of a French journalist visiting Lebanon, Said stated that "...the main thing for the European visitor was a European representation of the Orient and its contemporary fate."[36] He quotes extensively from Lord Arthur James Balfour,[37] British dignitary from the early twentieth century, who, speaking about Egypt, insists that "Orientals" have no experience with self-government and that British rule yielded "far better government than in the whole history of the world they ever had before."[38]

Orientalism can be applied to urban planning just as it applies to other aspects of society and culture. The hegemonic theories and practices guiding urban planning and development around the world have their roots in Europe and the United States. Now followed almost universally, they favor the modern, rationally planned city imagined by professionally trained architects, engineers and planners, imitating the most powerful centers of global capital. The ideal planned city, the *formal* city, is contrasted with the *informal* city, the places built and managed by the people who live and work there, the "slums." The formal city aims for a "healthy" market economy and an efficient infrastructure to avoid major public health problems while encouraging growth and consumption. The informal city, we are told, is chaotic, dangerous, and dysfunctional. Since it is supposed that the informal city both breeds and concentrates poverty, we are led to believe that to achieve social justice we must eliminate the informal city and replace it with the planned, formal city.

This approach, *urban orientalism*, is rooted in colonial, post-colonial and imperialist thinking, and is deeply imbedded in the professions responsible for imagining and re-imagining the metropolis. It is an ideological underpinning for the expansion and accumulation of capital in cities, and an instrument of the global marketplace for land and resources. It is the justification for the displacement of tenants and working people living on land that is coveted for real estate development. Take for example Vila Autódromo, a livable and stable working class neighborhood in the Barra da Tijuca area of Rio de Janeiro which was recently targeted as a "slum" requiring removal. The real driving force was real estate speculation engendered by plans for the 2016 Olympics.[39] Or the aftermath of the 2010 earthquake that struck Port Au Prince, where Haiti's international rebuilding efforts, led by the most powerful nations, lagged amid thinly-veiled fears that "slums" would reemerge. Orientalism is also deeply imbedded within the wealthiest and most powerful nations; for example, the rebuilding efforts in New Orleans after Hurricane Katrina in 2005 gave priority to wealthier and whiter neighborhoods while many low-income African Americans were unable to return for lack of housing.[40] These are the real world consequences of urban orientalism.

As we face the challenges of metropolitan planning in the twenty-first century, orientalist dualism is a largely unrecognized problem. Though subjective, it has a profound influence on urban reality. It reinforces the continuing growth of urban enclaves fashioned to protect wealth and privilege. It demeans the multiple alternatives that arise from the everyday experiences and practices of people who live and work in the world's villages and cities. Orientalist urbanism fails to address the structural issues of global inequality, climate change and the long-term degradation of the natural environment.

Global Climate Change

Another problem with the urban fallacy is that neither the optimistic nor pessimistic version takes seriously the potentially game-changing role of global climate change, which could alter the shape of human settlements in fundamental ways no matter what economic and urban experts may or may not do. It is still unclear to what extent global warming will affect the urbanization process, but as global efforts to reduce greenhouse gas emissions each year fall short of even modest goals it is certainly premature to register optimism. It is not yet clear that technological and policy changes touted by reformers will be good enough or arrive in time. However, the apocalyptic predictions of doom for all big cities at the hands of climate change are surely premature, as are the claims that dense living in the green metropolis will save the planet.[41]

The twentieth century was a century of optimism for many, an optimism generated by the dramatic expansion of global capital. While founded on the deterministic Enlightenment belief in perpetual progress that sprouted at the height of European and North American hegemony, the optimism reached its peak after World War II, when perpetual growth appeared to be achievable in "the West." Indeed, monopoly capitalism was understood to be eternal and necessary to the achievement of progress, thwarted only by cultural "backwardness," resistance to modernism, and the threats of socialism.[42]

The inconvenient truth of climate change stands in the way of fulfilling the optimistic promise of linear growth in the twenty-first century. The scientific consensus is that the global climate is warming as a result of human development, resulting in sea level rise that could submerge large portions of existing metropolitan regions and threaten life as we know it. Global warming and sea level rise will directly affect many of the largest and most powerful urban centers in the world, and may have devastating effects in regions with limited reserves to mount effective responses. More significantly, however, unstable climate conditions could create major crises in food production and distribution, threaten the security of food for entire nations and regions, and lead to major political changes, even revolutionary ones. Extreme weather events could disrupt productive enterprises and the links between them that make up local economies. Climate change could displace billions of people and result in a catastrophic extinction of species comparable to other extinctions and collapses that have occurred since the earth was formed.[43]

It is therefore possible that global climate change could sharply alter the linear progression of urbanization before the end of this century. The total urbanization of the world is not preordained. The American hemisphere and European continent are already almost entirely urbanized. Asia, which accounts for the majority of the world's population, is rapidly urbanizing. But climate change and sea level rise could slow or reverse the urbanization process, or change the size, form and functioning of metropolitan areas even if it does not rule out the dominance of the metropolis.

City planning in the twentieth century played an important role in fostering global climate change. The carbon-intensive form of urbanization that now prevails throughout the world is a major contributor to global warming as well as serious pollution and urban public health problems. One hundred years ago, nurtured by the industrial revolution and the expansion of monopoly capital, the metropolitan revolution began with the private automobile, energy-intensive building technology, and urban rail transportation.[44] Will the next hundred years of human settlement change radically as a result of twenty-first century technology or will the trends from the last century prevail? While information technology and the internet are often said to be revolutionizing forces, so far they have only helped accelerate the metropolitan revolution without altering the trend towards global warming, greater pollution and urban health crises. "Green" technological fixes such as hybrid vehicles, energy-efficient buildings, and "alternative" fuels only expand the possibilities for the production and consumption of new products, many of them petroleum-based, and waste—indeed, the commodification of everything.[45] The use of newer energy sources such as solar and wind power, though gradually expanding, may not be sufficient to reverse course and supply the energy needed to drive the economic machine that demands expanding consumption.[46]

The promise of the metropolis was that it would be more energy efficient due to scale economies in production and infrastructure, and that its higher densities would lead to more efficient transit-oriented development. This promise has yet to be fulfilled. On a per capita basis, the metropolis contributes more than the small town and rural area to the global carbon footprint—not because it is inherently unsustainable (due to its size or density) but because of the way it has developed in the twentieth century. Let's call it *really existing urbanization*. The metropolis is the geographical center of capital accumulation and the consumption of goods and services needed for the growth and reproduction of capital; it is the center of the consumer society and consumerism. Its economy thrives on the production and consumption of commodities, especially the economies with the most powerful metros, which benefit from the post-colonial outsourcing of manufacturing and labor reproduction that makes continuing growth possible.

The preferred vehicle for urban transportation in the metropolis is the private automobile, the major reason that 25 percent of global greenhouse gases come from the transportation sector. The industrial food system serving urban areas combined with the transportation sector together account for over 50 percent of greenhouse gas emissions. The carbon-intensive food system mostly serves the metropolitan population even though its raw materials may originate and be processed in rural areas. The metropolis is a giant waste manufacturer yet is so far unable to recycle most of its waste to reduce energy needs; most of it ends up in landfills or as toxic smoke and ash from incinerators, creating risks for humans and other species who live nearby. Most important of all, per capita energy consumption tends to be highest in metropolitan areas, suggesting that there are enormous "diseconomies of scale" that outweigh the great potential for efficiency that comes with higher densities and larger cities.

Capitalism, the Original Game Changer

The metropolis did not emerge from a mysterious urge of people to live in big cities, an expression of the power of the "free will" of humans. The metropolis grew out of capitalism, and to understand the metropolis, including its environmental and social problems, we cannot avoid understanding the role of capitalism. Global capital since the early twentieth century has been based in the metropolis, its natural habitat.

It continues to extract resources from the hinterlands of the world and concentrate them in its financial centers, where a large portion invariably end up in the growing global real estate network taking shape in the twenty-first century. In order to grow, monopoly capital needs to extract natural resources, and encourage conspicuous consumption and planned obsolescence in its interminable pursuit of profit. The waste, pollution, species extinction, deforestation, and greenhouse gases left in its wake are seen as "external costs" to be paid by others. Capital is an engine driving economies across the globe by measuring progress largely in terms of growth in capital and not improvement in the quality of life for humans and the planet. As we discuss in the following chapters, it is responsible for the sharp divide between urban and rural life and perpetuation of the modern myth that improved human welfare requires the domination of humans over every thing, living and not, on the earth.

Many of the energy and environmental problems of the modern metropolis, and many of its benefits, are unintended consequences of growth driven by capital accumulation. Investors deposited large portions of their surplus earnings in the metropolis because that is where they expected it to be safe and to multiply. They created mountains of real estate using energy-intensive materials such as concrete and steel. They contaminated and paved over the earth to avoid the costs of preserving it in its natural state. Their development produced significant temperature increases in cities (the heat-island effect), destroyed flora and fauna, and both required and encouraged waste-producing mass consumption so that local markets would feed off and recirculate global capital. In the pursuit of real estate profits investors squeezed out and circumscribed human activities such as food production, and any species that did not serve the immediate needs of human production or reproduction, yielding a consumption machine dedicated primarily to the absorption of surplus capital.[47]

Despite the reckless waste of resources in today's metropolis, in principle it could still become the most energy efficient human settlement form. For example, in some more densely developed urban areas rates of domestic consumption of energy for heating, electricity and water are consistently lower than in lower-density suburbs. However, the number of people living in sprawled suburbs far outnumbers those in the higher density urban cores. Scale economies for some infrastructure like water and sewer systems might be greater, but there may also be diseconomies of scale beyond a certain size.[48] More energy efficient modes of transportation—rail and trolley, for example—are often not feasible in smaller settlements and achieve maximum economies only in the large metropolis. However, they are not the predominant modes of urban transportation in the world.

We in the U.S. are acutely aware of the generalized taboo against criticizing capitalism, even after the disastrous situation it has left us in due to the latest round of overproduction, overconsumption, speculation and near-depression. As a nation we have accepted the notion that there is no alternative to capitalism. The solution to the crisis of capitalism is, well, more capitalism. Given the collapse of twentieth century socialism, and the significant environmental and social problems it had been responsible for, we keep our eyes closed to the important lessons learned from the attempts to build socialist cities (this is the focus of Chapter Six). The major capitalist powers have boxed themselves into a logical and political cul-de-sac where the only choice is to rescue and make the best of capitalism even while it remains chronically ill and unable to recover.

There are surely different regimes of capitalism and much competition among capitalists. But the mainstream regimes are driven by "free-market" ideology and mired in neoliberal orthodoxies. Others call for a kinder, gentler capitalism including an important place for public goods and a wide social safety net. This latter option, however, no longer appears realistic. Many in the U.S., the home of free-market capitalism and short-term thinking, look at Europe, with its welfare states and tradition of labor organizing, as a possible way out. Yet Europe has adopted free-market and neoliberal ideology, though unevenly, and the European Union is now struggling with the consequences. There has yet to develop any serious, large-scale alternative.

Capitalism has been the game-changer in urban development and the foundation for modern urban planning in the twentieth century. The experience of the United States is most important because of its leading political and economic role in the world for at least the last half century. As we show in Chapter Seven, in the U.S. economic growth is the most important principle of urban planning and the role of the public sector is to stay out of the way and facilitate the free choice of urban consumers. People "choose" where to live—they supposedly prefer the single-family American Dream home. The inefficiencies and inequities that go along with millions of dream homes and suburban sprawl are simply "external costs." People "choose" the private automobile over mass transit, the bicycle and walking. They "choose" the whole array of individual products from computers to cell phones. Governments are powerless to stop the buying frenzy and can only help organize it. Thus the free-market metropolis is a fragmented one in which any attempt to regulate and control are denounced as against the free market, individual choice, and freedom. In a nation that has never seen a major socialist political trend but retains a deep Cold War philosophy, all non-capitalist futures are suspect.

If the production and reproduction of capital have something to do with the metropolis and its problems, then the answer to a free-market sprawled metropolis cannot simply be the creation of a free-market unsprawled one. It could change the geography but not the depth of the problems. Instead, we will need to probe more deeply the roots of urban problems in the economic and social relations underlying them, particularly the relations between capital and labor. At the center of this is the way humans live their lives collectively in a global economic system geared towards producing an endless stream of commodities for profit and in which progress is measured in terms of quantitative growth in production and consumption. At the center of the urban question, therefore, is *really existing capitalism*, not the abstract free-market utopia that is celebrated as myth. It is the foundation for urban orientalism and the most important structural contributor to urban inequalities, environmental problems and climate change.

A major theme of this book is that metropolitan regions, as developed in the twentieth century and as they continue to develop in this century, have been created and planned following theories and practices born in the colonial and imperial centers of power—Europe and North America in particular, and increasingly in new centers of global capital, such as China, Brazil and South Africa. The economic foundation of urban growth is the accumulation and expansion of capital in cities, appropriation and extraction of valuable resources from rural areas, and the generation of an unending consumer demand that sustains and expands the appetite for commodities. This occurs unequally throughout the world and is part of a global pattern of *dependent urbanization* (as discussed in Chapter Three). These are the roots of the environmental and social problems affecting the entire world, both urban and rural.

The Urban–Rural Divide

Another characteristic of the modern metropolis is its brutal divorce from rural areas. Large cities now rely on rural areas only for food and natural resources; there is very little contact and interaction with rural areas beyond this crude extraction of value and profit. Tourism is an urban-oriented industry in which landscapes, both urban and rural, are consumed as commodities. Indigenous cultures and ways of life in rural areas are objectified and commodified for consumption by urbanites. While the metropolis might have integrated city and countryside had it developed differently, urban–rural divides are becoming more pronounced as metropolitan areas grow.

One aspect of this sharp division is a global crisis in food security affecting large portions of the world dependent on capital-intensive industrialized agriculture. Most urban consumers have no control over food supply because their choices are strictly limited. Multinational corporations own and manage factory farms that produce huge monocultures. This has created increasing vulnerability to changes in supply due to global market conditions, and growing uncertainty with the advent of climate change. Industrial agriculture is carbon-intensive and a major source of greenhouse gases, toxic waste and pollution. It reinforces economic dependencies and global imbalances in political power. Centuries-old cultural traditions in local food production and consumption are disappearing and control over food is increasingly in the hands of a small number of financial and corporate institutions. In the twenty-first century, this has created the crisis of food sovereignty and it is fundamentally related to global climate change and metropolitan growth.[49] We will return to the critical role of food sovereignty and the urban–rural divides of the world in Chapters Four, Eight and Nine.

Enclave Urbanism and Environmental Justice

The two versions of the urban fallacy—one that says cities are the problem, the other that says they are the solution—tend to obscure, though in different ways, the growth of unequal urbanization and planning practices. They overlook what we call *enclave urbanism*—the tendency towards the fragmentation of cities by class, race, gender and other social dividers, producing not an integrated metropolis that can be subject to democratic planning but a sharply divided one that may easily reproduce and expand existing global and local inequalities. The free-market model of urban development that evolved in the U.S. is a leading example of enclave urbanism because metropolitan regions are fragmented and driven by a mania for individual free choice, consumerism and private over public space.

Praise for the greater and greener cities by Glaeser and others helps to obscure social and environmental inequalities. While the metropolitan revolution of the twentieth century created for the first time large, complex cities with many economic and cultural opportunities, it is not good enough to simply celebrate the city without looking at who benefits and who loses. We can boast of the environmental and public health benefits enjoyed by those living in dense urban cores like Manhattan, or praise the greening of Leipzig, or the return of bicycling and windmills in Copenhagen. But these are privileges enjoyed by the wealthy and they are unavailable to the vast majority of the world's people, both urban and rural, who are exposed to growing environmental and health risks. We are moving towards an environmentally and socially unjust world sharply divided into the centers of privilege and health and peripheries of poverty and pollution.

Just as colonial and post-colonial urban planning promised an orderly urban future, just as urban renewal and new town development in the twentieth century promised to build the healthy city of the twentieth century, now free-market solutions promoting green technology are the panacea for twenty-first century planning. This is not to say that good planning and design cannot make a difference in the quality of life for all people who live and work in cities. However, if current trends continue the deeply imbedded historic trends providing the benefits of design and planning to the privileged few will continue.

The showcasing of green urbanism evades the central issue of *land*. Under oriental urbanism, land is dealt with as a thing, a commodity, and not a nexus of relations between people, place and environment. Land is a profit center, or an object to be used and thrown away, like most other natural resources. If there is not a drastic change in the way that humans relate to land and use the resources of the earth and other species, a fully urbanized world could create more wastelands, pollution, climate change and economic collapse. We need to place a huge question mark over the rosy pictures of a global urban future in which free markets, new technology, and human intelligence guarantee an inexorable and linear advance along a one-way street towards progress and development. It hasn't worked so far. Urbanization has not solved environmental problems or diminished social inequalities. It is not likely to do so unless something fundamental and systemic changes going forward.

Enclave urbanism is at home in North America, the most metropolitanized region in the world. In Chapter Seven, we will visit the U.S. and look in greater detail at how enclave urbanism is closely connected to global climate change, capitalist growth, the urban–rural divide and urban orientalism. A few key points are worth mentioning here.

The U.S. has the highest per capita consumption of energy.[50] Apparently the strict emission controls and environmental regulations of the U.S. serve to rationalize expanded consumption rather than greater energy efficiency. This is a major contradiction of urban growth in the U.S. In 2006, however, China overtook the U.S. as the single largest greenhouse gas emitter in absolute tons of cardon dioxide, showing the ecological impacts of its rapid expansion and urbanization.[51]

The metropolis in the U.S. is one of the least efficient forms of human settlement in the world and its sprawled, low-density, auto-dependent regime of urban development has become the leading model around the world. The U.S. uses vast stocks of materials to build its detached single-family dream house. Detached housing requires more energy for heating and home appliances than attached, multi-family housing. The sprawled suburb requires that 25–30 percent of its land be surfaced for streets, sidewalks and parking, increasing surface runoff and water contamination from lawn chemicals, petroleum products and debris (and in the northern climates, vast quantities of road salts). The U.S. metropolis is ringed and crisscrossed with highways that, contrary to the orthodoxy of twentieth century traffic engineering, increase congestion, auto use and pollution. This model extends the working day unnecessarily by requiring lengthy commutation, and puts more people in front of steering wheels and electronic devices than in public squares or fresh air.[52] The rare exceptions, such as New York City's mass transit system, are unintended consequences of dynamic real estate development, and are lacking many of the efficiencies found in Europe's planned intermodal transit networks.

One of the world's major polluters is the private automobile and its natural habitat is the sprawled metropolis. The U.S. model of metropolitan growth is driven by a loosely regulated real estate market and conspicuous consumption of land, building materials, and privately-owned vehicles. It is premised on the seemingly unlimited availability of capital, energy resources and land, and the maximum mobility for capital and labor—basic ingredients of the U.S. regime of economic development since the eighteenth century. The sprawled auto-centered Los Angeles region is the supreme American model of the suburban metropolis and is now being reproduced, however imperfectly, across the globe.[53]

Suburban sprawl in the U.S., though rooted in an economy dependent on oil and auto, reflects historic social patterns and anti-urban ideological traditions that encourage the establishment of urban enclaves. The nation of the "crabgrass frontier"[54] was formed by the appropriation and development of large tracts of land forcibly removed from the stewardship of indigenous people and placed in the hands of individual settlers and profiteers. On this land, the ideal homestead, a single-family house on a separate tract of land, was the means for maximizing private space, minimizing public space and creating settler enclaves separate from dark-skinned people. Throughout the first three hundred years of settlement in the American hemisphere, there were so many opportunities for the development of new land that developers could take profits quickly and move on to other opportunities. Land, like all commodities produced in this regime of conspicuous consumption, was something to be used and thrown away. This approach profoundly influenced twentieth century urban planning, which fostered wasteful suburban sprawl as well as the disposal of many central city neighborhoods to promote the use and reuse of land.

While mass transit is capable of providing accessibility for many more people than the auto for the same expenditure of energy and capital, in the U.S. metropolis it is utilized mostly to abate the worst vehicular congestion in some central cities or to serve a small proportion of suburban commuters. The auto is responsible for 60–80 percent of the ground-level ozone and particulate matter in the air, and a major contributor to global warming and the greenhouse effect. Pollution from autos contributes to cancer and lung diseases, and it is one of the most dangerous modes of transit, costing over 40,000 lives a year in "accidents" (which are not really accidents but "crashes" because most are preventable with safe street design, strict laws, and alternative modes). Auto dependence also contributes to the nation's growing epidemic of obesity.

There are now some two billon motor vehicles in the world, twice the number in 1990.[55] Auto production and consumption is a key element of all developed and developing economies. In the United States, there is one car for every two people and transportation is responsible for 9.5 percent of the Gross Domestic Product.[56] While it accounts for only 5 percent of world auto production (Europe and Asia produce 84 percent of the total),[57] the U.S. remains the largest consumer of cars.

The inefficient U.S. metropolis was made possible because at the time the metropolitan revolution began at the turn of the nineteenth century, North America possessed seemingly unlimited amounts of land, building materials and energy. This was supplemented by the vast resources available on favorable terms from the dependent nations of Africa, Asia and Latin America. An unequal international division of labor allowed the U.S. to thrive on low-cost energy and labor from across the globe. With the end of colonialism and the rise of U.S. hegemony among capitalist powers after World War II, the U.S. was able to capture markets formerly dominated by Europe and Japan even as the centers of global capital became more multilateral. U.S. industry has profited from the export of its auto-centered regime of sprawled development to the developing nations, which suffer the worst consequences of energy inefficiency because they have the least ability to regulate or cure the pollution and public health problems that result from it. Less developed countries are flooded with the most polluting motor vehicles. If all megacities were to conform to the U.S. paradigm, doomsday predictions about the catastrophic metropolis could come true. If China, Russia and India pursue the goal of mass auto use in this century, there may be little the rest of the world can do to stop global warming, even if they were to utilize the latest "green technologies."

Thus the prevailing approach to metropolitan growth reinforces economic, social and environmental inequalities. We return to this theme throughout the remaining chapters with examples from across the globe. Before moving on, however, we will stop for a moment to define in greater detail what we mean by urban orientalism, since it is a central concept in this analysis.

Chapter 2

Urban Orientalism, Planning and the Metropolis of "The Others"

The various doomsday, anti-urban visions of the metropolis—that it is too big, too dense, environmentally unsustainable, etc.—are an essential component of *urban orientalism*, the way of thinking that sees the metropolis through the lens of the powerful, dominant economic and political forces in the world. As shown in the previous chapter they rely on the *urban fallacy*—the notion that the problem is with the city and not the social and economic system. In this chapter we will go deeper to understand how the urban fallacy comes from a more complicated and intricate system of thought. Urban orientalism presents an oversimplified picture of life in the metropolis and magnifies problems opportunistically to maximize control by the powerful over land and people. It sensationalizes "slums" and objectifies the people who live and work there, making them more vulnerable to exploitation and displacement. Orientalist spatial utopias are also advanced as panaceas for metropolitan ills—these include urban enclaves, malls, gated communities, and new models of the modern, sanitary and violence-free city. Urban orientalism has been the philosophical underpinning of Victorian urban planning of the late nineteenth century, twentieth century metropolitan planning and strategic urban planning of the twenty-first century.

As noted in Chapter One (p.17) Palestinian scholar Edward Said used the term *orientalism* to describe an approach to the "Orient" that was born in Europe during the late eighteenth century as an integral part of its colonial empire.[1] Orientalism is founded on the many myths invented about the inferior and invisible "other," the Oriental, the barbarian, the "slumdweller," the stereotyped and historically irrelevant object that is different from the "civilized" and peaceful European subject. Orientals are seen through the eyes of the imperial masters, producing convenient simplifications that legitimize their subjugation, oppression and segregation. One of the surest signs of the triumph of orientalism is the internalization and adoption of orientalist thinking by intellectuals who emerge from the native populations, particularly those trained at the centers of empire.[2] Indeed, with the waning of colonialism, the principal practitioners of orientalism are elites of the former colonial nations.

Orientalism is problematic on two counts: political and epistemological. Orientalism plays a powerful role in global politics and is used to reinforce structural imbalances in power. It also divides the world into artificial dualisms, based on arbitrary and subjective binaries. These are used to rationalize existing hierarchies of power by suggesting, for example, that the "west" is more important than and even superior to the "east"; the "modern" city is better than the "Third World City"; and the "civilized world" is threatened by "terrorism." This presents critics of orientalism (and urban orientalism) with two challenges: addressing the deep inequalities created and perpetuated by orientalist discourses and exercises of power and simultaneously challenging orientalism's epistemology. As an alternative, we use dialectical and historical materialism, which provides a framework to address issues of urban political economy—the material basis for ideas and ideologies—with an appreciation for their role in the processes of change—dialectics.[3]

I define *urban orientalism* here as an application of the concept of orientalism to cities and city planning. Following Said's work, we begin to see that orientalism advances a *dualist* vision of the urban world—a world divided into ideal, polar opposites of east and west, south and north, rural and urban, slum and community, irrational and rational, unplanned and planned, periphery and center, informal and formal, *gemeinschaft* and *gesellschaft*, bad and good.[4] This world is devoid of complexity and diversity. Contradictions are opaque and time stands still. Urban history is rewritten as a series of events that does not change the universal and always static categories that describe the universe. Cities are understood as examples of universal ideal types that are labeled in accordance with the static, dualistic values of the most powerful—they are either developed or underdeveloped, rationally planned or chaotic, sustainable or unsustainable.

In a present-day world made smaller by global communications and technology, historically simplistic dualisms dominate. For example, press reports often refer to the agency of "Western nations" as if they all think alike and act in consort. United Nations reports and scholarly works refer to the "global North" and the "global South." The World Bank refers to the rich and the poor. Asia, a continent of more than 4 billion people, over half the world's population, is still "the East," one of the components of Samuel Huntington's *Clash of Civilizations*.[5] These dichotomies fail to distinguish differences within the west and north; ignore the peripheries in the center and the centers in the periphery; conflate the divisions between clans, classes, ethnicities, and other social dividers, everywhere. Above all, they manufacture and reproduce the "other" as always occupying one pole in a bipolar system.

The other is the slum-dweller, the poor, the object, and the outcast seen from the vantage point of the legitimate urban citizen, the denizen of the developed, planned city. The other is dark-skinned and a woman. The other is an indigenous person, a "primitive," underdeveloped, uneducated, and undisciplined. The other is dirty, unsanitary, and a victim of its own uncivilized behaviors. The other is prone to violence and terrorism. In today's cities, the other is to be feared, segregated, and controlled. Urban planning is needed to organize and civilize the other. The other has no lasting value and will eventually wither away as a result of the inexorable march of "progress."

In the twentieth century, these prejudices against the other became part of the comprehensive system of orientalist thought that forms the basis for the dominant regimes of urbanization and urban planning. Urban orientalism was rooted in European and North American ideas of the city, themselves based on regimes of economic growth and development that were tied to dynamic global empires. Orientalism oversimplified the complex urban world and continues to rationalize pervasive and growing systems of unequal economic and political power. Thus, the orientalist view of the "underdeveloped" city as one with "mass poverty" classifies the vast majority of the population in a category of despair so it can be the target of "poverty-reduction" and economic growth strategies designed and financed in the imperial centers.

For example, from the vantage point of North America, Lima (Peru) is an "under-developed city," a city of boundless slums. In a story entitled "Squalid Slums Grow as People Flood Latin America's Cities," *The New York Times* quotes an urban scholar as saying, "The city has grown like a wild animal without any kind of planning ... Lima is a time bomb."[6] To many Limeños, such terms would be perplexing, insulting, or downright ridiculous. The upscale residents of Lima's Miraflores neighborhood might consider their community to be more like upscale Manhattan, and see the rest of Lima as "underdeveloped." Residents of the *barriadas*—the majority of Lima's population—are more likely to see the city as a complex array of economically and socially distinct districts even if they may know only a few of them well, the areas where they live and work.

In a recent front page *New York Times* article, the city of Gurgaon, India is introduced as a place "Where Growth and Dysfunction Have No Boundaries."[7] In contrast with the nearby New Delhi, which has grown thanks to enormous public and private capital investments over decades and has become a showcase for the potential of a "modern," Western-style, functional urban India, Gurgaon is presented as an example of chaotic, disorderly India. In fact, as we discuss in Chapter Four, cities like Gurgaon are products of the brutal imposition of orientalist urbanism that leaves the people who live and work in the city powerless and unable to effectively practice on a daily basis their deep traditions of stewardship of the land. New Delhi's wealthy areas are only elite enclaves whose prominence obsures the reality for the majority of the Delhi region's population which lives in conditions like those in Gurgaon.

Figure 2.1 New Urban Enclave in Hanoi, Vietnam

Urban orientalism is not simply problematic as theory. In practice it underlies policies that make conditions worse for the people who live and work in cities and reproduces the most undemocratic and unjust elements of the metropolis. Thus, if the problem is "the slums" of Lima then the orientalist solution is to eliminate them— by displacing residents, tearing down their shantytowns, and putting in their place shining new examples of rationally-planned cities. This results in the bulldozing and displacement of entire neighborhoods to make way for "planned" enclaves and, not coincidentally, valuable real estate deals. If cities are too large and dense, then the solution is to thin them out and deconcentrate the population. If the problem is poor environment and public health, the solution is to sanitize and sterilize the environment and build green. Thus, the formal, planned city is presented as *the answer* to the informal city that grew incrementally, built by "the others"; like a medieval morality play, the good city must replace the bad one. And if that doesn't work, it can be blamed on the failures of "the others."

Modern Town Planning and Colonialism

Many of the earliest empires on the earth sought to strengthen their control over colonized people by reorganizing physical space through city planning. They built new towns and rebuilt old ones so that the occupying armies would be able to exercise control over the resident population, facilitating access by laying out a street system easily understood by the occupiers.[8] Athens commissioned formal plans for the layout of settlements in its colonies. Rome implanted its imperial axes, the *cardo* and *decumanus*, at the center of cities to maximize access and control. This practice continued and expanded with the rise of European colonialism. For example, the Spanish crown created a blueprint for the cities it founded in the Americas: the Laws of the Indies set out formulas to be applied to the physical development of towns (see Chapter Eight). England planned enclaves, sometimes fortified, for its settlers, and trained native professionals in the empire's approach to city planning.

While historians of city planning in the centers of empire dote upon the ways that cities were laid out by colonial powers, they treat the habitats of colonized people, both before and after foreign occupation, as unplanned, chaotic, and unhealthy. As part of a historic narrative justifying colonialism, the prior traditions of urbanism are devalued or, at best, relegated to static museums with static museum objects. It has been quite easy to ignore entirely the powerful urban traditions in Africa, Asia and Latin America that preceded colonial occupation because many of the most developed cities were sacked by war and devastated by famine and diseases that followed occupation by settlers. After relics of art and urban culture are carted away to the museums of the imperial center, well-financed archaeological explorations uncover sites that then become valuable tourist destinations around which to build orientalist conceptions of "the ancient cities." The people who lived and worked in these places then become *objects*, much like the urns, statues and ruins that are uncovered. They are not *subjects*, have no agency, nor do their descendants in modern, post-colonial development.

Most historians who have studied the matter know that the cities of the Incas, Mayas and Aztecs were extensively planned.[9] Their cities were the products of conquests over large territories, and used sophisticated building technologies and

Figure 2.2 Post-Colonial Philanthropy in India

engineering techniques. To those reshaping urban space for the Spanish settlers, however, the ancient imperial cities were either invisible or downright inferior. One homogenizing empire replaced another. To read the modern skylines of the cities in the lands of the former Inca, Maya and Aztec empires, the past was vanquished.

Victorian Planning and the Metropolis

Orientalist thinking underlies the two major urban planning theories that emerged from the Victorian era in the late nineteenth century and shaped twentieth century planning for metropolitan regions around the world. The first was the Garden City theory. Proponents of this approach posited that the solution to the crowded, polluted industrial city was the newly-planned suburban town, designed to create a harmonious relationship between humans and their living environment. While these principles were laudable and progressive in their time, they eventually rationalized suburban development that was driven more by speculation in land than the original ideals of urban reform or social welfare. Still, the reformers treated existing communities as inherently problematic and in need of total transformation. The Garden City idea was to solve urban problems by moving away from the unruly city towards a tamed countryside.[10]

The second major idea in twentieth century planning was the City Beautiful, which posited the inverse solution to urban problems: bring the countryside to the city.[11] The City Beautiful would consist of magnificent new civic places in the center of industrial cities, with pleasant vistas, tasteful landscaping, and attractive buildings.

To create the new city, it was necessary to remove unsightly working class neighbor-hoods and create a *tabula rasa*, or a "clean slate." This became an underpinning for the massive displacement of urban neighborhoods in the twentieth century. The promise was that rational planning and design would improve the urban environment and replace the old and ugly with new spaces encouraging the "civilized" society.

The birth of the movement for modern architecture in the early twentieth century laid the foundations for the theory and practice of city planning throughout the century. Modern architecture's most prominent institutional expression was the International Congress of Modern Architecture (CIAM), founded by Walter Gropius in Germany. Modern architecture sought to integrate and balance physical form and socioeconomic function in ways that created new opportunities for the production of buildings on a large scale, using industrialized building methods. It emphasized the social function of architecture and city planning; urban development would be driven by social objectives and not simply the need for individual buildings with aesthetic value (particularly for wealthy patrons). In this sense modernism was progressive and even revolutionary in its time.

However, modernism was at the same time a powerful driver of *physical determinism* in planning—the notion that design and planning of the built environment could address and resolve social problems. This would legitimize the growth of a new technocratic elite responsible for the growth and development of cities by imbuing their professions with the mission of making a better world, a world envisioned by the most advanced professionals, the architects, engineers and planners.

Modern architecture relied on the notion that there needed to be a "rational" process for building in the sprouting metropolises, and in this sense it was aligned with the dominant way of thinking in the centers of global capital, where markets

Figure 2.3 Store in Tokyo

were "rational." In the U.S., modernism debuted at the Columbian Exposition at the 1893 Chicago World's Fair. Designed by architect Daniel Burnham, the American advocate for the City Beautiful, the Exposition was a precursor to Chicago's influential 1909 Master Plan.[12]

Le Corbusier made a special contribution to modernism with his "tower in the park" proposal. This rationalized the construction of the emerging central business districts around the world where enormous surpluses from financial investments were building new shrines to capital accumulation. Finance and real estate merged (producing what became known as the FIRE sector—Finance, Insurance and Real Estate). Le Corbusier's towers were high rise commercial and residential spaces that maximized the return on capital due to rising land values and formed the iconic skylines of the new downtowns. The "parks" were to be, according to Le Corbusier, empty spaces and not really parks, since his ideal city was designed for communication between buildings via the private automobile and other motorized vehicles. "Kill the street," he declared, a dictum that was echoed in planning the U.S. metropolis throughout the twentieth century, where the low-density suburbs, also envisioned by Le Corbusier, emphasized individual private spaces connected by motorways. Public spaces and the commons were erased. This was the city of mass, individualized consumption combined with the downtown centers of power, the twentieth century metropolis.[13]

Modernism, born in Europe and the U.S., rapidly permeated and overcame centuries of traditional city building and design throughout the world. Professional architects, engineers and planners from the four corners of the earth were trained in the citadels of modernism, in Europe and the U.S. When they returned they often created new markets for urban development following the paradigms advanced by the masters, or integrated elements of traditional city planning to produce new versions of the modern with superficial aesthetic highlights from the old. By the middle of the twentieth century modern architecture and planning became the "international style," suggesting a universality and applicability everywhere in the world. Powerful international firms such as Skidmore, Owings & Merrill, Turner Construction, and others were repositories of the modern tradition, incorporating professionals and ideas from many nations but producing homogenous and profitable urban products.

Two brief examples may help illustrate the power of this "internationalism." The first is the creation of modern Ankara, the capital of Turkey. Ankara was a small city located in the geographic center of the Turkish Republic, founded in 1923 after the collapse of the Ottoman Empire. Under the leadership of Kemal Atatürk, the new Turkey would seek to emulate Europe and "the West."[14] The new government debated a plan to restore and expand historic Ankara or build a new, modern city on land to be acquired by the government. They chose the latter and after a 1928 design competition entrusted the design of the new city to Hermann Jansen, a German professor. The national center of political power in the new Turkey became distinctly internationalist in style and appearance.[15]

Another example is the emergence of global "starchitects" like I.M. Pei, one of the most influential practitioners of modernist city planning around the globe in the twentieth century. Pei was born in China in 1917, studied at MIT and Harvard in the U.S., and became a protégé of Walter Gropius. After the Second World War, he worked for a decade with New York-based real estate magnate Howard Zeckendorf and then went on to found Pei Cobb Freed & Partners and become one of the world's most sought-after architects. Of special significance for twenty-first century urban planning and the future of the planet, Pei's modernist philosophy and deep engagement with high-value, profitable real estate development have been validated, emulated and surpassed by official planning in China, where the pace of urbanization in the last two decades has been breathtaking (see Chapter Six).[16]

Rational–Comprehensive Planning

Underlying modern architecture, Garden City and City Beautiful movements was the theoretical premise of rational–comprehensive planning. Following Enlightenment thinking, progress was seen as the product of human reason, which made humans superior to all other species and living things. At its extreme it also accepted as "natural" inequalities among humans, which made some humans superior to others—the premise for Social Darwinism. Orientalist interpretations of scientific advances in the world presume that superior technologies leading to the industrial revolution and modern urban societies were products of superior minds—people with the unique ability to understand science and nature, think in a logical, systematic fashion, and change the world. In the centers of colonial and imperial power, reason was a necessary component of capitalist economic growth and technological advancement. It determined the winners in the global competition for resources and power. It was also fundamental to the subjugation of all other living species which, lacking reason, would be dependent on humans. Thus, today's rationally planned cities have subjugated species (pets) and tamed flora (gardens and parks).

The notion of reason that prevailed in the practice of planning was reductionist; that is, it reduced planning to a simple set of cause–effect relations. For example, if you build a sanitary, modern housing complex you will solve the social problems of the old unsanitary housing. The urban reform movement prominent in the U.S. at the beginning of the twentieth century was committed to the idea of addressing troubled, unsanitary and disorderly urban growth by transforming the built environment with housing, building and health codes, new large-scale construction, and modern urban infrastructure including roads, water and sewer lines. Robert Moses, an engineer who transformed the face of New York City over a half-century, epitomized the physical planner driven by a social mission.[17]

This kind of rationality favors quantitative over qualitative analysis and concentrates on single points in time instead of looking at phenomena in their historical context. It is linear and not systemic and prefers simplistic explanations for complex phenomena. It ignores the huge diversity of systems of thought in the world, the incredible richness in urban environments, and the everyday practices of urban planning that shape cities throughout the world.

Perhaps these narrow views of rationality were balanced by the comprehensiveness in *rational–comprehensive planning*? By exercising reason, "advanced" civilizations are presumably able to "think big"—in a *comprehensive* systemic way about all aspects of urban development. This led to the production of *master plans* for cities and metropolitan regions. The physical master plan born in the Victorian era had the imprint of architects and engineers—there was no planning profession then. Many architects and engineers produced physical plans that did not question or propose to change underlying social and economic relations even if their implementation did indeed do so. The professionals were trained to create new buildings and the new city, not to preserve or rehabilitate the old ones. Throughout the twentieth century, small towns and cities of all sizes developed comprehensive physical plans. Some were fully implemented, some were partially implemented, and some were forgotten the day after they were produced—the proverbial "plan that sits on the shelf." As a whole they were a giant experiment in making conscious determinations about the future of the city through state intervention.

By the end of the twentieth century, however, the master plan had lost much of its legitimacy. It may have had (and still has) some practical application in smaller cities with less than a half million people. But when cities became large and complex metropolitan regions, and it became increasingly difficult to both understand their present status and plot out their futures, the master plan began to lose its utility. The dramatic growth of global finance and real estate around the world also undermined many of the independent mechanisms of state involvement in land development. With the growth of the neoliberal city in the latter part of the twentieth century, master plans based on long-term visions were discredited in favor of short-term development proposals acceptable to global investors.

The criticism for focusing only on the physical city was intense, especially in the U.S. where architecture and engineering were more constrained by economic and political factors.[18] Architects and engineers began to share the stage with urban planners and social scientists, who were often trained in the "rational" methods of citizen participation so they could construct a path leading to legitimation and approval of the plan. Urban planning arose as a distinct profession separate from architecture and engineering in North America, where traditional master planning was the weakest because of the power of the FIRE sector; in centrally-planned socialist economies master plans, the rational–comprehensive orthodoxy, and physical determinism lasted longer and produced more concrete results.[19]

Towards the end of the twentieth century, *strategic planning* began to overtake the physical master plan. Strategic planning began as a planning and management tool in the Pentagon, migrated to the business world, and then was adopted by government and non-profit sectors. It was still, however, founded on the principles of rational–comprehensive planning. Planners would analyze in systematic fashion the city's strengths and weaknesses, look at opportunities and obstacles, imagine possible future scenarios and then make proposals. The planners were facilitators of discussions about planning that brought "stakeholders"—everyone with some material interest in the outcomes—to the table. The planning process remained linear and deterministic. It faithfully obeyed the narrowest principles of rationality and aspired to comprehensiveness. Strategic planning became an instrument for local governments of vastly different political stripes.[20]

Rational–comprehensive planning is a supremely technocratic approach to planning because it places the professional planner at the center of the process. It is presumed to be value-neutral and serve the "public interest" instead of special, individual or group interests. This is particularly important for orientalist planning, where there is no place for the untrained "other." Indeed, for planning to be rational and comprehensive the other *must* be invisible or objectified, and may be represented only in terms of cold statistics.

In cities sharply divided by race and class, rational–comprehensive planning avers that there must be only one plan for all. Race and class are not supposed to matter; even if they are acknowledged as factors, to envision a future where race and class matter is to perpetuate these differences. A plan that seriously discusses race is racist and one that talks about class is an invitation to class warfare. In cities where women do not have equal rights to public space, there must be only one plan for all and gender does not matter. In cities with diverse immigrant cultures, there must be only one plan for all; culture or nationality should not matter. In metropolitan landscapes constructed on land that was confiscated from indigenous people, there must be only one plan for all and to follow indigenous cultural principles would be to exclude and discriminate against the majority of the population. Indeed, the liberal supporters of rational–comprehensive planning must argue that any injection of difference is actually an invitation to expand differences, possibly racist and sexist, and not in the public interest. However, in practice, since it leaves in place the structures of unequal power, this orientalist thinking serves only to manufacture consent for the existing systems of power.

Incrementalism, Pragmatism and the Role of the State

Another important element of urban orientalism, emerging particularly in the latter part of the twentieth century, is the incrementalist and pragmatist approach to planning. Faced with the many challenges of large-scale rational–comprehensive planning, a typically North American pragmatism has entered the global scene. After the Great Transformation[21] ushered in North American capitalism at the turn of the century, the ideological battle against the more rigid structures of European classicism entered the field of urban development. With the rise of finance capital and real estate, zoning was enshrined as the premier incremental approach to land use planning. After the Bolshevik Revolution and during the Cold War, the ideological battle against centralized, state-directed planning intensified. While the landmark Chicago Master Plan of 1909 reflected a powerful appreciation for rational–comprehensive planning, New York City, already emerging as the financial and real estate capital of the world, explicitly turned away from comprehensive planning and adopted instead a regulatory system geared towards promoting incremental growth in ways that favored landowners and investors. New York became the prominent exception that proved the rule: planning should provide "rational" order to incremental growth, be limited to regulations governing the physical city (zoning), and—true to Social Darwinism—leave the social and economic order to regulate itself.[22] Incremental decision making became a landmark of municipal governance and reform. At best it was short-term planning—still somewhat "rational" and "comprehensive" and controlled by technocrats—and assumed to be the only viable approach to cities just as capitalism was the only way to organize economies.

At the height of the Cold War, some in the U.S. attacked master plans as a Soviet plot. However, there were many obvious parallels and convergences between planning in the two systems. The enormous federal interstate highway and home mortgage financing programs in the U.S. literally mapped out and determined the shape of expanding metropolitan regions; in practice it was a giant national blueprint for the organization of urban space, and it accomplished its objectives much more thoroughly than all the physical master plans that local governments managed to prepare in response. While the nature of the state on both sides of the Cold War divide differed drastically, both had approaches to the city involving substantial central direction. In the U.S., huge public subsidies and a national regulatory framework stimulated private investment and privately owned enterprises. In the socialist camp, most of the investment and enterprises were established by the state.

Contrary to many myths suggesting that there was once some invisible unplanned process of spontaneous urban growth, human settlements have always grown as conscious products of the social groups and individuals that dominated them. Planning— *the application of human consciousness to the built environment*—predated the modern metropolis and also shaped it. Thus, cities in both the capitalist and socialist camps did not evolve organically, on their own, but mostly followed the path taken since the earliest human settlements: state directed planning in one form or another. The state plays a decisive role in urban development, though that role varies widely depending on the nature of the state and its relationship to class, race and all other social dividers.[23]

As a result of the financial crises of the 1970s, neoliberalism replaced Keynesian political economy as the main foundation for capitalist development. Neoliberalism's credo called for limiting the power of government, reducing regulation, commodifying public goods and public space, reducing the role of organized labor, and downloading responsibilities from national to local governments, non-profit organizations and individuals. The hollowed out state promoted by neoliberal orthodoxy has been promoted as more rational and efficient. It claims that increased private involvement operates in the public interest.[24] Neoliberal advocates repeat well-deserved critiques of planning by the state; however, in the three decades since President Ronald Reagan and Prime Minister Margaret Thatcher declared that government was the enemy, the neoliberal claim that "There Is No Alternative" to capitalism has helped to *expand* government's role in the growth of private wealth and the protection of power and privilege by means of expanded police and military powers—fundamental elements of the modern capitalist state.

Particularly since the collapse of the socialist camp, the incrementalist/pragmatist approach advanced in the U.S. has contributed to the neoliberal reengineering of state-directed planning. Official master plans have less impact on urban development, and strategic planning is far more common. Public–private partnerships promote case-by-case short-term planning. The U.S. experiences with participatory planning are adopted to build support for and legitimize private initiatives, making the structures of representative democracy seem even more irrelevant and out of touch than ever. This has happened in the former Soviet Union (see Chapter Six). It is happening in the European Union under neoliberal leadership, which promotes an approach to governance that favors local participation and economic development, bypassing the stronger national states.[25]

Perhaps the most important change ushered in by neoliberal planning, however, is that the grand ideas of modernist town planning that promised social transformation have been largely forgotten. Indeed, post-modern urbanism consciously avoids any approach that engenders top-down, monumental or state-directed plans. As we will discuss in Chapter Seven, post-modern urbanism is still not much more than an eclectic set of pragmatic and local solutions and tends to downplay the need for fundamental, structural reforms at both local and global levels. Its critiques tend to dwell on modernism as a social and cultural phenomenon while downplaying modernism's organic link with global capitalism. For example, one of the most important post-modern trends, The New Urbanism, contributes to the suffocation of progressive utopias by limiting future visions to physical models of the built environment and the reproduction of aesthetic symbols from the past.[26] In Chapter Seven, we will show how orientalist planning that is uniquely made in America, involving enclaves, malls, gated communities and the classical "American Dream" home in the sprawled metropolis, is now a powerful new paradigm.

Planning and "The Other"

Since the emergence of modern town planning in the late Victorian era, the most widely read experts on planning history have focused on the leading role of the mostly male, European city builders—architects, engineers, political leaders and urban planners. Leonardo Benevolo's classic work, *The Origins of Modern Town Planning*,[27] while carefully linking the achievements of planning with dominant class and national interests, is Eurocentric and exemplifies the dominant narrative in planning. This was followed by other grand Eurocentric narratives, in books by Lewis Mumford and Peter Hall, for example.[28] However, even when histories included "pre-modern" urban development, the protagonists who were profiled were the rich and powerful who provided the resources to build the centers of urban power, and the technically trained elites who they contracted to build them. The ancient citadels at the center of the earliest human settlements were the subject for most discussion, particularly since the vast majority of the places where ordinary people lived and worked were built of the least sturdy materials and unable to last through the centuries to be analyzed by archaeologists and historians.

This situation changed dramatically with recent challenges to the prevailing narrative. One of the first and most important challenges to the official story was made by Jane Jacobs. Her classic work, *The Death and Life of Great American Cities*,[29] begins with a scathing attack on the arrogance of rational–comprehensive planning traditions and practices. Her critique follows firsthand engagement as an activist fighting with neighborhoods against officially-sponsored urban renewal plans. Jacobs was one of many women activists who confronted the practices of planners and sharply criticized their underlying assumptions. What many admirers of Jacobs do not know is that in some of her other less-known works she reconstructed pre-modern urban history to emphasize the powerful role of women in urban history and the relative integration of urban development and food production.[30] The latter point is critical for present-day strategies to reintegrate city and countryside, and I will return to it in the following chapters.

Leonie Sandercock has done an excellent job of outlining the challenges to rational–comprehensive planning in her powerful introductory chapter to *Making the Invisible Visible: A Multicultural Planning History*. She summarizes "the official story" of planning history and then systematically punches holes through it. Following John Friedmann, Sandercock outlines five main claims of modern planning: that it is rational, comprehensive, based on science, a function of the state, and operates in the public interest. The "invisible" others who have been protagonists in urban history include indigenous people, women, African Americans, immigrants from former colonies, and LGBT[31] communities.[32] After expanding the narrative of urban history to include all those who have shaped the city, Sandercock also expands our notion of what counts as urban planning. Instead of narrowly defining it as the technocratic or academic pursuit of order and efficiency in governance and infrastructure, Sandercock expands the realm of planning into the everyday, considering the city to be the accumulation of many small struggles, choices and rebellions.[33] Following James Holston, she calls attention to the rich history of insurgent planning that has occurred outside of the dominant, state-initiated planning and often in conflict with it. Sandercock is far from alone in this pursuit. She is joined by other critical urbanists, including June Manning Thomas, who has explored the racism imbedded in postwar urban renewal planning and the centrality of social justice to economic development planning,[34] and Dolores Hayden, who critiques the limited way urban histories are reconstructed and celebrated without including women, and connects this exclusion to the institution of urban sprawl.[35] In rejecting the totalizing discourses of mainstream urban planning theory and practice, these authors introduce elements of ethnography, historiography, and subaltern studies to the discipline, and significantly expand the boundaries of citizenship and planning.

Many contemporary theorists have explored the ways that orientalist ideas and structural inequalities around class, race, gender and sexuality shape the metropolis. Loïc Wacquant, for example, has identified the spatial and political nexus between the prison and the "ghetto" in the U.S. and elsewhere. Wacquant shows the exploding prison system to be an outgrowth of neoliberalism, and a force in the declining role of the state as a provider of services or a guarantor of rights. He is a leading critic of the "imperialist reason" behind a great deal of international research, and the hegemony of U.S. political debates in international affairs.[36]

Israeli scholar Oren Yiftachel has looked at the ways cities and states are planned and constructed to promote racial difference. His work has unearthed the orientalism behind the urbanization of Israel/Palestine, South Africa, Austria, Estonia and Sri Lanka, and demonstrated the way colonial mentalities are realized in space. His work in Israel also deconstructs the ways racial privilege is stratified within an "ethnocracy," where groups like Jewish Russian immigrants represent a "gray area," receiving privileges over Palestinians but facing discrimination by more privileged native-born Ashkenazy Israelis. In a broader sense, Yiftachel's work, like that of Sandercock and Jacobs, represents a return to the focus on issues of power, inequality and political economy. This moves away from another trend, "communicative planning," that emphasizes the planner's role in facilitating dialogue and consensus-building.[37]

After adding up the multiple critiques of modern planning history and theory, the question then arises—what really did happen in cities if planning was so weak? The truth is that most cities throughout history were built, managed and run by the people who lived there. Most housing has been built by residents, and calling them "slums" did not change that fact. Most of the exchanges between humans in settlements have not been commercial but personal. Most cultural life, except for that which is financed and manufactured by the ruling classes, is based in the lives of local and regional clans and communities, and expresses the joys and miseries of life as experienced by the majority of the population. The cultures and urban lives of people who have been colonized or whose nations have been occupied by others invariably change but also quite often survive. In other words, to have an accurate understanding of urban history we must understand everyday life as experienced by "the others." If the critical problems of cities in the twentieth century are to be unraveled we will need to undo urban orientalism, and that requires acknowledging the agency of "the other"—the African, Asian, Latin American, rural, feminine other, and all the others.

Many organizers and scholars working today toward a non-orientalist urbanism are inspired by the work of French philosopher and sociologist Henri Lefebvre. Lefebvre analyzed the "social production of space," and argued for a geographic analysis of class inequalities in urban life. He looked for evidence of these structural inequalities in the fabric of everyday life and the physical layout of urban areas. In a hugely influential work, Lefebvre argued that everyday people, and not just economic and political elites, have a "right to the city," and, crucially, a right to change and reshape the city.[38] This line of thought both came out of and helped inspire urban revolutions in France and elsewhere, and is today the common rallying cry among organizers throughout the world from disparate circumstances, fighting everything from eviction and foreclosure to equal access to public space.[39] However, it remains to be seen how deeply the right to the city analysis will go and whether it will move beyond its European origins and incorporate the diverse insurgent histories, cultures and planning practices around the world.

While the characterization of the majority of the world's population as an "other" is problematic, to say the least, it does suggest possibilities for organizing against neocolonial projects and orientalist frameworks for urbanization. In the last decade, as corporate globalization and technological interconnectivity flourished, the possibilities for global social movements grew in equal measure. While neoliberals argued that history had come to an end and alternatives to capitalism were dead on arrival, movements against structural adjustment and neoliberal shock therapy swept the globe. After the stunning disruption of the International Monetary Fund meeting in Seattle in 1999, the World Social Forum was born in Brazil in 2001, bringing together heterodox social movements from around the world under the banner, "Another World Is Possible." These movements have taken on international finance and militarism, while also fighting local struggles around urban land, food production, water, transportation and access to housing. Their decentralized, cosmopolitan influence can be felt in the rebellions currently sweeping North Africa and Persian Gulf nations, the Zapatista rebellion in Mexico, and the indigenous rebellion against water privatization in Bolivia, to mention only a few examples. In addition to challenging unchecked capital accumulation, militarism and racism, contemporary movements are confronting the way urbanization is taking place and asserting the right of all people to shape their cities and their futures. It remains to be seen whether and how they will evolve.

Left to its own resorts, orientalist planning is driving the human race towards catastrophe and possible collapse resulting from climate change. The orientalist system of urban planning has constructed a dualist world with the false divisions between east and west, the global North and global South, while ignoring the very real inequalities of wealth and power that separate the privileged from the global majority. It is absolutely necessary, as we argue in the final chapters, that "the others," in all their diversity and complexity, gain political power, learn from each other's everyday practices, and begin to cross the vast language and cultural barriers and engage in dialogues about the best methods for sustaining human life on earth. We will need to turn on its head the foolish modernist prejudices that traditional ways of life are by definition backward; we must learn from the many theories and practices that were for millennia premised on the unity of all life, human and otherwise; ecological and systemic thinking and not reductionist, dualist or linear logic. For this listening and learning to occur, there must also be a deeper change in economic and political power relations, a tall order but one that may be forced on us by climate change, a deep capitalist crisis, and the exhaustion of the current models governing human development.

Chapter 3

Urban and Rural Dependencies and Divides

Those of us living and working in the global North must struggle to look at the world from the vantage point of the majority of urban dwellers, who live in Africa, Asia and Latin America and are the objects of orientalist myths that permeate our discussions. These myths portray the "underdeveloped" metropolis as a collection of giant, chaotic, unsanitary, and dangerous "slums," a homogenous and undifferentiated landscape inhabited by "the other." The myths lead to policies that blame the other for urban problems and perpetuate structural inequalities (see Chapters One and Two).

Urban orientalism isn't just an ideological or cultural phenomenon; it has a material basis in the real world and helps shape that world. The actually existing foundation for urban orientalism is what we will call *dependent urbanization*. In the post-colonial world the myths of planning, orientalism, the city and metropolis are shaped by a consistent historical and material factor: economic dependency on the leading centers of global capitalism. The metropolises throughout Africa, Asia and Latin America have unique and diverse histories, cultures and geographies, but their development continues to depend in varying degrees on outside forces, much as it did under colonialism. This dependence, not cultural or individual behavior, explains most of the global inequalities between urban and rural areas, and among and within metropolitan regions. In the current era of increased global interdependence, dependent urbanization has been reconfigured and in some emerging economies reduced, but it nonetheless remains a powerful defining factor.

In this chapter we will show how and upon whom local capital and labor are dependent, how rural societies are underdeveloped and sharply divided from urban life, and how land and the reproduction of both labor and life itself are commodified, expanding environmental and social inequalities. These are evident in the global crises of food security and food sovereignty. Global and local social movements, however, are advancing progressive new approaches as they struggle to gain control of both rural and urban land and democratize them. This can be the basis for a new, independent and more environmentally sound and just approach to the city of the twenty-first century (for examples, see the following chapters).

Dependent Urbanization

Dependent urbanization is a product of economic and political dependency and an essential component of global capitalism. Contrary to the urban fallacy (see

Chapter One), the problem is not urbanization itself but economic dependency. Simply put, the local economy depends on the export of a limited number of products and services. The cities where this production for export is located attract large numbers of migrants from rural areas who are seeking work, resulting in greater inequalities between urban and rural areas and within urban areas. As "poor" as the new urban migrants may be, they are relatively better off than people living in rural areas where local subsistence production is undermined by industrialized agriculture that produces for the capitalist marketplace. These social differences are most acutely felt in the production and distribution of food; dependent urbanization leads to crises in food supply, food insecurity and widespread food-related health crises. Thus dependent urbanization is not simply the dependency of one group of human settlements on others; it is a reflection in space of unequal economic and social relations of power.

Dependent urbanization spans the history of colonialism, industrial capitalism and imperialism. It arose when cities, regions and nations, subject to the powerful influence or direct rule of foreign powers, specialized in the production of a small number of commodities for export to feed the markets in "the mother countries," which are today the centers of post-colonial and imperial power. This pattern is rationalized by the economic theory of *comparative advantage*, which basically says that nations should specialize in the production and export of the products they are endowed with (by nature) and that get the highest prices on the global marketplace. This theory rationalizes the stereotypical banana republic that sells itself for a single global commodity. Thus, Honduras, for example, will do the right and natural thing by producing bananas in huge quantities for export because it will supposedly increase the wealth of Hondurans.[1] That the banana market is monopolized by a U.S.-based corporation is also considered natural and necessary to the realization of Honduras' comparative advantage. The theory of comparative advantage was hatched by European economist David Ricardo in 1817[2] and rationalized the plunder by the European powers of gold, spices and exotic foods from the colonies. After formal independence of the colonies new elite groups sympathetic to and financially engaged with Europe continued to give priority to a small number of export products. Comparative advantage ignored and undervalued the subsistence needs of the population and assumed that the greatest values would be achieved in a global market, which was of course controlled by the wealthiest and most powerful nations. In short, dependent economies are organized first of all to maximize income by exporting selected products and only secondarily to meet the needs of their own populations. This very simple and basic historic truth has had a determining effect on the location and growth of cities. Most of the major metropolitan areas in Asia, Africa and Latin America, for example, grew up around ports that were established by colonial powers to facilitate international trade. The new cities often replaced or overtook in importance pre-existing settlements. The ones that developed into large metropolitan areas today—such as Lagos and Lima, for example, have assumed economic livelihoods of their own in local and national markets, however limited, that today often define them as much as their global trading function.

Dependent urbanization did not spring up from nowhere in the period of European colonialism. It began with and followed the concentration of capital throughout history, before the emergence of capitalism. In the earliest towns and cities, in Mesopotamia and the Indus Valley, wealthy families and individuals stored agricultural surplus in their private enclaves, thereby controlling access to food. They built fortifications to protect their wealth and financed groups of loyal supporters to administer distribution of the bounty and armies to protect it from attack. They supported the ideologies and religions that made their rule appear to be natural and even eternal. The majority of the urban population depended on them for survival and protection. However, as trade expanded and became globalized through thousands of years of human history, dependencies were also globalized.

With the rise of modern capitalism, the structure of these economic dependencies changed. As cities developed specialized craft, industrial and commercial activities, more and more people left their villages seeking out the promise of higher incomes and better living conditions in the cities. This movement from the countryside to the city, however, was not simply a product of individual will or economic growth; it was and remains a feature of systemic economic inequality, particularly in regimes with relatively flexible, dynamic and unregulated capital flows. For example, the mobility of capital and labor, and the level of urbanization, has been exceptionally high in the U.S. as compared to many parts of Europe. There, and in the socialist countries of the twentieth century, levels of urbanization were lower than in the U.S. because powerful states, sometimes encumbered by feudal remnants, invested heavily in small towns and cities and migration to cities was minimized; or migration was limited due to government regulation of capital and land, and because of universal access to education, health care and other social benefits, which took away a major incentive for migration.

Socialist countries in the twentieth century regulated both capital and labor flows through central economic planning and universal social benefits. For example, during the 50 years since the Cuban Revolution in 1961, the capital city of Havana was the only major city in Latin America that remained fairly stable in size relative to other cities. This was the result of a consciously planned redistribution of state investments that established universal access to health care and education throughout the country and targeted urban investments to provincial capitals and rural areas, and relatively less to the once-favored capital city. Cuba's more balanced pattern of urban growth had less to do with the work of the professional urban planners and everything to do with the decisions made by economic planners.[3] This pattern closely followed that of other socialist nations in the twentieth century, where levels of urbanization were not as great as among capitalist nations (see Chapter Six).

Dependent urbanization is not just a function of population distribution and economic inequality. It is also a result of environmental inequalities and injustice. The dependent metropolis has the greatest environmental burdens and weakest regulatory mechanisms to control them. For example, Mexico City is filled with old polluting cars that would normally be banned from streets in U.S. cities, where in fact many of them come from; as a result air pollution and its health impacts are greater in Mexico than across the border in the U.S. where the auto manufacturers and their owners have their corporate headquarters. In Venezuela, a post-colonial nation with an economy dependent on oil exports, the cities are choked with traffic while the minority of auto owners benefit from steep public road and fuel subsidies and the lowest gasoline prices in the world. The majority of the population, who can't afford air conditioning in their homes or cars, breathe in the fumes since they do not own cars and are forced to make their way on foot through heavy traffic in cities designed for the car, or in loud, polluting buses.[4] Thus dependent urbanization appropriates environmental benefits for the most powerful and distributes the negative environmental impacts to the weakest. This raises a serious question about strategies to address global environmental problems and climate change: will they create safer and healthier environments only for wealthy cities and nations and leave others at the mercy of pollution and floods?[5]

There is an important difference between *unequal* and *uneven* development, as also noted in Chapter Seven. Since the establishment of the earliest human settlements, urban development has been *uneven*. It occurred first in certain parts of the world due to the convergence of a complex array of geographic and climatological factors that led to surpluses in agricultural production, active commerce and improvements in the overall standard of living. Uneven economic and spatial development are inevitable because differences in climate and resources throughout the world are the norm. Plagues, natural disasters, and limits on the supply of resources have produced widely uneven outcomes for cities.

But *unequal* urban development is quite different. It is an outgrowth of the social, economic and political divisions that emerged as cities began to develop. Unequal distribution of the surplus produced more lasting territorial divisions based on class and ethnicity, and these are institutionalized through the use of force. These inequalities have evolved over centuries into the global system of dependent capitalism.

The reality of dependent urbanization is obscured by the myths of urban orientalism. Orientalist mythology sees cities with mass poverty as unfortunate victims of time in societies that just haven't caught up yet with the developed world. Following U.S. economist Walt Rostow's development theory, which breaks the process into five phases that more or less replicate the development process in the U.S. and Europe, post-colonial nations are thought to be stuck in an early stage of economic growth and waiting to "take off" in the inevitable march of capitalist progress, just like the colonial powers themselves did.[6] Others see them as suffering from a "culture lag" or a "culture of poverty," crippled by tradition and moral inadequacies.[7] Orientalist planning is consistent with and flows from such theories. It ignores durable and structural economic and political inequalities that underlie urban patterns and focuses instead on "the poor" and the behavior of people who live and work in "slums." As a result, the problems of cities can be solved by waiting until the "slums" become obsolete and naturally disappear as "development" trickles down to them; or the whole process can be accelerated by getting rid of the "slums" using public and private redevelopment schemes, thereby forcing people into "better" habitats that make them behave differently. The new, modern, rationally-planned and sanitized enclaves, created in the image of the metropolis of the dominant world powers, are thus presented as evidence of the inexorable march towards the ideal of urban development without poverty or the "slums."

One of the most critical elements in dependent urbanization is the way land is treated. Even in countries that have powerful indigenous systems of communal land tenure, dependent urbanization transforms all land into a commodity to be sold on the market. Thus in African nations that have traditions that associate urban places with ancestors and family histories, the globalized metropolis has converted them to real estate. While the conversion is never complete and remnants of communal land tenure do linger, dependent urbanization brings land into the circuit of capitalist reproduction. This makes possible the development of new enclaves and the full transformation of urban space into a commodity. The commodification of land is most intense, however, in the global centers of financial capital, where surplus capital seeks local places for safe keeping and reproduction. Outside these centers many other practices and traditions continue to function at the margins of global capitalism.

Dependent Labor: The Metropolis as Flexible Labor Reserve

As mentioned in the first chapter, the movement of surplus capital across the globe is one of the main determinants of the size and pace of urbanization. In general, labor follows capital to and from cities. At the same time labor shapes cities through its everyday practices, organizing and bottom-up planning, and constrains the movement of capital.

While labor generally migrates with capital, capital also creates huge *labor reserves*, much larger than the labor force it needs at any given time. This reserve army of labor suppresses overall wages and increases the power of employers to hire, fire and control the labor force. This is not what is commonly called "urbanization without industrialization," a misnomer because industrial economies have been behind all urbanization for over a century; it is urbanization with more labor than can be gainfully employed in salaried, relatively permanent jobs. This creates what is often called an "informal" sector of the economy, which is nothing more than the large pool of people working in services at low pay. The informal sector supports workers in the "formal" sector and also helps depress wages overall. Dependent urbanization breeds excess labor and is one of the main reasons why metropolitan population grows even faster than its local economy, and why so many of the world's largest cities are in less "developed" nations. The unequal distribution of capital produces an unequal distribution of labor, and also creates an excess of labor in the metropolis.

The reserve labor pool suppresses wages across the board. It suppresses wages in export-led industries, thus reducing costs to global and local capital. However, it also affects wages in the much larger service sectors, including local retailing and personal services. The large excess labor force in services further reduces wages in all sectors of the economy. A large labor reserve helps reduce both the cost of labor and the cost of reproducing labor. Low costs for housing, food and clothing, for example, reduce the amount employers need to pay for labor. Widespread environmental, public health and quality of life problems further devalue labor but for capital these are "external" costs paid for with the lives and well-being of a cheap workforce.

Women make up a disproportionately large segment of the labor reserve. They are generally among the lowest paid sectors of both the formal and informal workforces. Their unpaid labor is essential for reducing the costs of labor force reproduction and lowering overall wages. Women are at the core of the labor reserve and therefore struggles for women's rights are critical to the right to the city movement.

Dependent urbanization thus thrives on the maintenance of poor living conditions because they reduce the demand for higher wages, especially for women. If people are living in shacks that were pieced together with cheap building materials and unpaid labor and they pay no rent, employers can pay them less. If they don't have to pay for basic municipal services because there are no services, then employers can pay them less. Thus capital thrives in cities where the majority of people live without adequate housing and public services—that is in most of the cities of the world.[8] The problem is not that they lack for capital; the problem *is* capital! "Slums" and "mass poverty" are quite useful for global capital, contrary to the handwringing of their charitable institutions (that is until the land occupied by the "slums" becomes valuable real estate and removing poor people becomes the preferred solution). The World Bank's "pro-poor" strategy and the UN Millenium goals aim to mitigate the negative effects of a global economy whose basic functioning they fully support and never question.[9]

The latest wave of globalization beginning in the latter part of the twentieth century helped to intensify the *transnationalization* of the surplus labor force. Modern communications and transportation technology now make it possible for capital to access labor reserves in a flexible way, for short periods of time from a few months to a few years.[10] The more "developed" nations of the world can temporarily tap into labor reserves by encouraging immigration whenever their own labor costs rise due to unionization and improved living conditions for workers. Outsourcing in manufacturing and services is a way to maximize benefits to private capital from global labor reserves, which are basically "economy rentals" parked in metropolitan regions across the world.[11]

One product of transnational labor mobility is *the remittance economy*. Immigrant workers, particularly those who migrate without their families, send large portions of their earnings back home. These remittances make up the majority of national income in several nations. For example, remittances account for 30 percent of Haiti's GDP, three times more than all foreign direct investment and foreign aid combined; remittances to Latin America total $58.9 billion annually.[12] The remittance economy works because of the suppressed standard of living for both the migrant workers in the wealthy nations and their families in their home countries.

The transnationalized system benefits both capital and labor in the "developed" nations, though unequally. For example, the outsourcing of computer services from the U.S. to India helps to lower the cost of certain goods and services in the U.S., benefiting both producers and consumers. The cost of educating Indian engineers and computer scientists is mostly paid for by the Indian taxpayers so that outsourcing effectively appropriates these expenditures to benefit Western companies and consumers. The unpaid labor of women and the relatively low cost of housing and urban amenities in Indian cities reduce labor reproduction costs. However, while consumers in wealthier nations may benefit in the short term by having access to cheaper goods and services, in the end these benefits are illusory. The price savings eventually boomerang and effectively reduce the cost of reproducing labor in the wealthier countries, lowering overall wages there. For example, Wal-Mart, the largest corporation in the world, competes with other retailers to keep prices low, but low prices from big retail increase pressures to lower wages overall. It is no coincidence that wherever Wal-Mart goes wages also go down. When Wal-Mart enters a local labor market they actually reduce the number of jobs and overall wage levels. Wal-Mart's employees are poorly paid, prevented from forming unions, and subject to gender and racial discrimination.[13] Wal-Mart and its competitors enter a race to the bottom. All consumers end up paying the high price of cheap imported goods when they see their wages decline. Thus, as we have argued consistently, *it is the relationship between capital and labor, not just their location in different cities or nations, that really matters.*

To maintain the system of transnationalized labor, the wealthier nations are increasingly concerned about keeping tight control over migration and the conditions immigrants live in. Anti-immigrant and xenophobic movements arise from the competition for jobs and housing and have become convenient instruments for insuring state control over immigration flows. The Northern League in Italy, the National Front in France, and The Tea Party in the U.S. are important political movements affecting immigration policies in their respective nations. They advocate limits to immigration, services, and rights, all of which keep down wages and benefits.

Workers who migrate to Europe and North America, and increasingly to less "developed" nations where they work in transnational industries, are the most prominent of urban "others." They work under the most precarious and difficult conditions without basic human rights. For example, 400,000 children work as laborers on U.S. farms without basic rights and protections guaranteed to U.S. citizens. They are subject to ethnic and racial discrimination, excluded from many places in the metropolis, and lack any rights to the city.[14]

Rural Dependency and the Urban–Rural Divides

If the world continues to urbanize at the current rate, by the end of the century most people will live in cities. Very few will reside in rural areas. This assumes, of course, that global climate change or other environmental challenges will not change everything. With our rose-colored glasses tightly fixed over our noses, we might celebrate such an urban world. We might consider the disappearance of villages and towns a victory for human progress and the triumph of modern development. The huge social inequalities between urban and rural areas will disappear because there will be practically nobody left in rural areas. After all, isn't it true that the standard of living, life expectancy, and access to education and health care are generally better in cities? Cities offer an array of diverse economic and cultural opportunities not found in rural areas. Even with a population of more than 10 billion by the end of the twenty-first century, concentrating that number of people in metropolitan areas would still only use up less than 1 percent of the earth's surface for human habitation. And if the full economies of scale in resource use could be achieved as a result of new technologies, metropolitan regions would consume fewer non-renewable resources (per capita and per square mile), thereby averting more serious environmental and resource problems. In this optimistic future scenario, the outsized carbon footprints of metropolitan areas would shrink thanks to solar and wind technology, biofuels, electric vehicles and a host of other, yet undiscovered, technological innovations.

With these bright prospects for an urban future why would we not want a world of metropolises? Why would we not encourage it? Surely this would be a more practical and realistic approach than dispersing and deconcentrating urban populations and going back to small town life? In any case, in the nearly two centuries since the Industrial Revolution in Europe, all efforts to disperse urban populations have produced minimal results and instead fed suburbanization and the expansion of metropolitan regions at their peripheries. Far from favoring or repopulating rural areas, metropolitan growth has consumed them.

If we take off the rose-colored glasses, however, we find many unrealistic assumptions leading to this urban panacea. First, climate change continues to proceed while the world's largest greenhouse gas producers are moving extremely slowly towards corrective measures. International efforts to reduce carbon emissions following the 1997 Kyoto Protocol have faltered and even its modest goals have not been achieved.[15] The most urbanized nations in Europe and the Americas continue to be the largest sources of greenhouse gases, and rapidly urbanizing nations in Asia—China in particular—are increasing their carbon footprints. Sharp economic and political divisions led to the breakdown of recent climate talks in Copenhagen (2009) and Cancún (2010). The pioneering launch of an alternative initiative at the 2010 climate justice summit in Cochabamba, Bolivia, focused squarely on uniting the less powerful nations and people behind a more ambitious agenda, but has yet to be recognized by the most powerful nations and global institutions.[16] Meanwhile, the polar ice caps are melting. Temperatures could rise beyond five degrees centigrade by the end of the century (a modest estimate). Severe weather changes and a rise in sea level could result in the displacement of urban populations in some parts of the world (top candidates are coastal cities, in both the centers and peripheries of global capital). In 2008 and again in 2011, crises in food security that were partially fed by severe weather events possibly associated with climate change contributed to popular uprisings in parts of Africa, Asia and the Middle East.

Second, the technological fixes promoted by "green" venture capitalists as panaceas against climate change may yield only marginal environmental benefits and could make things worse. For example, the host of "alternative fuels" being proposed to power motor vehicles—including ethanol and other biofuels—only offer a new lease on life for the least efficient mode of urban transportation, the automobile. Ethanol from corn used to fuel autos, far from being a fix, is more carbon-intensive than regular gasoline.[17] Continuing public subsidies of all fuels will encourage more auto use, exacerbate air pollution and public health impacts, make the quality of life in cities worse, and expand the likelihood of catastrophic climate changes.

In sum, the combination of global climate change and a declining urban quality of life could very well force even the pragmatic to confront other possible scenarios. Throughout history there have been unpredicted collapses of human societies spurred by climate change, resource depletion and unsustainable human practices. There have also been major shifts of population due to wars, uncontrolled epidemics, tribal and political conflict. Conscious human decisions can and have been made to prevent collapse, but it requires clear forethought about the long-term consequences to human society.[18] In a world dominated by short-term, pragmatic decision making, this is problematic. The notion that modern society has a built-in protection against natural disasters is not only a powerful human conceit, but it is built into the logic of inevitable urbanization in the metropolitan era and its capitalist and orientalist premises.

Rural Enclaves in the Metropolitan World

The industrial cities in Europe and America physically separated city and countryside but also led to giant inequalities between them. The dominant economic activity, agriculture, was subdued and pressed into serving producers and consumers in the modern city. Today, 70 percent of all food consumed in metropolitan areas is produced elsewhere; and in wealthier nations, where urban and peri-urban real estate pushes farming away, the food coming from "elsewhere" includes a relatively large proportion of cheap imported food. Urban industry needed large-scale agriculture to sustain and reproduce labor; banks financed capital-intensive agriculture to reduce food costs and thus the cost of reproducing labor. Consumers, themselves unable to affect the new world they were part of, also believed that they benefited from cheap food and freedom from the hard work needed to produce it.

Following industry and finance, urban planning turned its back entirely on the rural and singularly focused on the new urban society. Rural traditions, in which land retained significant use value and was a habitat for a diverse array of species other than humans, were left behind. The land became a physical object, the exclusive site for human activity, and a commodity. Urban land was alien and superior to rural land, rural life, other species and food production. In sum, rural areas became dependent and unequal.

The vanishing species and contaminated land in today's metropolitan world suggest the depth of *rural dependency*. Since the rise of the metropolis there has been a corresponding decline in the viability of rural areas as places for human habitation and the maintenance of biodiversity. The history of the vanishing village is filled with struggles to sustain livelihoods intimately connected to the land and other living species, the production of food and reproduction of living things. It includes many calls for alternative rural scenarios, from Julius Nyrere's *Ujamaa* in Tanzania[19] to the village in Gandhi's *hind svaraj* (see Chapter Four), and today's rural advocates belonging to organizations such as *Via Campesina*.[20] We will return to these in the final chapter. For now let us probe deeper into the past and present of rural areas.

Figure 3.1 Modern Tokyo and Rural Relic

If the recent past is any indication of the near future, rural land in the twenty-first century will become the nearly exclusive domain of a small number of large corporations and state-owned entities and even more alienated from the everyday lives of the human population. The experience of the U.S. may foretell the global future: less than 1 percent of the population works in agriculture and just 16 percent live in rural areas as defined by the U.S. Census. In Europe the proportion is less dramatic—4.7 percent work in agriculture and just over one-quarter live in rural areas.[21] In the Organisation for Economic Co-operation and Development (OECD) countries the proportion is 23 percent rural. The U.S. addiction to processed food with excessively high proportions of animal fat, sugar and salt, and the addiction to fast food (and fast cars, fast electronic devices, and fast living) is connected to rapidly rising rates of obesity (two-thirds of the population is obese or over-weight), diabetes, stress, and drug abuse. Most food sold in the U.S. is a product of a handful of monocultures—corn, soy, wheat and beef.[22]

In contrast, village life and village food is generally "slow." India, traditionally known as a nation of villages and today one of the last major rural nations, has a history of wide diversity in native seeds and products, farming for local markets, and minimum use of non-renewable fossil fuels. However, Raj Patel spells out the gloomy picture for Indian farmers in the chapter from his book, *Stuffed and Starved*, which he titles "A Rural Autopsy." Patel rejects any idealistic picture of bucolic village life and talks instead about the lives of hard work, food shortages, malnutrition, debt, despair, and suicide.[23] Some of these conditions were inherited but they got worse under British rule, and especially since India opened up to global capitalism in recent decades. Under this sustained siege, without drastic political change the village cannot possibly survive (see Chapter Four).

The commodification of rural land at the service of urban development is a major contributor to global climate change, species loss and desertification. Small-scale local agriculture almost invariably has a smaller carbon footprint than extensive, industrialized agriculture. Currently about 40 percent of the earth's land surface is desert and by 2025 predictions are that roughly 70 percent will be desertified due to the practices of global agricultural and forestry industries.[24] This will place even greater pressure on the remaining land to produce food for a growing world population. Today, only 31 percent of the land surface in the world is cultivable and 11 percent is cultivated.[25] There is potential for this to grow to meet future needs. Contrary to the alarmist neo-Malthusian predictions that the world's food supply will be unable to keep up with population growth, the more likely scenario is that an increasing proportion of food will be produced using capital-intensive systems of industrial agriculture requiring minimum human labor, using chemical inputs, mechanization, and genetically modified seeds. All of this will result in an even greater concentration of production in the hands of a small number of producers—corporations and global investors. The expanded proportion of food produced by the industrial system will make the food supply more vulnerable to climate disruptions, natural disasters, and fluctuations in commodity and capital markets. It will increase food insecurity.

The 2008 food crisis, in part a result of uncontrolled urbanization and the advance of industrial agriculture,[26] has also stimulated a dramatic new trend of post-colonial land grabs and economic dependencies that represent a major step towards the elimination of the remaining villages and rural life in the world. Equity funds and investor groups from Europe, the U.S., oil-producing nations in the Middle East, and China, among others, are buying up rural land in parts of Africa, Asia and Latin America, ignoring and displacing indigenous agricultural producers. They are producing a new generation of industrialized agriculture serving powerful urban markets and increasing rural dependency.[27]

Currently, only some 13 percent of the earth's surface (excluding water bodies) is preserved as wilderness areas and centers of biodiversity.[28] Preserved "natural" enclaves, often financed and run by the state or multilateral organizations, retain for capital the power to shape and contain nature and insure its long-term accessibility. One of the main mechanisms for this form of "fortress conservation" is the United Nations' Biosphere Reserve program. The program, active since the early 1970s, has set aside 580 sites in 114 countries. Nature preserves may be excellent "biospheres" that are internally rich and diverse with natural species. But they can also be used as highly controlled museums, recreation areas, and breeding grounds for marketable species, and leave vulnerable everything that lives outside these enclaves.

Already in the U.S., where the national government is the largest single property owner, public land reserves are a valuable resource for private land developers and leased to mining and forestry enterprises. Oil, gas, coal and mineral deposits serve the growing demands for energy in metropolitan areas, and the corporations that mine them are highly concentrated in Europe and the Americas and transnational in reach. Canadian mining companies, for example, control 60 percent of all mining in the world. In the latest rush to appropriate underground resources to feed the urban energy markets, mining companies in the U.S. and some places in Europe are using a new technology known as hydraulic fracturing—or "fracking"—that reaches deep subsurface deposits of natural gas by injecting a chemical-laden mixture to release the gas for extraction. This has spurred protest, especially in areas where fracking can pollute aquifers used for drinking water. It is but the latest example of how capitalist growth requires exploiting even more natural resources to feed the urban consumption machine.[29]

During the rise of the metropolis, the most important economic activities in rural areas were mining and agriculture. Mining has produced a fairly unstable and dependent form of urbanization in the countryside. Mining towns come and go as enterprising speculators and mining companies extract all that can be sold on the market. Market and technological changes can easily make mines and their communities obsolete. Mining became a leading economic sector in colonial and postcolonial regimes that had no stake in creating sustainable communities, only extracting valuable ores for export. The long histories of striking miners in Bolivia and South Africa, for example, show how politically conscious miners conclude that mines feeding foreign-owned industries create dependent development.[30]

The key to the growth of human settlements over the millennia has been a surplus in food production. Sedentary agriculture in the Neolithic era created abundant surpluses that consolidated village life and allowed it to grow. Food surpluses led to the expansion of commerce, including markets within cities and long-distance trading in those food items that could be preserved. Food production was essential to both rural and urban life for millennia until industrial capitalism transformed it into a relatively exclusive tool of global monopolies serving urban life.

Rural areas were abandoned to agribusiness, capital-intensive farming, and the green revolution in the age of the metropolis. John Bellamy Foster explains this process as a consequence of capitalist growth. He traces it to what Karl Marx called a "metabolic rift" caused by capitalist development—a sharp break in the relationship between humanity and nature resulting from the changes in nineteenth century agriculture stimulated by the growth of capitalism. Marx observed the depletion of soil nutrients in rural areas due to the production of larger volumes of food to serve the burgeoning industrial cities. The metabolic rift depleted the soil and left it unable to regenerate as it had after centuries of subsistence agriculture based on regenerative practices (though of course not all practices were regenerative). In addition, capitalist control over agriculture was responsible for the loss of the commons—the appropriation of land that was shared among villagers by private property owners who treat it as a commodity.[31] Agricultural land, therefore, became real estate. When it was at the periphery of expanding metropolitan areas it became very valuable real estate and used for condominiums instead of agriculture.

One of the most dramatic examples of the way that urban and rural dependencies emerged in tandem with soil depletion and neo-colonialism is the story, related by Foster, of *guano*. Guano, the excrement from birds living on islands off the coast of Peru, was mined by British companies able to take advantage of the weaker economic and political regimes that followed formal independence from Spain in the early nineteenth century. Guano was exported to Great Britain under favorable terms to replenish the soils of Great Britain that were depleted by extensive agricultural practices.[32] It distorted Peru's economy but eventually ended with the depletion of guano, leaving Peru without this important source of income and prodding Britain to seek other sources of fertilizer including chemical products. Guano, like gold before it, was Peru's "comparative advantage," to use Ricardo's orientalist theory. After the collapse of the guano market, Peru's oligarchy then substituted cane sugar (until that market collapsed) and petroleum.

Foster also calls attention to Marx's analysis of capitalism's tendency to devalue nature except when it can be turned into a commodity. This belies the unfounded claims that Marxist theory is thoroughly wedded to the Enlightenment conceit of human superiority over nature and blind industrialization. Foster cites a key passage from Marx's *Critique of the Gotha Program*: "Labor is not the source of all wealth. Nature is just as much the source of use values (and it is surely of such that material wealth consists!) as is labor, which itself is only the manifestation of a natural force, human labor power."[33] Foster also argues that Marxism departs from the mainstream labor theory of value which sees labor as the *only* source of value; Marx vehemently argued against this physiocratic view and affirmed the importance of use values, especially including the values found in natural life.[34]

Foster outlines three modern agricultural revolutions: a first revolution that evolved over centuries leading to enclosures, local markets, crop rotation and other regenerative practices; the second, between 1830 and 1880, was stimulated by the growth of artificial fertilizers; the third, in the twentieth century, was the most dramatic (coinciding, as we have noted many times, with the revolutionary period of metropolitan growth) and involved mechanization (tractors replacing animals, large-scale processing in factories), more intensive chemical fertilizers, herbicides and pesticides, and the production of monocultures.[35]

In the development and maturation of rural dependency, city planning played an important ideological and political role. City planning turned its back on rural life.

Most visions of the good city objectified, domesticated, controlled and tamed rural life, subordinating it to capital and real estate and the grand narrative of the human-centered city. This anti-rural bias was not simply ideological, or an unintended consequence of "progress," because it also served the political interests of capitalists, who created and required a mass of urban labor and had no use for an idle rural population divorced from the metropolitan machines of production and mass consumption.

The "green revolution" of the twentieth century claimed to solve the problems of global inequality, poverty and hunger by introducing modern farm machinery to increase productivity, artificial fertilizers, insecticides and pesticides, and promoting large-scale rural irrigation and development projects. The green revolution was to be a technological fix for the more profound economic and ecological rift generated by global capitalism. Instead it produced greater dependency by farmers on imported machinery and inputs and resulted in the decline of small-scale agriculture. The latest technological fix is genetically modified organisms (GMOs), introduced by a few global corporations (including Monsanto, Syngenta and Bayer). GMOs are promoted as boosting output, reducing the need for chemical inputs, and saving the world from hunger and malnutrition. However, as Vandana Shiva and many others have argued, GMOs are but the latest device to promote monocultures, monopolize seed production and other inputs, and secure monopoly control over agricultural production; in many cases they produce less than "conventional" farming in the village. Monsanto, the world's largest producer of GMOs, aims to patent seeds, including those now saved by individual farmers, to increase its control of the market and most reproductive plant life. It aggressively markets GMO seeds that are supposed to be resistant to its insecticide Roundup, but this has encouraged the use of chemicals, damaged crops, poisoned the soil, and raised serious questions about the long-term environmental and public health consequences of GMOs.[36]

Industrial agriculture and the "green" revolution have helped to make rural areas invisible to most of the world. The rural is becoming a factory for urban areas, a natural preserve for capital and a place for leisure enclaves. As argued again in the final chapter, one of the most important challenges for urban planning in this century is confronting urban and rural inequalities, developing new conceptions of both urban and rural, and radically rethinking the fundamental means for meeting basic human needs for food, housing and a quality of life. In an almost entirely urban world, every urban planner should also be a rural planner. Urban planning must incorporate planning for food systems and food sovereignty, which means returning control over the production and distribution of food to people who consume it. This is part of the unfinished business of national sovereignty in the post-colonial world and a part of breaking out of dependent capitalism and dependent urbanization.

Orientalist Metropolitan Planning

Over the years a host of orientalist strategies have emerged that propose to address the spatial inequalities resulting from export-led dependent urbanization. These strategies attempt to address what is often referred to as "imbalanced urbanization": the dramatic growth of large metropolitan regions with huge populations lacking basic urban services, the relatively limited growth of intermediate cities, and the rapid depopulation of the countryside. One symptom of this imbalance is the "primate city" phenomenon: a nation's largest city is many times larger than the next largest cities. For example, Peru's largest city, Lima, is about eight times as large as the second largest city, Arequipa. This is often compared to the distribution of city sizes in "developed" countries, which are more even and balanced. While the primate city phenomenon has been widely criticized as having little relationship to economic development, equity or the quality of urban life, and is contradicted by examples of primate cities in developed countries, attempts to reduce the relative disparities in size have still been touted as important economic development strategies. These fall into the trap of the urban fallacy by confusing urban and spatial phenomena with economic and social ones. They are orientalist because they present schematic solutions that originate in the centers of global power to address the problems as perceived by the powerful. Let us briefly take a look at two of these strategies: growth poles and balanced regions.

Growth Poles. The idea behind this strategy is to trigger economic development in "poor" regions by creating industries employing large numbers of workers, reproducing the model of industrial growth experienced by the developed parts of Europe and the U.S. The growth pole philosophy was famously practiced in Italy's post-World War II "southern strategy" in which public funds were used to build steel, auto and ship-building plants in and near cities in the less-developed south. In Venezuela, Ciudad Guayana was established in 1960 as a small, planned growth pole driven by new state-financed industries. In South Africa under apartheid, a national policy of "growth points" and "influx control" channeled financing for industry but also reinforced spatial segregation. All of these efforts were premised on the understanding that we outlined in the first chapter, that capital attracts labor and leads to urban growth; however, as planning strategies they have usually fallen short because they are dependent on piecemeal investments narrowly focused on industrial enterprises. Italy's southern strategy resulted in many "white elephants"—outmoded large-scale industrial failures in an age of flexible, small-scale production. Ciudad Guayana became a metropolis with levels of inequality similar to those in other Venezuelan cities. And the system of South African apartheid imploded. In sum, attempts to deal with urban imbalances in single regions without undertaking national economic and social reforms affecting all regions are problematic. They address spatial imbalances without addressing inequalities in the economy and society; they see the regions from the vantage point of the center and "the others" at the periphery are merely pawns in an orientalist game.[37]

Balanced Regions. Another approach that relies heavily on ideal, abstract spatial forms is the balanced region approach. Based on the work of Walter Christaller, central place theory claims that there is a natural hierarchy and pattern of towns and cities, and they are distributed across the land in some sort of regular, predictable pattern. The patterns are supposed to be based on market and transportation principles first "discovered" in central Europe. In "less developed" regions, however, the pattern is found to be incomplete or distorted. It then follows that government should intervene to correct imbalances by supporting local market functions and improving transportation, gradually reaching the ideal model. In practice, however, this has more often resulted in greater imbalances. For example, the World Bank and many bilateral aid programs finance road building and local markets in rural areas but at the same time support national programs of resource extraction so that the roads only drain resources and stimulate migration to large metropolises. Again, without addressing economic and social imbalances, attention paid to spatial differences may only lead to the reproduction of inequality.[38]

In the next chapter we will look at an example of dependent urbanization and urban orientalism in India.

Part II

Enclaves and Orientalisms

Last Chance for the Urban Village?

The Urban–Rural Divide and Food Sovereignty in India

India is the second largest nation in the world, with a population of 1.2 billion. As China rapidly urbanizes, India has become the last of the large nations where village life and traditional farm production survives. While weakened by neoliberal reforms many government policies continue to support rural institutions. Could India become the most prominent exception to the trend that over the last century transformed the United States, Russia, Brazil and most recently China from rural to urban nations?

India is rapidly urbanizing and it may already be too late to reverse course. Neoliberal economic policies favor the withdrawal of benefits to towns and villages and accelerated investment in urban infrastructure. Global and local investors promote industrialized agriculture, genetically modified seeds, forest development and large-scale irrigation and energy projects that push farmers and farm workers out of villages and into cities. If current trends continue, India could join the many other nations in Asia and Africa that have shut the door on the possibility of alternative development scenarios that integrate urban and rural life, promote food sovereignty and reduce their ecological footprints. However, if India's dynamic and diverse social movements have their way, another world may be possible.

Metropolitan India and Orientalist Planning

Three of the ten largest metropolises in the world are in India: Mumbai, Delhi, and Kolkata. Yet only a small proportion of India's total population lives in these mega-cities; most Indians still live in cities, towns and villages with a population of under a million. However, today there are 42 cities with a population of under a million compared to only five in 1951.[1] In the long run urban migration may be improving the living conditions for groups of impoverished farm workers who migrate, but it also makes them more dependent on the vagaries of the global marketplace. Most migrants live in poor neighborhoods with inadequate services, face food insecurity, and as urban land is redeveloped they face continuing displacement. At the individual and household level, therefore, they experience the consequences of *dependent urbanization*, the consistent historical and material factor shaping urban life throughout Asia, Africa and Latin America (see Chapter Three). India and other post-colonial nations have unique and diverse histories, cultures and geographies, but their development continues to depend in varying degrees on the leading centers of global capitalism, much as they did under colonialism.

Urban India is emerging as a poster case for orientalist urban planning—the way of thinking that sees the metropolis through the lens of the powerful economic and political forces in the world. The typical orientalist portrait of urban India today is one of chaotic cities with uncontrollable traffic, noise, odor and pollution. Three-wheeled vehicles and motor scooters with single-cycle engines clog the streets and sidewalks while pedestrians and bicyclists skirt and often dart in and out of the motorized chaos. This is not a product of endogenous development but, contrary to the stereotype, a result of the "rational" planning model imposed on the complex patterns of human relations that evolved over centuries in the Indian village. This has produced what to Westerners appears as an irrational, disorderly, noisy and unsanitary city. Shocking narratives of dirt and disease yield orientalist solutions that impose even greater doses of the more "rational" Western order that only makes things worse: it brutally separates public and private space, sidewalks from roadways, front yards from sidewalks, public from private transportation, destroying the traditional integration of everyday life and replacing it with an urban territory of fragmented private enclaves. The ecological values of the village are absolutely and brutally relegated to the past and given no chance to thrive in the engineered and commodified urban future.

Everyday life in the Indian village has a logic and order, but migrants to cities are forced to adapt to an entirely different order that devalues their own histories. The orientalist theory and practice of urban planning is responsible for the resulting "chaos" but planners claim that what's needed is *more* orientalist planning. Official urban planning continues to follow nineteenth and twentieth century British colonial traditions that reinforce the divisions within cities and the sharp divisions between urban and rural land use. *Neoliberal* urban policy is not a break with but a

Figure 4.1 Village Market in Kerala, India

Figure 4.2 Street Life in Dahanu, Maharashtra, India

continuation of this trend. It reinforces the notion that economic development and progress requires an unrestrained free market in production and consumption which is not to be encumbered by regulation or social spending. Government policies have favored large-scale rural infrastructure projects, many promoted by the World Bank and financed by powerful lenders, that displace rural producers in large numbers and make village and small town preservation difficult. Paradoxically, even as Western urban planning begins to incorporate food security and urban agriculture in its theory and practice,[2] the current trends in India are producing greater food insecurity and cities that severely reduce the historic ties of Indians with the land. Planning for food is still mostly absent from urban planning. This raises the question of food sovereignty for India: will the nation and its population, both urban and rural, gain greater control over the means of sustenance, or be increasingly subject to crises and dependent on global food monopolies?

India's Dependent Urbanization

The Indus Valley was the site of some of the earliest human settlements in the world and before the onset of global urbanization in the nineteenth century the Indian subcontinent had many important urban centers. During the century and a half of British rule until Indian independence in 1947, India's largest urban centers grew as sites of British economic activity and political rule. They were the most important centers of political power but were separate from the vibrant indigenous, rural economy. The British first made Calcutta (now Kolkata) the center of colonial India, then moved

Figure 4.3 Orientalist Order and Chaos

their capital to Delhi.[3] In recent decades, these colonial-era metros were joined in the top ranks by the Mumbai metropolitan region which in 2010 housed over 20 million people.[4] Mumbai is India's most important economic powerhouse, with a large and diverse industrial base and service sector, an important financial sector, and real estate matching some of the highest value properties in Asia, Europe and the United States. It is the fourth largest metropolitan region in the world after Tokyo, Delhi and São Paulo.[5]

In 2010, 152.1 million people—approximately 13 percent of India's population—lived in cities with a population of over a million.[6] This is far less than the metropolitan portions of other large developing nations such as Brazil (41 percent) and China (20 percent), and developed Asian nations such as Japan (29 percent). India's rate of urban growth (1.2 percent between 2000 and 2010, ranked 35th in the world) is relatively low, compared to other former colonial nations.[7] This may be related to the government's strong pro-rural policies in the period immediately following independence. But it is also worth noting India's relatively recent break with direct colonial rule and the continuing role of feudal relations. Thus, most Latin American nations became formally independent by the mid-nineteenth century, a full 100 years before India, and today Latin America is the most urbanized of former colonial regions.

Corresponding with a dramatic expansion in direct foreign investment in the Indian economy since the 1990s,[8] however, urban growth rates have mushroomed.[9] Two major industrial centers expanded in the last two decades due to substantial investment in information technology (IT)—Bengaluru and Chennai. However, investment also grew in other economic sectors of these local economies and in all of the expanding metros. The average size of metropolitan regions in India is around three million, one of the largest averages of over-million cities in the world, though similar to the rest of Asia. This is no doubt related to the diversity in economic functions: single-function factory towns rarely grow into metropolitan regions unless they diversify economically, a rule that holds throughout Asia and the world.

Neoliberalism and Dependent Urbanization

In recent years, the World Bank and International Monetary Fund have been giving greater priority to urban spending. This follows almost a half-century of their anti-urban policies that looked askance at investment in urban infrastructure, often claiming that those investments would spur rural-to-urban migration and stimulate the demand for higher wages and social expenditures. The earlier generation of anti-urban policies gave priority to investments in rural infrastructure—roads, dams, and irrigation systems—that promoted export-oriented resource extraction and extensive, industrial agriculture. While these megaprojects continue, the new priority for global investors is access to large sectors of the more educated urban working class (for example, in the IT sector), which requires greater investments in urban infrastructure and services.

Beginning in the late 1980s, the government of India began a gradual shift in economic policy in line with the World Bank's priorities. They embraced, though with many provisos, the leading tenets of neoliberalism: privatization, deregulation, contracting out services, and the downloading of central government functions to weaker local governments. Government subsidies to rural areas were gradually reduced and services once financed by central government were made the responsibility of local governments that raised revenues through partnerships with private firms. This gradual policy shift is formally acknowledged in India's most recent Five Year Plan.[10] Recent government programs to subsidize the rural labor force and sustain farm price supports serve as palliatives to buy social peace, support powerful local elites, and regulate immigration to urban areas rather than a serious counterweight to national policies favoring neoliberal urbanization.

Neoliberal urbanization policy shapes the growing metropolitan regions to accommodate global investment. Land use policy and regulation is mostly passive, guaranteed not to interfere with the real estate and finance sectors as the leading forces in urban expansion and local revenue generation. Thus, for the first time a real estate industry linking global and local capital is shaping India's metropolitan development. Neoliberal policies emphasize public–private partnerships that result in the expenditure of state funds for infrastructure development (including roads, mass transit, water and sewer systems) that serves economic sectors dominated by global investors. They include public programs to displace low-income neighborhoods in favor of profitable land development. They provide the conditions for the reproduction of the highest-value labor power and the growth of investment capital.

The imposition of neoliberal policies in India has been anything but linear and inevitable. The Indian state is a complex nexus of government bureaucracies, regional interests, powerful individuals, competing local economies, and conflicting ideologies. Interpretation and administration at the local level may differ substantially from the structural and legal skeletons established by executive and legislative authorities.[11]

The continuing influence of hierarchical and informal relations within government, themselves influenced by both the feudal and colonial past, may contribute to divergent outcomes. However, there is also a growing sense that urbanization and free-market capitalism are inevitable and, to use the phrase coined by neoliberal pioneer and former British Prime Minister Margaret Thatcher, "There is no alternative."

A major instrument of neoliberal urbanization is the Jawaharlal Nehru National Urban Renewal Mission (JNNURM). This program has allocated 50 billion rupees in low-cost financing to 63 local governments.[12] About half of it is going into road building, and a significant portion also goes into "slum improvement," which in practice usually means the displacement of people with limited incomes in favor of profitable real estate and infrastructure development. For example, in Delhi "slum clearance" resulted in the demolition of 45,000 homes between 2004 and 2007. In a ruling supporting the displacement, India's Supreme Court claimed that Delhi should be the "showpiece of the country" and poor people were encroaching on public land.[13] The JNNURM funds come with a set of conditions that include promotion of public–private partnerships (public money helps private investors), generation of local revenue (local taxes help pay off the loans), and the use of citizen participation (public discussions help legitimize unpopular programs).

Along with neoliberalization and deregulation came a boom in India's urban real estate markets serving the extremely wealthy. In Mumbai, between 40 and 50 million square feet of residential construction is underway, most of it targeted to the elite.[14] In 2005, a single Mumbai parcel—a vacant textile factory—sold for a record $160 million.[15] While India's real estate sector has been affected by the global credit crisis, even Bhopal, a city contaminated just 25 years ago by one of the most brutal industrial disasters in history, continues to experience tremendous real estate growth. In 2010, home sales in Bhopal went up by 42 percent.[16] The growth of India's real estate market is directly connected to the country's dependent urbanization. It depends on global trends in construction and development and the continuing privatization of land, which was promoted by the World Bank's 1991 structural adjustment program and has roots stretching back to the British Land Acquisition Act of 1894.[17] The real estate boom is both a symptom and a cause of the rapid changes in land tenure that are taking place across the country, and is creating a crisis for India's agricultural working class.

Orientalist Urban Planning Policy

The pattern of dependent urbanization that characterized India's colonial period continued after independence in 1947. Even though the largest cities maintained their dominant economic and political positions, the socialist policies of the Indian government put a damper on any significant new urban development. The five-year economic plans attempted to distribute more evenly the capital flows to the states and cities. But powerful elites at the state level often retained their powers and were able to control both public and private capital. And as the nationalist policies instituted by Jawaharlal Nehru wore thin and neoliberal policies filled the void, foreign capital began to flow freely to cities. In the 1990s, all major cities received injections of foreign direct investments, and several secondary cities mushroomed as well. Thus India's urbanization became even more dependent.

Perhaps the most dramatic example today of dependent urbanization is the much-publicized growth of Bengaluru (Bangalore). Beginning in the 1990s, the city saw the dramatic growth in the IT sector.[18] New industrial campuses sprouted throughout the city center and periphery. Jobs once located in the U.S. were outsourced to Indian workers at a fraction of U.S. wages. Bengaluru has grown as a *resource city*—a city that serves as a resource for the command and control centers of global capital.[19] Investments in the IT sector were attracted to the city's highly-educated labor force that was developed at Indian expense. The city was home to the Indian Institute of Science and a host of other high-level technical and research institutions.

While IT investments have sprouted in many other cities, particularly Chennai, the kind of physical, economic and social development occurring in Bengaluru is emblematic of the neoliberal model of urban planning. Bengaluru has traditionally been known as India's "Green City" because of its enormous tree canopy, wide boulevards, lakes and wetlands. It once evoked comparisons to Paris and London. Today the traditional oriental city is being transformed into the contemporary oriental city, fragmented by private real estate development and reorganized under neoliberal urban policies. It is becoming a city of private enclaves—shopping malls, commercial districts, gated residential communities, IT campuses, along with the previously existing enclaves for research and education. While the planning principles guiding official urban development in Bengaluru are similar to those in effect in other major Indian metropolises, the changes they are bringing are most dramatic in Bengaluru.

The private real estate market is the main force shaping Bengaluru. The more densely developed districts are being cut up for malls and commercial strips. Lakes and wetlands are being filled. And the traditional multi-use street space shared by pedestrians, merchants, bicyclists, autorickshaws, and scooters is slowly giving way to the monopoly of the car. This policy has prepared the way for massive car ownership, perhaps led by the new Tata Nano, a small car built in India that claims to be the cheapest in the world. This could have the same revolutionary impact on urban life that the Model-T Ford once had in the U.S.[20]

While real estate rules, public infrastructure and services are developed to serve it. To link the separated public and private enclaves, a new transportation system is needed. Priority is given to the transportation needs of the most active sector of the economy, the IT sector, and its relatively privileged (in the Indian context) labor force. The priority mode of transportation is now the private automobile. Bengaluru's wide boulevards are being re-engineered for higher speeds, often resulting in the removal of mature trees and intense protests by environmental and civic groups; the city's streets and boulevards are becoming highways.

This private transformation of Bengaluru and other Indian cities could not occur without the support of public programs, infrastructure and services. The Jawaharlal Nehru National Urban Renewal Mission (JNNURM), mentioned previously, is financing "slum clearance" that displaces existing neighborhoods in favor of upscale enclaves and new highway infrastructure. Residents of one neighborhood, Hosabala Nagar, are fighting the project and do not believe promises that they will be the beneficiaries of replacement housing.[21] Bengaluru is also building a new mass transit system similar to those in other Indian cities. The elevated rail system in Bengaluru will serve only 5–10 percent of total travel demand, mostly to the newly emerging business and elite districts.

As with the urban planning models developed in Europe and the U.S., the Indian approach brutally excises the ideas, traditions, forms and soul of life in rural India. The green and the gardens are now aesthetic options for the well-to-do, not essential elements of everyday life. There is no place for food production, only mass consumption. While peri-urban agriculture survives barely at the margins, wherever land has not been blacktopped or built on, the new city is rising as a center of consumption for the goods of industrial agriculture.

The Crisis of Agriculture and the Village

Over 58 percent of India's labor force was engaged in agriculture at the time of the 2001 Census: 31.7 percent lived on and cultivated the land and another 26.5 percent worked as agricultural laborers.[22] This population has sustained the Indian village, town and non-metropolitan cities. The agricultural labor force has dropped from around 80 percent at the time of independence but is still significant. If we look at the composition of the rural workforce alone, in 2005, 70 percent worked in agriculture.[23] The significance of this high proportion of labor in agriculture is tempered by the low rate of participation in the labor force (in 2001, 39.1 percent, and only 25.6 percent among women). The statistics do not reveal the true role of the "informal economy" in both urban and rural areas, but do underline the continuing importance of agricultural production for the majority of India's population. The continuing high participation of the labor force in agriculture may be contrasted with the declining share of agriculture in the Gross Domestic Product (GDP). In 1973, agriculture contributed 41 percent of GDP and in 2005 that proportion had been cut in half, to 20 percent.[24]

Another indicator of the crisis in agriculture is the dramatic decline in the size of the average agricultural holding. Between 1961 and 2003, the average holding plunged from 2.63 hectares to 1.06, an average which also conceals the disproportionately large number of small holdings and a small number of very large ones.[25] This drastic change in the pattern of landholding is related to a number of factors: the subdivision of plots within families, sale of a significant amount of land to the small number of large owners, conversion of farmland to other uses, and the taking of prime land for dams, forestation and other large-scale projects.

As a result of neoliberal policies, private investment in agriculture has grown much faster than public investment. In 1971, 60 percent of agricultural investments were private and by 2003 the proportion was 75 percent. Agricultural subsidies as a proportion of GDP have nevertheless grown, constituting mostly subsidies for fertilizers and food price supports, which disproportionately benefit the larger farmers.[26]

These changes in the structure of agriculture have not resulted in higher overall productivity. Compared to other nations with more heavily industrialized agricultural sectors, India appears to be less productive. According to the World Bank, value added per worker in India is $392 compared to $3,126 in Brazil, $23,967 in Italy, and $41,797 in the U.S. This low productivity is not mainly a reflection of a scarcity in arable land; India has 15 hectares of arable land per 100 population compared to 13 in Italy and 10 in the United Kingdom, though another large developing nation, Brazil, has 32 hectares per 100 population.[27]

The growing inequities in rural India follow inequities in the implementation of land reform legislation. After independence India enacted land reforms that aimed to limit the size of large holdings, redistribute land, eliminate exploitative sharecropping, and abolish powerful usurers and intermediaries.[28] They focused on reducing the power of the *Zamindar*—large landlords who the British relied on to collect taxes from the peasants. Initially the considerable economic and political power of a government that formally adopted central economic planning helped to stabilize small-scale agriculture through the provision of financial and technical assistance. However, the reforms were implemented unevenly by state governments in which landed elites had varying degrees of influence and control. The Chinese Revolution in 1949, and later the Vietnamese Revolution, also enacted vigorous agrarian reforms that reinforced rural development and gave a lesser priority to urban development.[29] Unlike China and Vietnam, however, Indian independence in many areas did not alter private property or the hegemony of the urban elites and upper castes who had economic and cultural ties to the former colonial power, and in parts of the country they left intact the power of large landholders.

Strong support by the Indian government for agriculture in the decades after independence helped to sustain the village economy and the political base supporting the ruling Congress Party. At the same time, however, government investments in rural infrastructure contributed to distress among farmers and exacerbated the problems facing villages and towns. The most damaging of the investments were in dams. In the span of 62 years, the government launched 4,291 large dam projects and displaced between 21 and 56 million people (there is no official data about the number displaced or where they went).[30] Once an area is designated for dam construction, no government investment occurs in that area, even if construction is delayed or prolonged. This encourages greater distress and migration. Those without land rarely get compensation and when they do it is limited. 40 percent of displaced people are members of tribes, who account for only 8 percent of the population.[31] In the era of neoliberalism, private companies are often the main developers and they are less vulnerable to appeals by villagers. As mentioned later on, the vibrant struggles against dam construction have brought to light alternative and sustainable strategies for rural development.

Most of the regions that have the highest levels of participation in agricultural production are the poorest in terms of gross income.[32] Poverty is most deeply felt by those who live in rural areas but own no land. The relationship between agricultural production and poverty is borne out in the sharply declining per capita incomes of agricultural workers compared to other sectors of the economy.[33]

Neoliberal reforms in agricultural policy have led to an overall decline in loans and subsidies to farmers[34] and an increase in spending for research and development and extension spending, which tend to favor expansion of large-scale industrial agriculture. This is leading to the privatization of the seed industry, making more farmers dependent on industrially-produced seeds and experimentation with genetically modified foods that would further increase the dependency of rural producers on corporate suppliers.[35] Chemical fertilizers and insecticides have already caused extensive pollution of the land and ground water, and poorly designed irrigation systems increase soil erosion. The environmental and public health problems of industrial agriculture are growing along with the economic problems for farmers.

Urban Food Insecurity

In the large metropolitan regions of India, food production tends to be limited in scale and mostly confined to peri-urban areas that have not yet been consumed by real estate speculation. Household gardens and livestock are common wherever land is available, but they are largely used to supplement a food supply that is generally provided through wholesale markets. These markets still include fresh produce, most of it brought from within the local region, but they are gradually giving way to fast food, processed and packaged goods, and goods produced far away in the industrial food system. This contributes to the new urban epidemics of diabetes and obesity. There are currently over 35 million diabetics in India, and this is predicted to rise to 75 million by 2026.[36] The World Health Organization warns that in India's urban areas, obesity rates approach 40 percent.[37]

One of the consequences of the uneven development of Indian capitalism and the uneven implementation of reforms by Indian states is a wide divergence in levels of food insecurity. A recent study found significant problems in 16 states; using a composite index, three of the poorest states were rated "extremely insecure": Jharkhand, Bihar and Madhya Pradesh. The most secure included Kerala, Punjab and Himachal Pradesh.[38] The proportion of poor and undernourished people in India has grown since the 1980s. One source claims that while the number of poor people doubled, the number of undernourished farmers increased nearly six-fold.[39]

The case of the southern state of Kerala, one of the most food secure, is worth noting. Kerala's food production is integrated throughout its unique urban and rural settlement structure, often characterized as rural–urban sprawl. The state extends along the western coast of India, and is characterized by many gated household plots,

Figure 4.4 Disneyland in Kozhikode, Kerala, India

a pattern originally established by migrants from northern India fleeing economic hardships. This sprawl has helped sustain household food production. There are 4.32 million home gardens totaling 1.33 million hectares. Census data report that only 7 percent of all workers cultivate the land,[40] so household food production is an important supplement in the food system and enhances food security in times of scarcity and economic recession. Low-density sprawl in Kerala, while increasing transportation time and costs, may also have some environmental and health benefits. Kerala's relative prosperity is also reflected in long life expectancy, high literacy and low infant mortality. Radical social reforms in Kerala have helped to protect the population from crises of insecurity.[41]

Kerala has the second highest population density among Indian states and its agricultural holdings are relatively small (0.24 hectares on average). This calls into question the proposition that higher densities are incompatible with agricultural production and food security. Also, Kerala's small plots and gardens tend to grow multiple species for home consumption, a practice that is more likely to sequester carbon than monocultures; this helps explain the relatively small carbon footprint in Kerala compared to other Indian states.[42] Nevertheless, the relative prosperity of Kerala may be changing as global capital sweeps the state to turn the lengthy coastline into a major tourist destination and take advantage of the highly educated labor force.[43]

People's Struggles: Looking to the Future with Gandhi

Current trends are leading to the rapid growth of large metropolitan regions and the transformation of India from a diverse nation of villages, towns, regions, religions, cultures and languages towards a homogenized nation integrated in the post-colonial Anglo-Saxon empire. This is much more than a belated modernization and it is resulting in the destruction of sustainable production and consumption practices, with all their problems and contradictions, and replacing them with new forms of dependent development. Sixty years after independence India is gradually falling into the arms of global capitalism. This is the backdrop for the current crises of food sovereignty, Indian farm communities, and food insecurity.

Fortunately, however, there are powerful counter-trends. The overall rate of urban growth in small cities remains relatively low and agricultural production is still a major source of economic livelihood despite sharp regional differences and inequalities. More importantly, however, the revolutionary spirit that animated the struggle for independence survives in the diverse social movements that are contesting the destruction of the village, in both its material and spiritual form, the displacement of people, and environmental degradation. They include the movements to protect local agriculture and the people who farm from giant infrastructure projects, industrialized agriculture, and GMOs. Today many in these movements are creating new systems of thought and practice[44] as they rediscover the seeds of sustainable living that Mahatma Gandhi helped to plant during the struggles for independence.

At the time of India's independence almost the entire population of the nation lived in rural areas and small towns. The largest cities were the former British strongholds of Kolkata and Delhi. The leaders of the independence movement that came to power enjoyed a wide base of popular support in the villages and towns even if they themselves were prominent individuals from the urban elites. The rulers of independent

India were modernizers to differing degrees but they faced an overwhelmingly rural nation filled with deep suspicions of urban elites who seemed to have greater affinities with the English rulers. At the same time the continuing influence of the caste system and feudal relations tended to reinforce local conservatism. Thus the political space for any government stimulus for urbanization was limited and the demand for government action to improve rural life was intense.

Inspiration for the new government's program favoring investments in the country-side came from Mahatma Gandhi, whose earliest writings reinforced traditional values of local self-reliance and implicitly rejected dependent urbanization. In Gandhi's seminal work, *Hind Swaraj*,[45] we find a philosophical basis for India's policies promoting rural development. A re-reading of this seminal work, however, suggests new approaches to the urbanization and food security problems of today.[46] Gandhi's critique of Western civilization laid the basis for independence not simply as a political act but a matter of liberation of both body and soul; not an act of expelling foreign rulers but of rejecting their "civilization." He begins with the individual as the basic unit of society, promoting self-reliance, village life, the local economy and decentralization. According to Gandhi:

> [India] ... has 750,000 villages scattered over a vast area ... The people are rooted in the soil, and the vast majority are living a hand-to-mouth life.... Agriculture does not need revolutionary changes. The Indian peasant requires a supplementary industry....[47]

The above is from a longer response by Gandhi to charges that he was against technology. Far from being a Luddite, Gandhi favored what we might call today sustainable technology that did not threaten to throw people off their farms or put them out of work. His advocacy of *khadi*, locally-produced cloth, over imported textiles was not a "Buy India" campaign but a rejection of the inevitability of the global marketplace and its dislocations. These were not abstract dreams but part of a popular resistance to British colonialism and the havoc reaped by its technology on India's local economies. His thinking reflected the *swadeshi* movement that arose in the early part of the twentieth century in Bengal; *swadeshi* is understood as the soul of *swaraj*, and *swaraj* means self-reliance.

Gandhi's views, put forth in *Hind Swaraj*, included a passionate belief in the need for bottom-up democracy in post-independence India, where individual freedom is linked to community power:

> Independence must begin at the bottom. Thus, every village will be a republic or *panchayat* having full powers. It follows, therefore, that every village has to be self-sustained and capable of managing its affairs....[48]

Jawaharlal Nehru, India's first prime minister and the central political figure in post-independence India, rejected Gandhi's radical approach and became a major advocate for modernization and scientific strategies of development.[49] In 1945, Nehru explicitly rejected Gandhi's approach in *Hind Swaraj*. But he could not help but be influenced by Gandhi and the very practical political fact that most Indians lived in small towns and rural areas. Thus, Nehru stated that, "Personally I hope that heavy or light industries should all be decentralized as far as possible...." He also saw the need to restrict urban growth: "Many of the present overgrown cities have developed evils which are deplorable. Probably we have to discourage this overgrowth and at the same time encourage the village to approximate more to the culture of the town."[50]

Nehru and Gandhi perhaps understood with prescience the importance of rural life to India's urban development, and the importance of urban India to rural life. Without an integrated, holistic approach to human development the metropolis would develop and be divorced from the land and its productive capacity, a dependent metropolis that makes development of the independent village as impossible as the integration of nature, and food production, with the city. In parts of rural India today, for example, food is plentiful and locally produced, nature is still worshipped as a god, and self-built mud houses last four times as long as new concrete structures.[51] This is not to say, however, that village life is idyllic or free from serious economic and environmental problems or to deny the extreme deprivations in most rural areas. To do so would be to essentialize and orientalize. Our purpose is instead to argue against the orientalist prejudices that consider rural life to be, by definition, backwards.

Gandhi's views on food and health were also related to *swaraj* (i.e., self-reliance). His critique of Western medicine came long before the urban epidemics of obesity, diabetes and asthma, and the notoriously ineffective system of public health promoted at the global center of neoliberalism, the United States, where huge expenditures fail to yield better health outcomes and food-related illnesses are on the rise. Gandhi criticized Western food and medicine as a set of practices that both encouraged and claimed to combat food-related problems. The business of doctors, he said:

> is really to rid the body of diseases that may afflict it. How do these diseases arise? Surely by our negligence or indulgence. I overeat, I have indigestion, I go to a doctor, he gives me medicine, I am cured. I overeat again, and I take his pills again. Had I not taken the pills in the first instance, I would have suffered the punishment deserved by me, and I would not have overeaten again. The doctor intervened and helped me to indulge myself.[52]

The continuing strength of *ayurvedic* and other holistic systems of health care in India is an indication that holistic approaches are surviving in contention with the linear, reductionist, cause–effect practices that dominate in Western medicine. Most Indians are still vegetarians and have yet to suffer the health consequences of consuming industrial beef and livestock. However, Indians are now learning to reject traditional ways and love fast food and fast medicine, even while Western tourists visiting India consume idealized, sanitized and orientalist interpretations of the Indian village. According to Raj Patel, India's newfound dependency on industrial monocultures in the food system has resulted in one of the highest rates of type 2 diabetes in the world.[53]

While Gandhi may well have failed to recognize some of the benefits of Western medicine and technology, his cautionary approach suggests how India might avoid dependence on the addictive medicines of the drug monopolies, the predations of the Green Revolution engendered by the industrial food conglomerates, and the epidemics like obesity, hunger and malnutrition that they foster.

Grassroots Resistance

The powerful impulses towards local and national independence reflected in Gandhi's philosophy and political work have reemerged in the extensive grassroots efforts to resist the "development" projects promoted in the neoliberal agenda for rural and urban areas. These movements, often dispersed and fragmented, nonetheless represent a serious obstacle to neoliberal and dependent urbanization.[54]

The first and most important aspect of the popular movements is their resistance against *displacement* in both rural and urban areas. The largest struggles against displacement in rural areas were triggered by government and private measures to implement the Green Revolution. These include plans for dams and irrigation systems designed to appropriate water for both industrialized agriculture and urban development. They include resistance to reforestation projects that would replace native forest with commercially attractive monocultures—for example, the eucalyptus groves planted with World Bank support that bankrupted local producers.[55]

Vandana Shiva has played a role in and written eloquently about many of these struggles and highlighted the central role of women.[56] The struggles have slowed down considerably the government's ambitious plans to control rural land. They led to significant changes in law that opened up access by local groups and individuals to India's complex and arcane postcolonial bureaucracy, such as the 2005 Right to Information Act.[57] In addition, over the decades farmers have managed to sustain influence as a political bloc on the formulation of national and state-wide agricultural policy.[58]

The struggles against displacement include the urban struggles against government-sponsored redevelopment programs that bulldoze working class neighborhoods to make way for new real estate development and the highway infrastructure to serve it. In Delhi alone at least 45,000 homes were demolished between 2004 and 2007, and fewer than 25 percent of displaced households received new homes;[59] in many cities no new housing is provided for displaced people. Urban environmental movements in the large metropolitan areas are also protesting the destruction of the natural environment to create new cities that emulate the modern concrete and asphalt paradises of the developed nations. These protests in cities from Delhi to Bengaluru include challenges to roadway expansion and the destruction of public space, the displacement of older neighborhoods, and the damage to the environment wrought by new urban infrastructure. In the larger cities, the middle class appears to dominate the most prominent activist organizations, and the Gandhian spirit contends with Victorian and Western notions of environmental sanitation and planning.[60]

Perhaps one of the most widely publicized rural struggles that also had strong links to urban movements and issues was the successful defeat in 2008 of a proposal to build an automobile factory in a fertile rice-producing area of West Bengal. The Tata factory was to have produced the Nano, heralded as a popular mass-produced economy car. The proposed factory spurred fears among villagers that the industrialization of the region would threaten small-scale agricultural production (itself a product of a relatively successful agrarian reform) and food security.[61] It highlighted growing conflicts within the popular movements and the declining hegemony of the traditional left in West Bengal.

One of the most notable of many support organizations for the local movements is the People's Science Movement (KSSP), which started in 1962, now has some 40,000 members and is a central element in the All-India People's Science Network. This grassroots network brings together scientists, educators and activists and provides information about the environment, energy and public health. Its activists have contributed to the movements to save the forests and bring to environmental issues an approach that incorporates social justice. They produce and disseminate environmental information through workshops, publications and other media that are accessible to a wide audience. They are one among many local movements that have alternately criticized and allied with the political parties and government agencies supporting independent development.

One of the most powerful insurgent movements spanning both urban and rural areas emerged in the struggle for food security—the struggles against GMOs (the most recent addition to the menu of the Green Revolution). Here again Vandana Shiva has played an important role in spreading awareness of the way that the introduction of genetically modified organisms in India threatens food security.[62] Shiva demonstrates how genetically modified mustard seeds were threatening public health and gives examples of local, sustainable alternatives promoted by organized farmers and consumers.

GMOs are reinforcing the monocultures of global agribusiness—soy and corn in particular—and undermining the diversity of local species. A small number of multinational food conglomerates have introduced genetically modified seeds to which they own the patents. This creates an even greater degree of economic dependency as farmers give up the traditional practice of saving their own seeds and must buy seeds after every harvest. This leads to greater reliance on credit, itself a major cause of bankruptcy, despair and suicides in the countryside. Anti-GMO activists have spearheaded legal efforts to prevent global corporations from appropriating and monopolizing native seeds and thus colonizing the very building blocks of life and local culture.[63] The Indian government was forced to establish a committee that must approve new genetically modified products before they are introduced in the market (the committee recently postponed a decision to approve BT brinjal, or eggplant, which would likely force out of the market the scores of local eggplant varieties). But the government allows imported packaged products and many local processed foods that contain GMOs since there are no labeling requirements.

In the end food security is a land issue. Land reform in India after independence was far from complete and the agenda for genuine reform is still a long one.[64] The fundamental question remains: what is the relationship of people with land in urban and rural areas? Who controls the land—the people who live on it and depend on it for sustenance or those who alienate it as property? In post-colonial societies this is critical to the struggle for national independence, but it is also central to the survival and independence of each individual and household and, in India, to *hind swaraj*.

In India as elsewhere, the neoliberal agenda may not be quite so new.[65] Instead it appears to reflect a resurgence of classical liberalism after the hiatus of Keynesian capitalism. In India, the new public–private partnerships that undermine local self-reliance recall similar arrangements that were hallmarks of the British colonial period. According to Randeria:

> Like the transnational corporations of the contemporary world, the British East India Company, which began the process of introducing British law into India

prior to its becoming a Crown colony, was a private trading company. The relationship between the state and private trading companies in European countries has been unclearly delineated in the past and present. Powerful, partly autonomous from the state and seeking to escape from government control and metropolitan law, private trading companies in the nineteenth and twentieth centuries, like their transnational counterparts today, always relied on their respective governments to further their interests abroad.[66]

As Arundhati Roy points out, the legacy of British imperialism remains:

India's freedom struggle, though magnificent, was by no means revolutionary. The Indian elite stepped easily and elegantly into the shoes of the British imperialists. A deeply impoverished essentially feudal society became a modern, independent nation state. Even today, fifty-seven years on to the day, the truly vanquished still look upon the government as *mai-baap*, the parent and provider. The somewhat more radical, those who still have fire in their bellies, see it as *chor*, the thief, the snatcher-away of things.[67]

In sum, orientalist theory and practice continue to dominate rural and urban areas, private and public life. Gandhi's call for self-reliance should not be interpreted as nostalgia for village life. It might instead help inform the search for new ways forward as global climate change and widening inequalities force more of us to understand the past while seeking answers for the future. The majority of the world's population already lives in metropolitan areas and India is the largest rural nation. Can India chart a new course that integrates urban and rural, achieves independence, and establishes food sovereignty?

In the following chapter we will look at one of the most explicit and iconic orientalist urban planning experiments, by Sir Patrick Geddes in British-controlled Palestine a century ago.

Chapter 5

Orientalist Roots
Palestine and the Israeli Metropolis

Edward Said's trailblazing *Orientalism* looked in detail at the ways that European, particularly British, interpretations of history and culture reflected imperial positions of power. The concept of urban orientalism (see Chapter Two) has special meaning in Palestine, the place where Said was born and that he sought to free from Israeli occupation. Orientalist planning in Israel and Palestine was not simply a byproduct of the establishment of the state of Israel in 1948 but has strong roots in colonialism and the British Mandate that preceded Israel's founding. It has evolved and sustained itself until today, mediated by the resistance of the Palestinian people.

Urban orientalism in Palestine starts by making traditional Arab urbanism invisible, the product of a non-European "other." European settlers considered Palestinians to be "strangers" in a land that was "empty," to be settled and urbanized by the rightful owners.[1] European settlers in early twentieth century Palestine encountered a society deeply rooted in small towns and villages. Many of them adapted to this society and sought to integrate with it. But when settlers from Europe began to emigrate in large numbers, especially after 1948, they mostly went to larger towns and cities; most of them came from relatively urbanized European nations even though discrimination had forced many of them to live in rural areas. Still, their leaders brought with them faith in a rational, scientific and orderly approach to urban development and settled in cities, where Palestinians were largely invisible to them.

While this chapter focuses on Israel and Palestine these are far from the only examples of urban orientalism in the region. In Dubai and Abu Dhabi, for example new orientalist enclaves are being built at alarming speed. Following many earlier urban projects in Saudi Arabia, towering modern cities of concrete and steel are sprouting in the desert, absurd experiments in mega-development that use some of the world's most energy-intensive designs and oppressive labor practices. The patina of wealth and progress in Dubai and Abu Dhabi masks brutal realities. The majority populations (low-wage construction and service workers, many of them migrants) are strictly segregated from the primary benefactors—wealthy local elites, often connected to royalty or extractive industries, and the professional workforce tied to global finance capital. Parts of the cities are ghostly concrete shells without life; Dubai features the world's tallest skyscraper but there is little urban life behind the skyline or on the street. Dubai has extensive new roadways, but they are constantly clogged with traffic, and there are few alternatives such as sidewalks, bicycle infrastructure or rail. Dubai brands itself as "sustainable" and is a co-sponsor with the United Nations of the "Dubai International Award for Best Practices to Improve the Living Environment" but this is little more than green washing. This is a desert city that includes an enormous indoor ski-slope in one of its many luxury malls. Abu Dhabi is now building a model city that seeks to address some of the absurd wastefulness by sharply reducing energy consumption, but this will likely be an elite "green" enclave and rein- force the sharp social, political and environmental inequalities. If Israel/Palestine is a prominent example of urban orientalism, surely Dubai, Abu Dhabi and other cities in the region can share the distinction.[2]

Another urban orientalist project was adopted by the U.S. in occupied Iraq. Eight years after the 2003 U.S. invasion, Baghdad is a deeply divided city. The majority of the city's infrastructure was destroyed in the invasion and not sufficiently replaced, and its population lives in chronic insecurity. Within a small enclave known as the Green Zone, however, U.S. diplomatic and military personnel, contractors and a small number of Iraqi workers have lived in relative comfort and safety, with newly built infrastructure, commercial services, and regular shipments of goods from the U.S. and Europe. This Baghdad is wholly separate from the more humble and vulner- able city most Iraqis know. This is urban orientalism at its most brutally efficient: an enclave created and maintained through overwhelming military force to sustain an occupation.[3]

Orientalism in Palestine

The checkpoint, the gate and the wall are the most visible signs of enclave urbanism in today's Palestine. One of 500 military checkpoints is located between Bethlehem, which is in the Palestinian West Bank, and Jerusalem. It takes as long as two hours

Figure 5.1 Dubai: Duplicates of New York City's Chrysler Building in the Desert

every day for Palestinians to cross the checkpoint so they can work in Jerusalem. Once they are in Israeli territory, they are confronted with gated communities that are off-limits to them. The Palestinian commuters from Bethlehem, mostly men over 30, are herded through turnstiles and fences, run through metal detectors, surveillance cameras and document checks. They are the "lucky" ones, the small minority that got permission to enter Israel to work, because there are fewer jobs and lower pay in the West Bank. But the commuters have to go back to Bethlehem the same day or they will be hunted down. Every worker has a magnetic card they must swipe in the morning and again in the evening so the Israeli state will know if they miss the return trip. Palestinians are, in effect, prisoners of a powerful security state able to engineer the movement of people and their use of public space. Israel is the world's leading innovator and producer of high tech military and surveillance equipment, and a major contributor to the strategy and technology of the U.S. occupation of Iraq.[4]

Some checkpoints divide Israel and the West Bank but most of them are within the occupied territories. To get an idea what this means to Palestinians, imagine having to pass a military checkpoint to commute between San Francisco and Oakland. The Israeli army controls all movement between West Bank towns, within some towns, and also between Israel and the West Bank. Jewish citizens are not allowed to enter the West Bank, except for those living in settlements in the West Bank built in violation of United Nations declarations and international law. They take exclusive Israeli-built and protected roads to get to and from their homes. These roads are off-limits to Palestinians. This is one of the most developed examples of apartheid urbanization in the world, with separate settlements, separate roads, and separate standards of living.[5]

The Israeli settlements in the West Bank are designed and function as exclusive gated communities. Some have physical gates but many do not have to because they control access through other means. The "gates" are often symbolic and take the form of electronic surveillance perimeters. Israel's Former Prime Minister Ariel Sharon engineered the location of settlements with the strategic thinking of a military planner. They are placed on hilltops where they can oversee the daily lives of Palestinians and, should the military need to intervene at any time, provide them with the most strategic locations. The architects and planners charged with developing the settlements blended military and urban planning so as to create a symbolic and real sense of superiority and control over the land and people below. Palestinians are not allowed in, though exceptions are made for service workers. In his brilliant book, *Hollow Land: Israel's Architecture of Occupation*, Eyal Weizman shows how Israel's control of the high ground and monopoly of the underground water supply, constitute a "vertical occupation" that resulted in the destruction of Palestinian agriculture and the displacement of entire villages.[6]

The system of checkpoints and gated communities is enclosed by the Wall—what the Israeli government calls the Separation Barrier. Israel started building its giant Wall enclosing the West Bank in 2002, after the launch of the second *Intifada*, the Palestinian uprising against the Israeli occupation. While Israel claims the purpose of the wall is defensive, a careful look at the route it takes shows that it was planned as a land grab that would further shrink the boundaries of a future Palestinian state. The Wall, like the Israeli settlements with over 500,000 settlers in the occupied territories, aims to create "facts on the ground" that would dictate the parameters of an eventual negotiated settlement with the Palestinian Authority. Most of the Wall has been built on Palestinian land. It takes huge loops that incorporate illegal Israeli settlements built on Palestinian land. If completed, the 760 kilometer Wall would effectively turn the Palestinian territory into a handful of isolated *bantustans* and make a viable Palestinian state with a unified economy and infrastructure impossible. Following the example of Gaza, Palestinian towns would be prisons and all exchanges between them would be subject to surveillance and Israeli military control. This would result in one of the most technologically sophisticated apartheids in the history of cities.[7]

In the remainder of this chapter, we will trace the roots of urban orientalism in British-controlled Palestine and the important role of Victorian urban planner Patrick Geddes. We will then look at the process of gentrification and "Judaization" of Palestinian land, and the role played by orientalist planning.

The Birth Of Urban Orientalism In British-Controlled Palestine

After World War I the Ottoman Empire collapsed and ceded Palestine to the British. At that time the majority of the population was Arab but the population of European Jews began to expand. The Zionist organization began in the late nineteenth century among European Jews and had close ties with some factions of the British government, which looked favorably on the Zionist idea of establishing a Jewish nation in

Figure 5.2 The Israeli Wall

the Middle East. To the Zionists, Palestine was the historic homeland of Jews, who had been expelled some two thousand years earlier, and Palestine was now "empty" land occupied by "strangers."[8] The Zionist project was to create "a Jewish nation for the Jewish people" and the Palestinian people were essentially invisible: Palestine was "a land without people for a people without land." Lord Balfour, whom Edward Said referenced as a major proponent of orientalism, was the author of the 1917 declaration that promised a homeland for European Jews in Palestine. The Balfour Declaration opened the gates for their settlement in British-controlled Palestine.

In its African and Asian colonies, the British Empire was proficient in the art of exploiting ethnic divisions. "Divide and conquer" often described British imperial strategy. They chose one ethnic group as a preferred elite that enjoyed special privileges and the confidence of the masters. They favored the more educated groups and encouraged their assimilation into British culture and the colonial bureaucracy. The British did not create social and religious divisions but exploited them to enhance Britain's own role. This often helped to deepen religious conflict, as for example the divisions between Hindus and Muslims that led to the partition of India.

The British saw in the small European Jewish population of Palestine a willing partner and client whose ideological and political objectives fit in with Britain's strategy in the Middle East, where they vied with the French for hegemony. The British saw Jewish migration to Palestine as a useful way to deflate anti-Semitism in Britain and other parts of Europe, and this became a selling point used by Zionists to encourage migration. For a time, some elements within the Third Reich endorsed the idea of a Jewish return to Palestine as a way of hastening Jewish expulsion from Europe.[9]

Patrick Geddes and Tel Aviv

During the British mandate noted British urban planner Patrick Geddes introduced a comprehensive plan for a Jewish settlement that would become a central portion of the future city of Tel Aviv, Israel's largest. It was laid out in accordance with Garden City principles established in Great Britain. The Garden City was a planned alternative to the tightly-packed industrial cities of the time, a suburban model that would bring the city and countryside closer to one another.[10] The low- to mid-rise residential community in Palestine was designed to be integrated with the natural landscape and would maximize opportunities for social interaction among residents.

Geddes first went to the area in 1919 at the invitation of Chaim Weizmann, then president of the World Zionist Organization. He also visited Haifa and set forth principles for the future development of that city. His approach of building around the natural topography influenced the design of future hill-top settlements in the occupied territories, where the military objective of controlling high points merged with the city planning ideals of Geddes.[11] Geddes is considered one of the founders of Western urban planning and his ideas continue to shape the discipline. He believed that the plan should be based on the natural and social characteristics of an area, starting with a detailed examination of the "natural region" as determined by the topography and shaped by human interactions and culture. A famous eccentric, his political beliefs approached anarchism and socialism but he stood apart from organized politics.[12] While most of his work was conducted in England and Scotland, Geddes spent ten years, from 1915 to 1925, in Asia. In addition to his work planning the garden city in Tel Aviv, Geddes also introduced Western urban planning techniques to Indian cities. While his work contained the same orientalist assumptions as many other classical urban planners, Geddes opposed the British colonial administrators' slum clearance and boulevard development schemes. One of his most noted Indian plans revolved around preserving clean drinking water and preventing malaria and plague in Indore.[13]

Urban planners and designers today may marvel at the liveability of the community that Geddes planned in Tel Aviv because of the contrast with the ostentatious modernist high-rises that now clutter the landscape. As central locations in Tel Aviv increase in value, the planned community is becoming a desirable location and portions are turning into upscale cultural sites and tourist destinations. But the casual observer can miss one uncomfortable historic fact. The Geddes plan was located outside and separate from the largest populated area of the day, the Arab city of Jaffa. At that time Jaffa was a thriving port on the Mediterranean coast and had been an active urban center for centuries. The Geddes new town was intended to be separate from Jaffa and was to be built for the European Jews as the first modern urban expansion in Palestine. This was the beginning of Israel's urban apartheid.

The Geddes plan for Tel Aviv was *orientalist* in conception and execution. The Palestinian population was detached and invisible. Elements of Palestinian urbanism were not included in the plan. The Geddes new town effectively turned its back on the city of Jaffa and its people, who were invisible, despite Geddes' own philosophy of starting from the existing environment and cultures.[14] The development later became the point of departure for the growth of the new Tel Aviv metropolis. By the 1970s growth was sprawling far beyond the Geddes new town, towards new growth centers in the north and east. More recently it began to sprawl back to the south where it threatened the remainder of the Palestinian community still residing in Jaffa.

Tel Aviv and Jaffa Under Israel

After World War II, the British Empire was forced to downsize and the U.S. emerged as the leading imperial power. This provided an opportunity for the Zionist leadership to attempt fulfillment of its goal of establishing a Jewish state in the land between the Jordan River and the Mediterranean Sea. With support from Europe and America, and aided by the worldwide sympathy for the victims of the Holocaust, the settlers took control of Palestine by force. Scattered resistance by Palestinians was no match for the superior arms and technology employed by the settlers. They violently expelled a million Palestinians, destroying entire towns and villages. This is thoroughly documented in Ilan Pappe's *The Ethnic Cleansing of Palestine* and many other sources.[15] What became Independence Day to Jews is known as the *Nakba*, a sorrowful and tragic event, to Palestinians.[16] After 1948, the ethnic cleansing of Palestine continued as Israeli leaders undertook the "Judaization" of the land, further discussed in the sections below.[17]

Orientalist ideology reinforced the new system of power; Israel was defined as a democratic, peaceful and Jewish state and Palestinian resistance as undemocratic, violent and anti-Semitic. Discrimination by the Zionist settlers developed against Sephardic Jews who had lived for generations in the area, but both groups increasingly treated the Arabs in Palestine as "the others." Since Palestinian culture and society was seen as having no significant value, there was a collective denial of any responsibility for its displacement. The "empty" land was occupied.

Israel and the Occupation of Palestine

After creation of the state of Israel in 1948, most Palestinians fled or were forced out of their homes and villages and became refugees. But many stayed, and today Palestinians within the state of Israel account for about 20 percent of the population. The 1967 Middle Eastern war left Israel in control of 74 percent of the territory; only the West Bank and Gaza were recognized by the United Nations as occupied territories with an uncertain future status. Over the six decades since the foundation of the state of Israel, there has been a sometimes gradual and sometimes violent displacement of Palestinians.

The more gradual and less visible displacement might be called gentrification or, to use the term of some Israeli leaders, Judaization. In either case it adds up to a continuation of the process of ethnic cleansing. Urban planners play their role, often unconsciously, by facilitating continuing displacement and gentrification.

The Palestinian minority, Christian and Muslim, remain second-class citizens in the Jewish state. Many live in segregated residential enclaves with inferior services. Half of all Palestinian households are under the poverty line compared to the national average of 18 percent. They are vulnerable to eviction, displacement and gentrification. It is here that Israel's orientalist urban planners play their role, often unconsciously.

The Palestinian population in Israel is concentrated in the Galilee region in the north, the Negev desert to the south, East Jerusalem, and in "mixed towns" like Haifa. In all of these areas exclusive planned Israeli hilltop settlements are part of a conscious policy of "Judaizing" areas with Arab populations. This is essentially a policy of ethnic cleansing implemented through government land and housing policy. The Israeli government owns almost all of the land in Israel—around 93 percent—and leases it freely for the construction of new Jewish settlements; they also provide the infrastructure and subsidize services. The Palestinian population, however, is rarely given permission to build or expand.[18] To meet the needs of a rapidly growing population, Palestinians often build without legal approval, but they are subject to heavy fines and/or demolition orders. Over 18,000 Palestinian homes have been demolished by the Israeli government.[19]

There is a situation of extreme overcrowding in many Palestinian areas, where 91 percent of all land is used for housing compared to 55 percent in Jewish areas.[20] Since 1948 the Palestinian population has grown tenfold, mostly due to natural increase, and Jewish population increased eightfold, mostly due to immigration. This situation has contributed to a lack of opportunities for voluntary mobility by Palestinians. Only 4 percent of land in Palestinian areas is used for industry and infrastructure compared to 30 percent in Jewish areas.[21]

The planning paradigm for the Israeli settlements in the West Bank has been reproduced within the state of Israel and is now deeply imbedded in the urban structure. We see it in the gated Israeli communities that have sprung up on hilltops in the mixed Arab–Israeli regions and cities. There too the exclusive neighborhoods reinforce economic and social dominance through segregated living and work environments.

Thus, urban planning throughout Israel is firmly rooted in Israel's long-term geopolitical strategy of controlling all of the land between the Jordan River and the Mediterranean Sea, the dream of Israel's Zionist founders. Its realization was interrupted by the resistance of the Palestinian people who owned, lived on and worked most of that land. Israel now directly controls 78 percent of it, and the rest is under limited Palestinian control in the West Bank and Gaza (where Israel can and does intervene militarily and take land when deemed in their interest). Incredibly, if a settlement is ever reached between Palestinians and Israelis, Palestinians are likely to end up with less than 14 percent of the land between the Mediterranean Sea and the Jordan River.

In the remaining sections we will consider four examples of gentrification and Judaization: the transformation of Palestinian Jaffa into a Tel Aviv neighborhood; the conversion of Palestinian Galilee to northern Israel; the division, occupation and gentrification of Jerusalem; and the Judaization of the Negev. All of this is wrapped up in the Wall.

From Palestinian Jaffa to Tel Aviv Neighborhood

We return now to Palestinian Jaffa, which lies hidden in the shadows of Tel Aviv's phenomenal growth after the birth of the state of Israel. During and after the 1947 war, almost the entire population of 120,000 Palestinians were expelled from Jaffa and surrounding areas. The 3,000 who remained were moved to a separate fenced-in area (Hajami and Jabali). When the fence around the camp was taken down Palestinians became part of a "mixed city" in the new state of Israel. But in this mix Jews overwhelmingly dominated in number and controlled the land; Palestinians lived in both separate and integrated neighborhoods but did not have access to housing in most of the newer areas.[22]

Today Jaffa is one among many neighborhoods in the city of Tel Aviv. It has about 50,000 people, of which only some 20,000 are Palestinians. As land values rise more Palestinians are being pushed out and Jaffa is becoming both gentrified and Judaized. Those Palestinians who were able to remain in Jaffa after the 1947 war could take advantage of progressive tenant protections in the new Israeli state. They were considered "protected tenants" on the land, which was owned by the government. They could not be (easily) evicted. But this protection was valid for only the first two generations under a 49-year lease. The third generation had no legal right to stay and the Israel Land Authority (ILA) could refuse to renew the lease or remove them for any infraction. In light of economic pressures from rising land values and political pressures from Jewish gentrifiers, the Land Authority often demands that the Palestinian tenants pay market price for lease renewal. Given the steep differentials in household income between Palestinians and Jews, Palestinians often cannot meet the purchase price or qualify for loans.

The Land Authority will typically refuse to grant permission for building additions to Palestinian tenants. But when their leases come up and inspectors find illegal additions, the tenants are faced with demolition orders. Now that the Authority is promoting privatization of state property in general, places where Palestinians live are especially vulnerable to pressures from private real estate interests. Thus neoliberal urban policies reinforce ethnic cleansing—though in some cases wealthy Palestinians are able to buy and move into the gentrifying Jaffa.

Figure 5.3 Jaffa Today

According to one community organizer in Jaffa who was fighting gentrification:

"My family was from a [Palestinian] village north of here. It was confiscated by Israel. My family had papers showing they had owned the land since the Turkish period. They came to Jaffa. I am a citizen of Israel but we can't get our land back. Everything for me starts with that."

The organizer described the recent case of a Palestinian who couldn't get official permission to add rooms to his house, and now faces eviction for a building violation. He has an option to buy but with current real estate prices, can't afford to. In another case, a renter facing eviction is willing to buy the property valued at approximately $160,000, but the government will only accept cash and no bank will lend the family money because they do not have sufficient income. The organizer said that while Palestinians struggle to hold on to their homes, gentrifiers move in with ease and have no problem getting permission. They include Jews from Europe looking for second homes by the sea, and Israeli settlers from the West Bank who bring with them both an ideological mission to separate themselves from Palestinians and guns that are publicly displayed to make sure their mission is known. He described groups of settlers walking down the streets of Jaffa carrying guns, which he interprets as a public declaration of their control over the land.[23]

Despite the efforts of Patrick Geddes and other planners, Tel Aviv's growth as a modern metropolis is mainly due to large-scale real estate investments and not state-driven plans. Talia Margalit shows how over the last century the city grew as public land was sold off piecemeal for private development and zoning changed to facilitate it. While the initial priority of the city's planners was expansion to the north (and this was to have created the potential for an urbanized corridor reaching the northern city of Haifa), in the latter part of the twentieth century greater emphasis was placed on development of the relatively impoverished areas in the central and southern parts of the region, including Jaffa and other Palestinian settlements. But by and large new development was located wherever land was valuable and available for development, not where the planners thought it should be. A government-sponsored urban renewal program was also driven by market forces and it facilitated upscale private development on publicly-owned land, including Palestinian villages that were emptied of their original populations.[24]

As a result of market-driven growth, the original Geddes conception of organic planning tied to a comprehensive vision of the city is but a historical footnote. Yet the Zionist project of a Jewish metropolis remains. The new high-rise development is almost entirely made up of modern residential and commercial projects responding to a Jewish market. Much of it has taken place on sites that were formerly occupied by Palestinian communities, as well as industrial and commercial locations which did not maximize returns on land values. Thus, despite substantial public ownership of land, and the separation of land and building rights, Tel Aviv has developed largely in response to the private real estate market. As in many U.S. cities, the market is ethnically coded by investors, developers and landlords, and produces segregated neighborhoods, cities and suburbs.[25] Government has stepped in to subsidize housing, but mostly for new European Jewish immigrants, mostly from Russia.

From Palestinian Galilee to Northern Israel, Rural to Urban Enclaves

Sixty percent of the Palestinian population of Israel lives in northern Israel, in the Galilee region and the city of Haifa. There Palestinians are the majority in the towns of Nazareth and Sachnin, among others. But Jewish settlements, limits on the expansion of Palestinian communities, and the outright expulsion of Palestinians from some towns are re-branding the territory as Jewish.

Especially since the 1967 war Israel intensified its efforts to Judaize the Galilee. The Palestinian farmers in the valleys were surrounded by Israeli hilltop settlements, following the political/military strategy outlined by Ariel Sharon (who went from a career in the Israeli Defense Forces to become Prime Minister). Palestinian farmers were forced off their land by a combination of forces: competition with state-supported Israeli agriculture, the actions of the Israeli military, intimidation by Israeli settlers, or land use regulations. In the scores of Palestinian towns in the Galilee, regulations prevent them from expanding their homes and often lead to their eviction. Palestinians living in towns have been unable to get approval for new housing development and as their families grow their housing becomes increasingly overcrowded. Many are forced to emigrate and join the millions of Palestinians in the diaspora.

The northern Galilee became strategic militarily because of its border with Lebanon and, more importantly, because of its large Palestinian population in close proximity to the West Bank. The Israeli state adopted a policy of ethnic cleansing that used both the iron fist of military action and a velvet glove of bureaucratic land regulation to

Figure 5.4 Israeli Settlement in Galilee

change the balance of demographic forces. Some Palestinian towns were overrun and converted to mostly Jewish towns—for example, the present day Tsfat and Tiberias. Larger Palestinian towns were hemmed in by new hilltop Jewish settlements. After Palestinians were evicted from their homes and communities, Israel preserved selected sites, including mosques, as "heritage sites" to be visited by tourists. Many of them are now "artist colonies," where virtually all art is European or Jewish, such as the former mosque at Tsfat. Symbolic relics of Palestinian heritage may be found at other places such as Jaffa and Jerusalem where the Palestinians themselves are under siege.

In Nazareth, the largest Palestinian town, state control over land development helped to encourage new divisions among Palestinians that could be exploited to weaken political and social cohesiveness. Yosef Jabareen shows how the Israeli government intervened in a dispute between Christians and Muslims, exacerbating tensions between groups that had lived in the town without major conflicts for centuries. A plaza near a Christian church was the site of clashes between the two groups in 1999, and led to a four year occupation of the site by Muslims.[26]

The Israel Land Authority does not generally provide land for the expansion of the Palestinian population (the notion of "Palestinian settlers" never appears in the Israeli lexicon). With a rapidly increasing population this has produced extremely high densities and land prices in Palestinian areas. In 1961 the average population of the Palestinian town was 2,506; in 2025 it is expected to be 19,841. In 1961 the average population of Jewish towns was 2,268; in 2025 it is expected to be 6,901.[27]

In Palestinian communities, land available for public and open space is limited because most of it is used to meet the needs for household expansion. Most growth is inward, creating more crowded ghettoes. Since people tend to build their own homes and the average building is three stories, Palestinian communities tend to be tightly packed. Because Palestinian households are under intense pressure to build housing on a relatively limited amount of land, municipal governments in Palestinian areas are reluctant to take private land for public infrastructure. Thus infrastructure remains inadequate and open space deficits are growing. New schools and public facilities tend to be located where land is available and not necessarily where they are needed, often resulting in excessive demand for transportation.

Outside the towns in the Galilee, the Israel Land Authority has used its sovereign powers to take Palestinian farmland, often claiming it is fallow when Palestinian farmers are unable to farm intensively or continuously. Israeli farms, including the *kibbutzim* and *moshav*, are by comparison stable, highly productive and profitable, and benefit from subsidies, advanced technology, seeds, fertilizers and, above all, irrigation water, which the Israeli state controls. Israelis also have freer access to export markets; Palestinian goods must pass through Israeli checkpoints. The land taken by the ILA is often given to Jewish settlers, most of whom do not use it for production. In the late 1970s and early 1980s about 28 small Jewish settlements were established in the Galilee and these continue to grow.[28] The Israeli government has recently proposed a new town for some 50,000 "religious Jews" outside Nazareth.[29]

Israel is relatively "food secure" and exports some 20 percent of its production. The shift to industrial agriculture over the last two decades has reduced the number of agricultural jobs so that only 6.3 percent of the population now works in agriculture and agricultural services.[30] Palestinians, who relied heavily on agriculture first as direct producers then as laborers on Israeli farms, are now largely separated from the land. After the Second Intifada less than a decade ago, Israelis gave seasonal agricultural jobs to migrant laborers instead of Palestinians.[31] Israel also contributed to the decline of Palestinian farming by refusing to make more land available for growing by Palestinian farm families, who have relatively high birth rates and traditionally divide their land equally among all children. This leads to inefficient *minifundia*. Agriculture was both a major source of subsistence and a pillar of the local Palestinian economy and society; it is no longer.

Palestinian memories of connection to the land are sharply at odds with the settler's urban myth. The olive tree is of real and symbolic importance. When Palestinian farms are taken over, olive trees which may be hundreds of years old are often uprooted, wiping out both history and livelihoods.[32]

Jerusalem: The Layers of Holy Land Apartheid

The 2005 master plan proposal for Jerusalem set the goal that no more than 40 percent of the population of Jerusalem would be Palestinian; this represented a change from the previous goal of 30 percent.[33] While recognizing the high rates of growth in the Palestinian population, the plan still holds that the majority of the city's population should remain Jewish and European. While most Palestinians call for Jerusalem to be the capital of a future Palestinian state, and accept the reality that it will also remain the capital of Israel, the Israeli government has offered no such compromise. As a result, the struggle to control local territory continues by other means, and land use planning is one of them.

Israeli statistics show that the City of Jerusalem currently has a population of 720,000, about one-third Palestinian (mostly in East Jerusalem) and two-thirds Israeli Jews and European immigrants.[34] Jerusalem is the site of the most intensive demographic warfare, where the contradictions of Judaization are also most apparent. Jerusalem has hosted large religious communities of Jews, Christians and Muslims, all of which claim the city as a holy place. Judaization has further fragmented the city and region and created new configurations with enclaves defined by religion, ethnicity and class.

The 40 percent threshold for Palestinians set by Israeli planners is reminiscent of the *tipping point* philosophy that arose in the United States in the 1960s.[35] The idea of the tipping point was that in communities where white residents are leaving and black people are moving in, something needed to be done to prevent these communities from becoming segregated and all black. The tipping point philosophy asserted that there is an objective threshold of black to total population beyond which communities become all black. To preserve integrated communities, the black population should be prevented from growing beyond the tipping point, or so the theory went.

The civil rights movement was divided over the tipping point philosophy. Some claimed that it was a scheme to keep blacks out, and was based on the racist and assimilationist premise that all-black communities were not viable or desirable, and the myth that black people lowered property values and contributed to the decline of neighborhoods. Many also felt it reinforced a range of public policies that resulted in the neglect of and disinvestment in black communities. There was little confidence that government was able and willing to implement it. And there was no proposal to apply the tipping point philosophy in new, exclusively white communities; attempts to set objective goals for integration of white schools or neighborhoods were denounced instead as a quota system.

Others in the civil rights movement saw the tipping point as a practical way to support the small number of developers and landlords, both public and private, that were committed to the goal of racial integration. Following the Supreme Court victory that struck down the principle of "separate but equal"—which had claimed that blacks and whites could have equal education even if they were in segregated schools—the tipping point could have been one way to achieve integration. However, defenders of the existing system of urban apartheid opposed every practical measure for change including school busing and quotas to achieve integration.

Whether or not the proposed 40 percent tipping point in Jerusalem is actually used as a guide for government policy, it raises important questions about land use policies. In the face of a higher growth rate among the Palestinian population, it may serve as a justification to further limit housing expansion by refusing permits. It is consistent with the Israeli narrative of Jerusalem as an Israeli city and the refusal to consider East Jerusalem as the capital of a future Palestinian state. It is a form of urban orientalism because it views the city from the point of view of the most powerful and dominant majority and subjects development in communities of "the other" to an arbitrary statistical threshold articulated by the majority. Behind the impersonal number is the state-sponsored dehumanization of a minority population.

At different points in its history Jerusalem has been a center of Jewish, Muslim and Christian worship, and at the time of the establishment of the state of Israel it was relatively integrated and diverse. The walled city of Old Jerusalem had a mixed population and there was relative fluidity between the Jewish and Palestinian sectors. After the 1967 war an Israeli military committee annexed Palestinian East Jerusalem, including 28 villages, and began creating Jewish settlements to fill the annexed space. It unilaterally expanded the boundaries of the City of Jerusalem, which now has an all-Jewish governing body. Palestinians have chosen not to vote in local elections or participate in the government because they believe East Jerusalem to be their land and refuse to be a powerless minority in a majority-Jewish government. Israel has rejected self-governance by Palestinians because it would contradict the Israeli claims of sovereignty over East Jerusalem. The 1993 Oslo accords left the Palestinian Authority with no jurisdiction in East Jerusalem and Palestinians rely on Israel for all services.

Eyal Weizman's brilliant analysis of the architecture and planning of the Israeli occupation focuses on the vertical dimensions of the occupation. To completely control the land, says Weizman, Israel has moved to control resources below ground, including the water table and archaelogical resources. Israel builds tunnels below ground to segregate traffic in the divided metropolis. Its hilltop settlements are meant to guarantee control over the valleys. And Israel's sophisticated air force and communications technology assure them control from above.[36]

Jerusalem's vertical apartheid resembles a huge layer cake of archaelogical ruins, with multiple strata built over the city founded in biblical times. The layers are physical, social and economic and intersect in complex ways. The physical layers start with the strategic high spots taken for exclusive Jewish settlements. High points such as Hebrew University, the Mormon temple, and luxury hotels allow for expansive views of the exclusive Jewish settlements housing over 200,000 people. These "facts on the ground" are visible from on high while the minority remains invisible.

Figure 5.5 Israeli Settlement in East Jerusalem

As with Tel Aviv, the early plans for a Europeanized Jerusalem had strong orientalist roots in British town planning. Weizman relates how in 1917 Colonel Ronald Storrs of Britain, perceiving the city to be overcrowded and unsightly, invited the British engineer William H. McLean to develop a plan. With typical colonialist self-confidence, McLean took only two weeks to formulate a plan. The plan required that all new building be of stone, similar to that of the old walled city. The requirement of the more expensive building material, then and in the city's 1936 master plan, would eventually prove a useful device for stimulating construction by the wealthier strata of the population while limiting more affordable housing.

The Israeli government uses the narrative of the complex layering of Jerusalem as a story of multiculturalism and tolerance. This is the official brand marketed to sympathetic Jewish and Christian visitors. In this imaginary, Jerusalem is a model of multiple religions and ethnicities though still the uncontested capital of a Jewish state. In reality conflicts among Jews, and between Jews, Muslims and Christians are frequent. However, the narrative of religious and ethnic harmony has contributed to a vibrant tourist industry. Jerusalem's Palestinian minority, when it is visible to tourists, is seen through the orientalist eye as a collection of quaint market areas, "slums," sacred relics, and dangerous mysteries.

Oren Yiftachel explains Jerusalem's layers as part of an *ethnocracy*, related but not equal to layers of class and social status. Ethnicity clearly intersects with class: 60 percent of the Palestinian population of Jerusalem is below the Israeli poverty level, compared to 26.5 percent of Israeli Jews.[37] The Jewish layer is multi-faceted, and includes Ashkenazi Jews (from Europe), a "middle layer" of Mizrahim (from the Middle East), and conservative and ultra-conservative sects. The growing Russian population occupies what Yiftachel calls a "gray area" between the Ashkenazi and the lower strata of the Jewish population. The Russians are beneficiaries of privileges and resources that Palestinians have no access to, akin to the white skin privilege that has benefited generations of European immigrants to America; upon arrival they moved quickly to the top of the social hierarchy, over American natives and dark-skinned people who had preceded them by generations. Immediately upon their arrival, the Europeans have full citizenship and privileged access to economic and housing opportunities. While the state evicts Palestinians and demolishes their houses, they build new houses for Russians.[38]

The immigration of Russians was part of the Israeli plan to win the demographic war in Palestine. Russian immigrants helped to counteract high Palestinian birthrates and reinforce the European majority. Yiftachel points out that many Russians "...were allowed to enter Israel because of their kin relations to Jews" even if they were not religious. This demonstrates, he says, "the relatively subordinate position of religion vis-à-vis ethnicity in the making of the ethnocratic society."[39]

The biggest divide between East and West Jerusalem is economic and social. Most of West Jerusalem looks and feels like a European city, arguably a bit like Istanbul in parts; East Jerusalem looks and feels like a "Third World city." The West has paved streets and sidewalks, the East has potholes and narrow or no sidewalks. The West has sewers everywhere, the East lacks sewers in places. Though both are under the jurisdiction of the Municipality of Jerusalem, the East lags in school funding, garbage collection, street repair, and water. Throughout East Jerusalem buildings have extra water tanks on their rooftops so they can save water and get through periods of low water pressure. Public water supply in Israel and Palestine is controlled by the Israeli government, another element in Israel's vertical occupation.[40]

Judaization of the Negev

In the southern region of the Negev, 76,000 Bedouins live in settlements that the Israeli government has designated as unrecognized, illegal and subject to eviction whenever the land is needed for infrastructure or the military, or simply at the whim of the Israeli government.[41]

In 1948, Israel attacked and destroyed Beer Sheva, a town in the northern Negev desert. Beer Sheva was then under Egyptian control and largely occupied by Arabs. Today the city of over 193,000 is 89 percent Jewish.[42] For centuries before the Israeli state the area was one of Bedouin villages—mostly regular settlements and not nomadic encampments. Today there are some 52 Bedouin villages in the region, only 16 of which are recognized by the Israeli government.[43]

As a result of the Judaization of the Negev since 1948, Bedouin Arabs now constitute 28 percent of the population but occupy only 2.5 percent of the land.[44] Most of the recognized Bedouin settlements are in government-planned and controlled townships. As military installations near larger Israeli cities including Tel Aviv are being downsized to facilitate real estate development, the military is now looking to the Negev as the preferred location for its larger facilities. Eyal Weizman describes the military's eerie reconstructions of Arab villages in the Negev where they practice the counterinsurgent "deconstruction" tactics utilized in Lebanon and Iraq.[45]

The Regional Council of Unrecognized Villages in the Negev[46] has documented the consequences of orientalist planning. The "invisible" and unrecognized villages do

Figure 5.6 Bedouin Village in the Negev

not qualify for basic services such as water, sewer and electricity. Their buildings are "unlicensed" and can be demolished at any time by the government. Israeli government plans for the area call for the relocation of the villages, but the plans were prepared without consultation with the affected communities and there is little confidence among Bedouins that the quality of life in the new villages will be any better.

In Beer Sheva, now home to Ben-Gurion University, European modernity and lifestyle predominate. Even the old town center put in place by the first wave of Jewish settlers has given way to a suburban-style, sprawled city that turns its European face away from the desert. It is the business and market center for a region with Jewish towns, *kibbutzim*, and profitable farms benefiting from state support for irrigation, technology and price supports, and large military installations.

Wrapping up Urban Apartheid in the Wall

In 2002, after the launching of the second Intifada, an extended act of resistance to the Israeli occupation of the West Bank and Gaza, Israel began building a giant wall intended to separate the Palestinian population from Israel and, more importantly, to divide the occupied territories into isolated Bantustans separate from each other. Combined with the system of military checkpoints and settlements in the West Bank, the "Security Barrier" would supposedly end the spate of suicide bombings and attacks on Jewish settlers and in Jewish cities. The 760 kilometer wall, typically 12 feet high and made of solid concrete, was justified as fortifying the dividing line between Israel and the West Bank and Gaza.

However, this turned out to be yet another land grab, and most of the wall was to be built in occupied Palestinian territory. When completed it will take another 6 percent of Palestinian land, reducing the total amount of Palestinian land between the Jordan River and Mediterranean to a mere 14 percent.[47] Most of that land is not even under the complete control of the Palestinian Authority because the Israeli military and authorities claim the right to complete access at any time. In some instances the Wall incorporates on the Israeli side Israeli settlements that were built in the West Bank, so it is also a device aiming to prevent dismantling of the settlements as a condition for a two-state solution. In many instances the Wall divides Palestinian farmers from their land, splits Palestinian towns, and generally adds greater burdens to the everyday lives of Palestinians.

Suicide bombers are no longer a threat, but this is as much a result of the exhaustion of the Intifada, the détente that followed it, and wide acceptance among Palestinians of a strategy of non-violent resistance to the Israeli occupation. The unprecedented level of military aggression and economic reprisals by Israel in the occupied territories during the Intifada no doubt played an important role. But the Wall also has gaping holes and anyone with a little ingenuity can find a way around it.[48]

The Wall in Jerusalem is particularly significant because it could make it extremely difficult for East Jerusalem to become the capital of a future Palestinian state. The Wall and checkpoints separate Palestinian East Jerusalem from surrounding West Bank towns, including Bethlehem, Ramallah, and Jericho. By incorporating illegally built Jewish settlements to the east of Jerusalem, which come within a mere 15 kilometers of the Jordan River, the Wall drives a wedge between the Palestinian towns, increasing the time and distance required to travel between them. Another expansion area is to the north of West Jerusalem towards Ramallah. And there is yet another to the south, an area currently only sparsely developed and with few Palestinian settlements. The effect is to give Israel control over most of the Jerusalem metropolitan area and isolate the populated centers of Palestinians in separate enclaves with all connections between them under the military and civilian control of the Israeli state. Jerusalem could not become a central place for Palestinians.

The extent of the land grab by the Wall in Jerusalem would be dramatic. The Wall goes east over 10 kilometers from the Green Line and within 15 kilometers of the Jordan River, enclosing an area planned for the expansion of Jewish settlements, including the area designated "E-1."[49] Due to pressure from the international community, implementation of the Israeli plan has been stymied but the plan remains. While the U.S. and European Union continue to publicly criticize Israel for its settlement expansion, as they have since 1967 (with a few exceptions), they have not used any of their carrots or sticks to stop settlement activity, the Wall, or other major aspects of the apartheid plan.

Israel's strategic long-term territorial plan, informed by both military and political priorities, includes stronger links between Tel Aviv and Jerusalem and a gradual merging of the two metropolitan regions into one giant bi-polar metropolis. This central axis is to be linked with a major infrastructure artery going north to Haifa and one going south to Beer Sheva. The highway and rail infrastructure is a key element in shaping this future.[50] Israel controls all roads between and within Israeli cities. They have built a separate system of apartheid roads serving the Israeli settlements and accessible only to Israelis (and Palestinians with military clearance). The Israeli government also controls the system of roads in the Occupied Territories, on the ground via the checkpoints and from the air. The Wall will wrap up the apartheid system, encasing the Palestinian Bantustans in isolated settlements that, like Gaza today, function as urban prisons (to use the term of the United Nations Rapporteur on Human Rights).

The Wall is both a political statement and icon, a symbol of Israel's power to control movement and flows, indeed all exchanges—economic, social and political. The political effect of the Wall and checkpoints on Israelis is as important as the effect on Palestinians. Israelis are discouraged from going to the West Bank and Gaza, thereby reinforcing the estrangement from Palestinian people and their daily lives. They never see or hear of the conditions which the security network has created on the other side of the Wall. They never have to feel any pangs of conscience over the conditions their government has created for "the others."

The Right to the City

Despite the apparent continuity of official policy, there are many hopeful signs of change. Peaceful resistance and struggles against displacement are widespread in Palestinian communities, and they work in partnership with human rights and social justice groups in Israel. The Israeli Committee Against House Demolitions (ICAHD) organizes protests and Planners for Planning Rights (Bimkom) brings professional and legal expertise to bear to protect communities from displacement. A host of organizations continue to challenge the Israeli checkpoints and Wall.

Even after the "Arab spring" of 2011, however, Israel has little incentive to change course or to agree to a two-state solution and the establishment of full rights for Palestinians. It has the most powerful military and only nuclear arsenal in the Middle East. It is one of the largest recipients of U.S. military aid. The Obama administration carried forward the U.S. policies tolerating the Wall, checkpoints, and gradual incursion of Israeli settlements in Palestinian territory even while issuing ineffective verbal protests. While the Obama administration has pursued a slightly more balanced approach, speaking more critically about settlements in the occupied territories and calling explicitly for a return to 1967 borders, the U.S. approach overwhelmingly favors Israeli stability over Palestinian human rights and their right to land. Urban orientalism and apartheid remain the structural barriers to peace.[51]

Israel is today one of the strongest capitalist economies in the Middle East and a player in the global marketplace. The state retains significant power in shaping development and Israel is a model of state capitalism. The vast majority of settlers, especially the latest wave of settlers from Russia, have been the beneficiaries of a powerful and exclusive welfare state that promotes and protects Jewish settlement wherever it fulfills the strategic needs of the security state.[52] The early predominance of European socialist ideology among some Israeli Jews influenced development of the collective rural settlements established as *kibbutzim* and *moshav*. But these were for the most part exclusive Jewish enclaves, represented a small percentage of the settler population, and today function more as locally-owned businesses than collective farms.

In his essay, "Inconvenient Truths about 'Real Existing' Zionism," Jacques Hersh shows how both Zionist leaders and their British supporters such as Winston Churchill understood that Jewish settlement in Palestine would be for "the good Jews" that did not support socialism or the Soviet Union.[53] Let us now turn to the attempts to build more substantial alternatives to the capitalist city in the twentieth century, particularly in the Soviet Union and China.

Chapter 6

Lessons from Twentieth Century Socialism

The USSR and China

Tom Angotti and Samuel Stein

Gore Vidal famously called the U.S. "The United States of Amnesia" for its collective inability to learn from the past.[1] A nation and culture that was founded by European settlers on boundless optimism made possible by a seemingly boundless frontier, boundless capitalist enterprise, and the boundless repression of labor (slavery) was among the first to "forget" the Soviet Union and Mao's China as soon as they melted away at the close of the twentieth century. In the 1980s, England's Margaret Thatcher gave the clue to the thinking that would prevail after the collapse of the USSR: "there is no alternative," she said, to capitalism. The deep-seated Cold War fears of socialism were retained long after the demise of these two giant states, and became part of the ideological stockpile used to destroy any remnants of the past and prevent emergence of other alternatives in the future. Seventy years of socialist city building was erased as global finance and real estate rushed in to join local oligarchs in the production of new orientalist enclaves. Short-term profit-making replaced long-term planning and the modern, carbon-intensive city multiplied the environmental problems left by the old regimes. Without looking back, the new regimes have failed to learn from both the good and bad of the past.

From the victory of the Bolshevik Revolution in 1917 until the 1990s—most of the century—global politics focused on a real, material alternative to capitalism—"really existing socialism" in the USSR and Eastern Europe. After World War II and the victory of the Chinese Revolution in 1949, it became the Cold War, even as the USSR and China took different positions in the global debate over the nature and character of socialism. This grand twentieth century struggle had deep and profound effects on urban trends and urban planning. To "forget" the experience of twentieth century socialism is no less absurd than writing off the history of Ancient Egypt, Greece, and Rome because we see their societies as flawed. No matter what our views of twentieth century socialism, if we are to seek alternatives in the twenty-first century, whether they be through different regimes of capitalism or a twenty-first century socialism, closing our eyes to the big lessons of the twentieth century—particularly to the "others" on the other side of the Iron Curtain—risks compounding the mistakes of the twentieth century going forward.

What, then, are the lessons to be learned from the "socialist cities" of the twentieth century? We now look in some detail at the Soviet Union, which had the longest experience, and then China during its rapid urbanization after Mao. Both the Soviet and Chinese revolutions brought their respective lands rapidly out of feudal backwardness and developed modern industrialized economies. Both revolutions followed the ideas of Marx and Engels and the previous revolutions against capital including the 1848 revolutions in Europe, the Paris Commune in 1871, and other uprisings of workers and peasants. However, the USSR began its trajectory from rural to urban in the 1930s while China heavily favored agrarian reform and rural development until some time after the death of Mao in 1976. Although the USSR even in the 1980s still had a smaller proportion of its population living in metropolitan regions than western Europe, it had a fairly developed practice of urban planning—orientalist in many respects like its European counterparts, but also unique in its attempt to chart a course distinct from the capitalist city.[2]

In the last part of this chapter we will look at the changes in these two nations after their turns towards capitalism—Russia after 1991 and China beginning in the 1980s. Their drastic turns have altered urban landscapes in only two decades, creating and reproducing new forms of urban inequality and enclave urbanism.

The "Socialist City"

The first lesson from twentieth century socialism is that central economic planning and powerful state-directed urban planning produced cities with characteristics sharply at variance from capitalist cities. Without private property in urban land, cities were not subject to speculative investments and market-generated displacement. Tenants were not subject to large rent increases—in fact, the average household paid no more than 10 percent of income on rent. Without a private labor market and large labor reserves distinct from the employed population, and with national guarantees of education, health care and other services, there was no significant movement of population that was not sanctioned by the state. A strong state, limited private initiatives and state-run enterprises were responsible for major large-scale urban growth, although they sometimes competed among themselves for prime locations.

In the first decade after the Bolshevik Revolution, there was widespread debate over the role of cities. Although the revolution was led by the urban proletariat, only 20 percent of Russia was urbanized and the majority of the population survived on agriculture. Since one of the fundamental Marxist critiques of capitalism was against the division of city and countryside, the question immediately arose of how to confront this division. In the *Communist Manifesto*, Marx and Engels state:

> The bourgeoisie has subjected the country to the rule of the towns ... The bourgeoisie keeps more and more doing away with the scattered state of the population, of the means of production, and of property. It has agglomerated population, centralized means of production, and has concentrated property in a few hands.[3]

Therefore, upon seizing power the proletariat would seek "gradual abolition of the distinction between town and country, by a more equable distribution of the population over the country."[4]

The debate over urban policy was constrained by preoccupation with a devastating civil war (until 1921) and the New Economic Policy (NEP) that followed it. The NEP consciously channeled resources into the countryside, including an ambitious rural electrification program to prevent the collapse of peasant farming. In this environment, a group of architects known as the "disurbanists" developed schemes to decentralize the population into small, planned towns throughout the countryside. Disurbanist Nikolai A. Miliutin offered up a proposal similar to the linear city of Spanish architect Arturo Soria y Mata and the Cité Industrielle of France's Tony Garnier. Miliutin also proposed common dining and laundry facilities. There were other experiments with collective living arrangements that sought alternatives to the atomization fostered by individual property ownership. Cities were to be made up of "social containers" instead of property subdivisions. The territory would be consciously organized in a hierarchy of communities, starting from the *mikro-rayon* at the smallest level—about 5,000–15,000 people—and a *rayon* of 100,000.

The disurbanist ideas were not implemented in any major way during the NEP due to a serious lack of resources. After the death of Soviet leader V.I. Lenin in 1924, the new leadership under Joseph Stalin confronted the stagnation and problems of economic development by turning away from the NEP and in 1929 beginning "The Great Turn"—towards rapid industrialization, mechanization and collectivization of agriculture, and the introduction of centralized economic planning. The Great Turn speeded up economic growth and led to the expansion of large cities. Moscow doubled in size. In effect, the accumulation of social capital by the state turned out to be as powerful a driver of urbanization as the accumulation of private capital. Labor followed social capital as it followed private capital, though in somewhat different proportions due to conscious social policies. The process for distributing and reproducing social capital was very different from in capitalist societies but in both cases they encouraged spatial concentration. This was a distinct policy choice by a centralized state that evolved into state capitalism; it was by no means inevitable and could very well have continued some or all of the NEP initiatives that distributed more social capital to the countryside.

The 1935 Moscow General Plan was a prime example of the emerging approach to Soviet city planning. Moscow's development had symbolic and political value as the center of the new socialist state, in contrast with St. Petersburg, which had been the seat of Czarist Russia. The new master plan for Moscow incorporated many leading ideas of city planning in the West—including Garden City and City Beautiful movements—and put a distinct imprimatur on modernist architecture. It followed the traditions of rational–comprehensive planning but did not have the power of private landowners to contend with when designing buildings and implementing plans, although competition among state-owned enterprises, and the power of large-scale industries and their managers, proved to be significant.

The layout of the region in the Moscow General Plan followed a regular geometry connecting multiple residential and industrial districts with a road and mass transit network composed of radials and concentric circles. The developed city was to be encircled by a green belt that would limit future development. Most of the plan's projects were implemented in a few short years, unlike so many master plans in capitalist countries that were held up by competing property interests. Moscow's grand subway system was built with substantial state investment and the help of volunteer labor. The building of a modern new metropolis was an amazing feat in the nation that was once considered a backwater in Europe.

The dramatic economic growth of the 1930s under five-year economic plans ushered in an entirely new approach to comprehensive region-wide planning. It was based on the principles of integrated development, standard services distributed equally throughout the metropolis, the preservation of green areas (a green belt), preferential treatment for mass transit, separation of heavy industry from residential areas, and the promotion of social interaction through physical form. This ambitious agenda included a goodly share of unrealistic idealism and physical determinism. But it was also a bold attempt to shape in physical space a new socialist society using modern industrial development and state-led planning. It sought to integrate complex urban elements through planning. The basic principles of Soviet planning, according to Vladimir Semionov, included the following:

1 Planned population limits based on demographic projections.
2 Planned community services within organically unified residential blocks, or "superblocks."
3 Basic infrastructure for rural areas, not new satellite cities, to eliminate the differences between city and countryside.
4 Continuous regulation of projects to insure conformance with urban plans.
5 The superblock as the basic unit of urban structure.
6 Inclusion of cultural and political needs in the programs for community services.
7 In establishing new urban areas, consider the unique environmental, geographic, demographic and historical conditions.
8 Architecture and planning should include national traditions.
9 The metropolis is a unified whole and each action should be part of a comprehensive approach.
10 In urban design, consideration of maximum comfort for housing; development of the city center as the heart of the metropolis; the use of standards; the principles of socialist realism, criticism and self-criticism.[5]

After World War II, the USSR embarked on one of the largest new city-building enterprises in history. Some 1,000 new cities were built throughout the nation, mostly around new industrial plants. This policy was not driven by urban planning, but was part of a decentralized industrialization and national security policy mindful of the devastation suffered during World War II, when the USSR lost over 20 million people, 1,700 cities and towns, and more than 70,000 villages.[6] It relied on central planning that distributed investments throughout the 15 republics and among the 100 nationalities making up the USSR.

   The new cities were planned for populations ranging from 50,000 to 250,000, and were only rarely planned to become larger metropolitan areas; this ultimately led to dissatisfaction of residents with the limited quality of urban life and made it more difficult to attract labor to these cities. The largest and arguably most successful was Togliattigrad, named after Palmiro Togliatti, leader of the Italian Communist Party, and centered around a giant Fiat factory. The city was planned for a maximum 500,000 people, but the current population is around one million (we will return to the question of planned city size later). This policy of decentralized industry continued until the collapse of the USSR. Writing in 1985, Morris Zeitlin noted that in the USSR "Most of the 3,200 new industrial plants built in the last decade ... are in small and middle cities of urban agglomerations."[7]

The Balance Sheet of Soviet City Planning

To very briefly summarize the experience of Soviet city planning and extract lessons for the twenty-first century, we might consider a balance sheet of accomplishments and serious problems. On the positive side, Soviet planning demonstrated that comprehensive planning can indeed produce reasonably large, functional cities. Most residents can enjoy a minimum basic standard of living and live without the fear of displacement. Soviet cities were not divided sharply into residential enclaves that separated people by class and race. However, each of these accomplishments had a serious problem attached to it. The integrated plan was implemented unevenly so that it was not uncommon for neighborhoods to lack basic services. Integration sometimes translated into monotonous design, without space for diversity and creativity. The low rents and stability of tenure were also accompanied by poor building maintenance carried out by overly centralized authorities with insufficient resources. Stability turned into stagnation, and there was limited access to new housing to meet the needs of growing and changing households. To sum up the balance sheet, we might conclude that the socialist city of the twentieth century was integrated but suffered for lack of diversity, while the capitalist city often had a great deal of diversity but lacked integration. As Jane Jacobs argued, both principles—her term was "integrated diversity"—should guide city planning.[8]

While the USSR's post-war urban development was significant for its scale and scope, the theory and practice of planning that guided it turned its back on the work of the disurbanists. Soviet planning's strongest roots were in the 1930s during the period of intensive industrialization and therein lay the seeds for the eventual crisis and collapse of the USSR. In the 1930s debates on urban policy were suppressed in order to meet the single-minded goal of quantitative economic expansion very much like the capitalist growth machine. The energetic debates between disurbanists and traditional planners were cut short. This privileged industrial growth and the application of industrial models in all spheres of society, including housing development, and later came back to haunt the Soviet system. Housing problems were one of the most important social issues leading up to the collapse of the USSR.

One of the hallmarks of Soviet urban planning was the principle of *optimal city size*. This is one aspect of Marxist theory and disurbanist practice that survived the 1930s. Planners consistently asserted that cities ought to have growth limits. These would be achieved by preserving the urban peripheries with green belts, calibrating and limiting the number of housing units to be built, and preventing unauthorized building or migration through strict regulation. Without a private land and housing market, it appeared that there would be no major obstacles to master plan limits.

Yet time and again growth limits were exceeded and then adjusted upwards. Planners did not pay enough attention to the powerful trend towards greater concentration of social capital in cities. They did not take into account the powerful effects of industrializing and collectivizing agriculture, which resulted in even greater migration to cities. The Soviet experience does not mean, however, that it is impossible to limit urban growth even with powerful state planning. It means that urban planning cannot control city size without close coordination with economic decision making, whether by private or state capital. At the same time that metropolitan regions in the USSR expanded beyond their plan boundaries, the smaller towns and cities that were planned without adequate social investments testify to the problems of separating urban planning and economic planning.

The most critical social issue in the Soviet city before the collapse of the USSR, however, was housing. Soviet housing policy proved that it is possible to guarantee stable tenure with low rents for tenants and that displacement, eviction and gentrification are not the products of natural laws but the result of a loosely regulated real estate market. They could be avoided. However, there was a serious housing shortage in Soviet cities, and it was much different from the typical shortages in capitalist cities. There was severe overcrowding in cities where supply never met growing needs. This was exacerbated by a high divorce rate which generated demand for new units for single-person households. Married couples often had to wait years for an apartment. New apartments were usually too small to accommodate changing needs. The standard minimum living space in the Soviet Union was only nine square meters per person in 1981, although it was increased to 14.6 square meters in 1985, still below the standards in other industrialized nations.

The economic model established in the 1930s favored investments in production over consumption needs. Yet even when there were aggressive building programs, from the 1960s to the 1980s, the planning apparatus treated housing as no different from any other sector of the economy, as a sector with quantitative goals to be achieved. In effect, performance in this key sector of city-building was judged on the basis of production goals, not whether the housing was creating a viable living space in a livable and resilient community. Serial reproduction of the standard housing unit became the goal, not careful planning to meet the changing needs of diverse households in livable communities. Economic planning based on quantitative goals clearly trumped physical planning and qualitative goals. Throughout the capitalist world, the 1950s saw a similar frenzy, although there it was driven by expanding capital surpluses and speculative real estate.

The emphasis on new construction to meet housing goals allowed government to claim success by the numbers; however, a large part of the housing problem was lack of maintenance and this required huge expenditures for rehabilitation of existing housing. Local authorities were technically responsible for building maintenance, but rents only covered about a third of maintenance costs. This is one example of how a highly centralized planning system was unable to address day-to-day problems of urban life. The planners might well have taken to heart the brilliant analysis of Friedrich Engels on *The Housing Question*. Engels argued against the proposal by the French reformer Proudhon to "solve" the housing question by basically giving workers their homes. Engels reminds us that someone has to pay for housing costs.[9] Even under socialism, having done away with labor exploitation and speculative land rent, the cost of building maintenance has to be covered from the economic surplus—which is, after all, produced by labor; thus whether labor pays with lower wages or higher rents is purely a policy choice, but either way labor pays. The (very un-Marxist) myth that housing is free became the basis for government and individual inertia, and led to a serious regime-threatening housing crisis.

The Soviet planners seem to have forgotten the original critique by Marx and Engels of capitalism's invasion and plunder of the countryside. In the 1930s social capital was enlisted to establish economic and political control over the countryside, expanding and reproducing the urban/rural divide. While there was significant material progress over the decades in rural areas, Soviet society became increasingly alienated from nature, resulting in some of the worst environmental disasters in the world. The comprehensive, rational economic and physical plans were part of a grand mission to extract Russia and the Soviet Republics from economic underdevelopment in the shortest time possible. However, Marx and Engels had some strong warnings against unbounded rational–comprehensive planning:

> The solution of the social problems, which as yet lay hidden in undeveloped eco-
> nomic conditions, the Utopians attempted to evolve out of the human brain.
> Society presented nothing but wrongs; to remove these was the task of reason. It
> was necessary, then, to discover a new and more perfect system of social order
> and to impose this upon society from without by propaganda, and, wherever it
> was possible, by the example of model experiments. These new social systems
> were foredoomed as Utopian; the more completely they were worked out in detail,
> the more they could not avoid drifting off into pure fantasies.[10]

The largest missing element in Soviet socialism was participatory democracy, for that could have put a check on the "rational" planners. It could have helped to thwart the one-way, top-down system of state power that led to the emergence of inequalities and a new bourgeoisie. The idealism underlying the administrative/command approach that dominated the Soviet regime reproduced ineffective planning and ran counter to the dialectical and historical materialist method propounded by Marx and Engels: "Men make their own history, but they do not make it just as they please; they do not make it under circumstances chosen by themselves, but under circumstances directly encountered, given and transmitted from the past."[11]

Russia after the Soviet Union

When the Soviet Union fell in 1991, calls rang out from Western leaders and conser-
vative academics for a new era of freedom and prosperity. Political scientist Francis Fukuyama famously referred to the collapse of the Soviet Union as "the end of his-
tory."[12] Then-president George H.W. Bush called on Russians to adopt the "American Dream" and embrace the notion of freedom as private property, claiming that "it is a dream that the Soviet people are now striving to make real themselves."[13]

The reality that emerged in the former Soviet Union, however, is much bleaker than the forecasts of triumphalist cold warriors. Russia today has many of the same prob-
lems it faced in the past—bureaucracy, corruption and limited democracy—but they are now compounded by an exponential growth in social and economic inequality. The socialist safety net disappeared and the capitalist dream world failed to materialize.[14]

In the immediate aftermath of the Soviet Union's collapse, international financial institutions, Western think tanks and orthodox economists called for a swift and uncompromising transition to free-market capitalism and retrenchment of the state. Supporters and critics alike referred to it as "shock therapy." Economist Jeffrey Sachs called for a swift transition to capitalism.[15] The International Monetary Fund authorized loans requiring "structural adjustment" programs that cut social services, liberalized financial markets, privatized enterprises and land, and committed nations to repay their debts with interest.

In the first decade of post-Soviet Russia, private wealth expanded as a new oligarchy appropriated state-owned resources. New consumer goods and services were created but access to them was limited. Social inequalities expanded. Without guaranteed employment, a new reserve army of labor grew and suppressed overall wage levels. The gap between blue collar and white collar workers expanded. For the first time homelessness became a significant phenomenon. While there is debate over the meaning and durability of these phenomena, alchoholism and its public health consequences grew exponentially and the average life expectancy went down—between 1990 and 2000 from 69.2 years to 65.3 years—a phenomenon unprecedented in a developed nation.[16]

The Russian state moved dramatically towards the privatization of public goods. Health care had been considered a human right guaranteed by the state but is now becoming a private health insurance system available to qualified consumers.[17] Mass transit systems are being sold off to private firms and independent billionaires. Public investment in Russian Railways, Sovcomflot (the public shipping fleet) and Aeroflot (the Russian airline) is being phased out, as each enterprise is being sold off in a staged privatization to be completed in 2015.[18] Russia's public energy utility, Unified Energy Systems, has been broken up and sold off to private bidders on the Russian stock market, following a pattern set by the U.S. deregulation and privatization of heat and energy services.[19] While each of these privatizations is important in its own right, they all represent the diminished role of the public sector and the end of the state's commitment to public services. They will make both economic and urban planning more problematic.

As the state retrenches and its ability and desire to successfully redistribute wealth fades, poverty and wealth expand together, creating massive inequalities. Immediately after the transition to capitalism, 40 percent of the country faced unemployment, underemployment or substandard wages. Since then the new monied elite is capitalizing on Russia's deregulated markets and disciplined labor pool, further widening the gap between rich and poor. Today, Russia's inequality levels compete with those of the U.S.[20] And while Moscow has long been the center of economic and political activity within the country, regional inequality has only deepened since the post-Soviet transition. Income in Moscow soared above the rest of the country and the city is being transformed into a secure enclave for global capital. Though it contains less than 6 percent of Russia's population, it has more than half of the country's banking industry, one fifth of its retail activity, and one third of wholesale trade.[21]

Urban Inequalities, Enclave Urbanism

Almost immediately after the collapse, foreign real estate investors landed in Soviet cities seeking bargain deals in land and buildings. They snatched up many centrally located properties ("location, location, location") from unwitting officials much the same way the Dutch "bought" land from the Indians in what would become Manhattan. Corrupt local officials became their partners and part of the new landed aristocracy in their own right. The U.S. Agency for International Development sent teams of technocrats to teach orientalist planning methods to local administrators. Urban planners were taught that land use planning had to be separate from economic planning, that comprehensive plans were unimportant except when identifying new areas for short-term development, that land development needed to be incentivized by public subsidies, and to achieve this local governments had to establish a modern system of land registration that would facilitate the growth of an urban real estate market.[22]

A new class of Russian capitalists, often referred to as "oligarchs," became rich by appropriating public enterprises and land and they are now establishing themselves as global players in real estate and finance.[23] For example, billionaire Mikhail Prokhorov is a major partner in the Atlantic Yards project, a giant, luxury enclave in Brooklyn (New York City) and Brooklyn's largest-ever development.[24]

The changes in post-Soviet Russia have visibly altered the landscape of Moscow, Russia's largest city. The center of the metropolis has now become a typical Central Business District (CBD), as large financial and commercial uses took over administrative buildings. Moscow now has a "downtown" with giant malls and boutiques. With increased land values, gentrification has led to the conversion of many housing complexes for luxury tenants. An advertisement in *The New York Times* recently announced the intention of the city's planners to double the size of Moscow by building a giant new CBD to the southwest of the center, following the path of Moscow's highest land values. While this area of the city had been somewhat better off than others, especially in the final decades of Soviet power, today the contrast with the rest of the city is growing.[25] Another obvious example of this inequality is the appearance for the first time of gated communities at the edge of the city.[26] These are much more luxurious and segregated than the cottages (*dachas*), some of them humble and others quite elaborate, that many top officials used as second homes during the Soviet era.

Another dramatic change in Russian cities is the expanded use of private automobiles. In the first decade after the collapse of the Soviet Union, the number of private cars in Russia nearly doubled, from 14 per 100 households in 1991 to 27 per 100 households in 2000. Today, one quarter of all adults in Russia own private automobiles, with analysts predicting the rate to rise to 30 percent by 2013.[27] This auto dependency was facilitated by the huge boulevards originally built in Soviet cities for public transportation, but with an enormous excess capacity that is now a magnet for the private automobile. Russian cities thus have acquired all the problems that go with massive auto use: more air pollution, dependence on fossil fuels, public safety issues, decline in the use of public space and the multiplication of enclaves reachable only by car. This has also created a powerful new constituency of car drivers to advocate for greater public support for expanding and maintaining the roadway infrastructure.

As inequality expands in Russia's cities, changes in the Russian agricultural economy are creating rural inequalities the likes of which have not been seen in Russia for almost a century. About one quarter of contemporary Russia remains rural or peri-urban. Since the transition to capitalism, decollectivization of agriculture has been an uneven but continuous process; some areas have resisted while others have moved completely into individualized farming.[28] Individual families and domestic and international corporations have been encouraged to buy land and maximize output. Black Earth Farming, a firm started by Swiss-Russian financier Michel Orlov, has been buying up land in southwest Russia's most fertile areas. This one firm now controls over 800,000 acres of farmland.[29] The transition to corporate and industrial farming has created new class distinctions and a small rural elite that earned the vast majority of their wealth from privatization.[30] Rural reforms have been met with protests over the growing poverty and inequality in rural areas, retreat of the state and the turn away from socialist ideals.[31]

In sum, Russia's post-Soviet transition has left behind huge sectors of Russian society, while embracing the most destructive and unjust elements of capitalism and orientalist planning. Instead of correcting the obvious shortcomings of the Soviet system and preserving its progressive elements, shock therapy was applied to wipe the slate clean and open up new opportunities for global and local capitalism. The theory and practice of Soviet city planning is worth more careful consideration for the lessons it offers in this century when global climate change, a new capitalist crisis, and a completely urbanized world require much more than "business as usual," short-term thinking, and a state dedicated solely to the expansion of material wealth.

China: Creeping Orientalism?

While Russia's transition to capitalism could be described as a brief shock treatment followed by gradual change, the change in China has been long and deep. In both nations there was a dramatic expansion of urban inequalities but in China it was accompanied by one of the most rapid and dramatic transformations from a rural to urban nation.

In the last decades of the twentieth century, China urbanized at a tremendous pace, as it moved from a relatively autonomous socialist nation with a large peasant population to an urban, industrialized nation and leader in global capitalism. China was a semi-feudal society at the time of its 1949 revolution but is now the second largest capitalist economy in the world. This astonishing progress was accomplished through a highly centralized state in a global neoliberal climate that permits the relatively free movement of Chinese goods and capital throughout the world.

China's urban transformation has been no less dramatic than its economic performance. In 1951, China was 10 percent urbanized; by 2010 it was over 47 per cent urban.[32] The United Nations predicts that positive growth will continue through 2030, when China will have an urban population of almost one billion. In 1980 China had 223 cities; just 22 years later it had 660, almost three times as many.[33] Every year, China's urban population grows by 10 to 15 million new residents.[34] China has gone from being a leader in rural development and peasant empowerment to an urban growth machine, building and expanding cities at an unprecedented rate.

In the following we will try to better understand this historic transformation, its relationship to twentieth century socialism, and the significance for alternative approaches to the metropolis in the twenty-first century.

Urban Planning in Twentieth Century China

At the beginning of the twentieth century, China's cities were largely the product of an inward-focused economy and society. At the same time, however, large urban settlements along the extensive coastline were engaged in global trade. In coastal cities such as Shanghai and Hong Kong the British had established a powerful stake in the opium trade. As global commerce expanded, the importance of these cities and Western influences grew. Several Chinese cities experimented with Western urban planning methods. In the 1920s, for example, the mayor of Guangzhou, Sun Fo, who was educated at Columbia University and the University of California, introduced Patrick Geddes' survey to Chinese urban planners, with the goals of building a communications infrastructure, improving sanitation, and creating open space for recreation. Urban planning was seen as a way to modernize the Chinese landscape and create order in an extraordinarily large and diverse country.[35]

After years of protracted struggle, Chinese revolutionaries overthrew the urban-based and Western-backed government of Chiang Kai-shek. China's 1949 revolution was won with substantial support from the peasantry, then the majority of the population. One of the first steps of the new government, under Mao Zedong, chairman of the Chinese Communist Party, was a sweeping land reform that abolished private property and created rural communes under the collective management of the people who worked the land. While there were unrealized goals and setbacks—especially during the Great Leap Forward (1958–1961)—in a matter of decades China made dramatic progress in social development.[36]

The new regime that took power in 1949 had waged a struggle for national independence from Western and Japanese powers and for a socialist society. They sought solutions from within amid strong suspicion of approaches that came from the imperial nations that had opposed them. Mao was a powerful voice for rural reform, and the restructuring of rural society around the commune was a top priority. Mao was openly hostile to urbanity and technocracy and suspicious of the loyalties of the urban proletariat located in coastal cities where imperialist influence was greatest.[37] However, Mao's second in command, Zhou Enlai, had been active in organizing the revolution in cities and helped to balance China's policy.

The new government's urban policies mostly focused on the creation of state-sponsored enclaves—*danwei*—in cities. These walled enclaves included state-owned enterprises and institutions, simple housing and medical, educational and recreational facilities. Very little attention was paid to physical planning and siting or integration within the metropolis, as urban design was not considered relevant to the goals of the revolution.[38] Urban master plans in the 1950s, though roughly following the rational–comprehensive approach widely used in European capitalist and socialist countries, aimed to industrialize without urbanizing. Indeed, the national priority was to disperse small-scale industry throughout the country instead of concentrating it in large factories in the cities. The goal was to provide work in rural areas so that peasants would not have to leave their communes and move to the city. As a result, there was very little internal or external migration, although there was a massive expansion in productive capacity.[39]

The Cultural Revolution (1966–1976) focused even more on rural areas. Many urban residents were sent to the countryside to work in villages and towns, further diminishing the importance of cities in national planning. After the Cultural Revolution and Mao's death in 1976 conservatives in the Communist Party under its new leader, Deng Xiaoping, effectively set the nation on the pragmatic road to capitalist development and rapid urbanization. The revolution that once shunned the modern metropolis and orientalist notions of urbanism ceded power to a new regime that embraced them.

Within cities, master plans began to create "foreign trade centers"—free-market enclaves in a socialist China that was now eager to accumulate capital.[40] However, the commitment to socialism rapidly eroded. Deng's reforms ended the Maoist policy of regional self-sufficiency in agricultural production in favor of specialized production for the national and global marketplace. The new "household responsibility system" drastically reduced the responsibilities of the state and created wage-labor and piece-work economies for small farmers. Finally, in the early 1980s, the rural communes were eliminated and their powers transferred to local government.[41] Under Deng, rhetoric about building socialism dissipated. As cities now became the focal points for China's opening to world markets, there was a gradual move towards acceptance of modernist urban planning. The plans were still pragmatic and short-term, now aimed at quickly expanding production for the market and creating new wealth. Deng famously summarized his pragmatic ideology and openness to capitalist approaches using the Sichuan proverb, "Whether a cat is black or white makes no difference. As long as it catches mice, it is a good cat."

After the Cultural Revolution urban development became a priority and in 1984 large cities were given the power to manage the surrounding rural areas and annex them for new development. In 1989, the City Planning Act initiated a process of devolution of urban planning powers to local agencies. Cities were required to create local comprehensive plans and manage land use and building permits. This gave cities new autonomy and represented a continuing commitment to rational–comprehensive planning methods commonly used in Europe and the U.S.[42]

China's Global Role, Orientalism and Enclave Urbanism

China's rush towards integration in the global marketplace led it to membership in the World Trade Organization in 2002. The prominence of Chinese products around the world and the vast influx of capital they generated have had important implications for everyday life in China. They have created a new era of enclave urbanism in China.

The Great Wall of China is an international landmark of monumental proportions built centuries ago and China's ancient cities have traditionally included many enclaves, but contemporary China is now building its cities as a collection of walled enclaves. No matter how much it may be rationalized by China's rulers as a national project, China's city building ironically bears the marks of "orientalist" city planning. Most of China remained independent and free from colonial occupation throughout its history, and perhaps this made it even more vulnerable to a "creeping orientalism" introduced by the rising urban elites in alliance with global capital. China's urban policy privileges the modernist metropolis severed from nature and the countryside, the city of concrete and asphalt with a motorized and high-tech transportation system, and the "rational" physical order achieved by planning from above. It sees both economic and urban growth in linear, quantitative terms while considering "external costs" to the environment and public health as factors to be mitigated and regulated. In a drastic shift from a rural focus in the early decades of the Chinese Revolution, planners today favor growth in the most urbanized regions. The regime privileges the urban over the rural, the city native over the migrant worker, and the formal sector over the "informal."

New shopping malls are popping up in cities around the country, including possibly the world's largest, Dongguan's New South China Mall. New CBDs are sprouting all over. China's new skyscrapers include six of the world's fifteen tallest buildings. The largest cities, including Beijing, Shanghai and Guangzhou, now feature brand new CBDs that attract global capital.[43] In less than a decade, Shanghai sprouted Pudong, a giant financial district, and is now on its way to creating another one of equal or greater scale. High rises are being built even in China's smaller cities, such as Wenzhou and Jiangyin.[44]

Housing prices in Beijing and Shanghai continued to rise above even American cities at the peak of the real estate bubble.[45] Between 2000 and 2010, Beijing's population grew by a quarter million people; Shanghai's grew by over 3.35 million.[46] As China's biggest cities expand and increase in density, some second-tier cities are growing at even faster rates. Foshan, a once-small city in Guangdong, grew by an astounding 19 percent between 2000 and 2010, by far the largest expansion of a single metropolitan area in the world during that period. Wuhan, China's ninth largest city, is enacting a $120 billion master plan that includes a new CBD, cultural district, 140 miles of subway track, and two airport terminals. Currently there are 5,700 individual construction projects underway in the city.[47]

China's central planners are enacting policies to create 15 "supercities" with an average population of 25 million each, and are forecasting an urban population of one billion by 2030. The Chinese government has hired the British engineering and design firm Atkins to plan 48 new cities the size of London in West China.[48]

China's rapid urbanization has had enormous environmental implications. Most of the energy for heating and cooling the cities is produced by coal-fired power plants, among the least efficient sources of power generation. Cities that were once filled with zero-emission bicycles are now overrun by cars and smog. Although China's powerful centralized regime has enabled it to move rapidly towards the creation of solar, wind and other less damaging sources of energy, there is still a great deal of catching up to do. Climate change is advancing rapidly with potentially grave consequences for China; temperatures in the coastal metropolises are rising at twice the global average rate and sea levels are rising at perilous rates.[49]

China's global role also has implications for urban and rural life in many other countries. Chinese capital is involved in "land grabs" in faraway places to fuel its own economy.[50] In Patagonia (Argentina), the Chinese state agribusiness company Beidahuang bought almost 800,000 acres of farmland, as well as the water rights for the area and a portion of the San Antonio port.[51] Similar deals have occurred in Brazil, the Philippines, Sudan and elsewhere. Chinese companies are buying land for agricultural production and new industrial enclaves in every region of the world to take advantage of low land and labor costs.

While China's approach to land and labor is basically the same as that of the other players in global capitalism, there are some important differences. Even in the areas in which capital has nearly free reign (the "special economic zone" of Shenzhen, for example), the land is still owned by the state and leased to corporations and developers. The country's labor and agricultural markets are still subject to regulation and centralized planning, even if some powers are ceded to market forces. There are enormous holes in China's welfare state, but the state has not given up entirely its role in both economic and physical planning.

Displacement and Enclave Urbanism

The "others" in contemporary China include millions of migrants without housing and basic services, those living in harsh conditions around special economic zones, and those left behind in neglected rural areas and towns. In addition, millions of urban residents have been uprooted by urban renewal bulldozers in Chinese cities.

The most vulnerable targets for demolition and redevelopment are the traditional low-rise neighborhoods—*hutongs*—many of which evolved through centuries of Chinese history. In global cities like Beijing and regional centers like Kunming, these neighborhoods are being destroyed in order to create "modern" cities. Old buildings are unceremoniously marked with a single, circled red character, signaling their imminent destruction (see Figure 6.1). Most *hutongs* are summarily destroyed but some have been preserved as tourist destinations and New Urbanist-style enclaves in the modern city. Once privatized and renovated, housing in the preserved *hutongs* is marketed to Chinese and foreign professionals, as well as businesses that cater to tourists in search of urban "authenticity." This preservation-chic aesthetic is a curious footnote to a process of massive redevelopment that has touched an incredibly wide swath of China and created enormous changes in the everyday lives of millions.

Periodic major events that capture global attention, such as the 2008 Olympic games in Beijing and the 2010 World Expo in Shanghai, have created opportunities for the state to pursue its redevelopment goals in fairly ruthless fashion. Entire neighborhoods were cleared, causing massive disruption and displacement, and the cities

Figure 6.1 Building Marked for Demolition, Kunming, 2005
Source: Will Rhodes.

rebuilt according to the state's new priorities and aesthetic. This phenomenon is by no means unique to China, but the concentrated power and enormous resources of the Chinese state make it particularly effective.[52]

These new inequalities reflect the biases of the nation's privileged leadership, but they are also the result of struggles, class divisions, and contradictions within the state. From a distance, the state and the Communist Party appear as monolithic entities, united in pursuit of a new social and economic vision for China. This, however, is inaccurate and oversimplified. Within the leadership there are both advocates of free-market ideology and bastions of Maoist thought; those insensitive to existing residents and those who defend their rights. In general the free market prevails but it does not prevail exclusively.[53]

China's reforms may not amount to a single plan or political program, but taken as a whole they point in the direction of increased privatization, urbanization of rural areas, industrialization of agriculture, massive migration to the cities, and the prioritization of enormous infrastructure and development projects. Three different processes characterize this new urbanization: conversion of agricultural land into urban spaces; construction of "megaprojects" that simultaneously connect and segregate the country; and a massive migration of workers from countryside to city.

Conversion of Rural to Urban Land

During Deng Xiaoping's tenure as China's leader (1978–1992), the state identified 424 "growth points" in China, first on the eastern coast and then throughout the country. These areas were relieved of many regulations and given a great deal of autonomy. They included Special Economic Zones (such as Shenzhen), Open Economic Areas (like the Pearl River Delta), free trade zones (similar to those in developing countries around the world), state tourist zones, and other forms for enclave development. Four cities—Beijing, Shanghai, Tianjin, and Chongqing—were given authority over their surrounding regions. These actions helped create internal competition for foreign direct investment, state funds and development projects.[54]

The primary mechanism for state-driven urbanization in both rural and urban areas has been the transfer of land development rights from the state to private owners. While land in China is still state-owned, local governments sell long-term leases that effectively give developers ownership rights. To maximize returns, developers then build large-scale luxury buildings or new industrial ventures on what was once farmland. The amount required for payment to a displaced rural farmer is relatively small compared to that required for displacing an urban resident; this price disparity encourages developers to seek out opportunities in rural areas, rather than already urbanized spaces.[55] This accelerates the conversion of peri-urban land from agriculture and reinforces the growing insulation of cities from rural areas.

Some of this speculative urban investment fails and results in vacant buildings. Where it is successful, however, the former farmers often build small houses further outside the new cities and rent them out to itinerant workers. Rather than proletarianizing the peasantry, this policy quickly turns dispossessed farmers into urban landlords. These clusters of new "informal" housing become "villages within cities," occupied almost entirely by young, single men without papers. Demand for this quasi-legal housing is extremely high, given the escalating prices of "formal" urban housing.[56] On several occasions, these "villages within cities" have been demolished by the state, with native villagers resettled and migrants left homeless or sent back to their home towns. The land is usually sold to real estate companies and the village committees are turned into joint stock companies for new private developments.[57]

This form of urban sprawl has occurred in China's most productive agriculture regions—the coastal and central provinces, which feature the best climates and most fertile soil. From 1985 to 1995 alone, these regions reported net crop losses on two to four million hectares.[58] This increases food insecurity and reliance on industrialized agriculture and imported foods.[59]

Rural agricultural land, once at the center of the Chinese political project, is now seen primarily as a wide swath of development potential and a means to feed a growing urban population. This turn towards urban domination over rural areas is not just a reversal of Maoist priorities, but a return to the capitalist techniques of rural land and labor exploitation and a negation of socialist notions of urban–rural integration.

Megaprojects and Infrastructure

China's rapid urban growth could not occur without the state's ambitious national and local infrastructure projects. These include, for example, the Three Gorges Dam, the 26-mile Jiaozhou Bay Bridge, and a high-speed rail network that could rival the European and Japanese systems. While the ruling class in the U.S. cannot even agree on a single high-speed rail line, China's rulers retain substantial power over resources and exercise tight control over internal opposition. Technocrats and planners are given significant powers.

China's national government uses its infrastructure funding to encourage local private development by favoring cities with greater potential to generate tax revenues. Coastal cities, for example, have access to many more basic services, including piped drinking water and sewer systems.[60] Around the 2008 Olympics, Beijing created 12 new sports centers, a cross-city subway, scores of office high-rises, a new airport terminal, and a gigantic, egg-shaped theatre.[61] Similarly, Shanghai, with a population of 13 million, managed to triple its economic output between 2000 and 2008 with massive construction and infrastructure projects, including some of the world's tallest skyscrapers.[62]

China's most famous infrastructure megaproject, and perhaps its most ambitious in terms of engineering and environmental challenges, is the largest dam ever built: the Three Gorges Dam over the Yangtze River.[63] The dam straddles one of the world's largest rivers and has created a reservoir more than 410 miles long. It was built to help power China's enormous urban growth and to prevent floods. The project has cost over $25 billion and is expected to generate 84.7 billion kilowatt-hours per year.[64] Planning for the Three Gorges Dam began in the early 1980s. Preliminary construction began in 1994, with large-scale construction taking place in 2003. Just six years later, the dam was complete. Over 1.3 million people were displaced by dam construction[65] and an additional four million could be relocated in the near future.[66] Entire communities and small towns were flooded.[67] Resettlement sites are increasingly far flung as the state tries to deal with ever-rising numbers of forcibly displaced migrants.[68] Despite the enormous ecological and social toll, many more dams are being built in China.

Chinese planning favors private and commercial automobile use, despite the known environmental and social consequences of auto-dependent urbanism. China has built an enormous and elaborate highway system that sprawls across the country. The National Trunk Highway System, currently 46,000 miles and still not complete, connects all cities with populations over one million and 98 percent of cities between 500,000 and a million.[69] The highways are toll roads, financed by private companies that float bonds and sell stock to pay initial costs. As every city and large town is being connected by highways, China is also building new, wide, high speed roads in and around its major cities. Road construction accounts for the largest percentage of infrastructure growth and most cities are now surrounded by ring roads.[70] While Beijing has been surrounded by a thin circular roadway since the 1920s, construction began in the 1980s on a second, much wider ring road. Beijing ring roads kept expanding and multiplying, and there are now six separate high speed roads encircling the capital city.

As China builds car-dependent cities, they are also leading the world in high speed rail, with more miles of track laid than the entire world's high speed rail lines combined.[71] The network stretches over 10,000 miles, half of which was built in the last six years. Trains reach speeds of over 190 miles per hour and connect most cities in the eastern half of the country. Despite its rapid growth, there are signs of stress in the system: a train crash in summer 2011 killed over 30 passengers; and fares are high and out of reach of the majority of Chinese workers. Work continues on new rail lines, however, with the network expected to be completed by 2020.[72] The simultaneous growth of auto dependency and mass transit is not contradictory but complementary—much as in New York City, for example, where feverish real estate speculation contributed to the establishment of America's largest urban rail system even as the streets were getting clogged with cars.

While the state in China spends enormous amounts of money on the construction of megaprojects, far less is paid for maintenance and upkeep. The state is constantly moving on to the next megaproject and fails to spend adequate resources on preserving what it has already built. This unnecessarily shortens the life span of new infrastructure, often leaving local communities and governments to pay for repairs. It creates even more pressure for local governments to sell land rights.[73] This also raises questions about the long-term prospects for these infrastructure projects and the cities they serve.

Rural-To-Urban Migration

As city borders are expanding and new construction rises across the country, urbanization is occurring in a far more personal way for millions of Chinese migrants who traverse the country in search of work and security. The number of migrants currently living in Chinese cities is difficult if not impossible to count, as their status is defined in part by their invisibility to the state. Leslie Chang, author of an ethnography of migrant women in Guangzhou, estimates that there are 130 million rural-to-urban migrants in China, accounting for the majority of the population in southern factory towns and a quarter of Beijing and Shanghai. These figures make China's internal migration the largest population shift in modern human history; there are three times as many rural-to-urban migrants in China as European émigrés to the U.S.[74] Eighty percent of construction workers and at least 35 percent of manufacturing workers are estimated to be internal migrants. Average wages for these workers hover around $100 per month, well below the legal minimum wage in Chinese cities.[75]

The enormous growth in the migrant worker population was enabled by three parallel phenomena: the shift in the Chinese labor market from agriculture to manufacturing and services; the decline in rural social and economic security; and the steady erosion of the *hukou* system which determined whether an individual was allowed to live and work in a city or the countryside.

While manufacturing has been a crucial part of the Chinese economy for all of the twentieth century, it is now more widespread, both as a share in the total economy and its geographic reach. Mao encouraged the dispersal of industry into rural areas both to increase regional self-sufficiency and to hide industrial targets from China's enemies. Deng Xiaoping established as priorities the industrial expansion in the west, raw material extraction in the center, and construction and trade in the east. Municipal governments are now allowed to give tax incentives to developers and industrialists in order to lure them to their towns, initiating the sort of "smokestack chasing" familiar in industrialized capitalist cities.[76]

The post-Mao reforms led to the decay of China's social safety net, which Mao called "the iron rice bowl." While scarcity was a reality for many before market reforms, the state provided some basic necessities. Employment was universal and social services such as healthcare and education were guaranteed. Conditions are far harsher in contemporary China, especially in rural areas, where access to basic necessities is no longer a given. Lifelong employment has not been guaranteed since 1996 and rural pensions are a rarity.[77] Township and village clinics have closed all over rural China, replaced by fee-for-service healthcare that excludes most peasants.[78] Rural towns have become dumping grounds for the most toxic industrial by-products, leaving land, air and water severely polluted.[79] These difficult conditions propel many young men and women to leave rural areas in search of steady—if substandard— work in China's growing cities.

The extensive rural-to-urban migration is also made possible by declining enforcement of China's *hukou* system. Instituted under Mao in 1955, *hukous* determine the status of an individual as a rural or urban citizen. Originally, entire communes or *danweis* were given collective rural or urban *hukous*. They were the "ticket" to social services, including medical care, a pension, education and non-primary food.[80] Many migrant workers do not have urban *hukous*, creating a two-tiered labor system similar to the citizen/non-citizen divide in the U.S. and European labor markets. This benefits employers by creating competition between workers, lowering wage levels and making worker solidarity more difficult.[81]

The state is beginning to realize that the migrant labor system is unsustainable and many observers believe that China will eventually do away with the *hukou* system entirely.[82] In the meantime, however, Chinese cities are experiencing phenomena more commonly associated with capitalist labor markets than planned economies: a competitive two-tiered labor system and a large reserve army of the unemployed. This is allowed and encouraged by the state and is as much a part of contemporary city planning as the monumental feats of urban engineering and city building.

Lessons from Twentieth Century Socialist Cities

Contemporary Russian and Chinese urbanization is often discussed in apocalyptic terms. The rapid pace of urban development is presented as catastrophic, the brutal remnants of communist perversion or the nightmare world of primitive capitalism unbound.[83] Neither of these simplistic notions are revealing and both tend to revert to facile dualisms. The early attempts in the Soviet Union and the People's Republic of China to plan for cities were based on a commitment to meet human needs instead of profit and eliminate the differences between city and countryside. These efforts were contradictory; they were partially successful and partially a failure. They brought two of the largest nations in the world out of feudalism and extreme poverty, constructed the outlines of a more just economic and social system, and created cities without landlords, evictions and massive displacement. Their cities had modern infrastructure and were not sharply segregated into social enclaves. However, they were sorely lacking in maintenance, mobility, diversity and participatory democracy. The USSR eventually abandoned the search for the socialist city before it dissolved and Mao's China never moved past its anti-urban biases.

After the demise of the USSR and Mao's China, twentieth century socialism became history and the myth of the socialist city died. Their successors disposed of many of the advances that had been made when they decided to enter the global marketplace and promote private land development. Contrary to the urban fallacy, the problem with urbanization in post-socialist Russian and Chinese cities is not population size, density, or design. The main problem is that urban growth now responds to the drive for profits, not the needs of everyday life for people who live and work in cities. The new capitalist economies with powerful centralized states breed structural inequality, social insecurity and environmental peril. These are real and pressing problems in these countries and around the world.

Both Russia and China have experienced rapid and uneven transitions towards market economies and integration with global finance capital. It remains to be seen how much further they can go without the implosion of their new political systems. New social movements have arisen in both nations; they stage regular protests that go largely unreported in the global media. In China, protests staged by independent labor groups and ethnic minorities have become daily phenomena. In 2010, 180,000 street protests were logged within China.[84] That same year in Russia, left social movements coalesced around a "Day of Wrath," with simultaneous street demonstrations in almost every Russian city.[85] Many movements are suppressed, bought off or co-opted, but dissent persists, and the Chinese and Russian states may be forced towards real change that learns all the lessons, positive and negative, of twentieth century socialism. In the twenty-first century they may have to confront the deep economic and ecological consequences of their passage from the socialist city through the gates of the free-market metropolis. It is time now for a new discussion about socialism for the twenty-first century, one that learns from the experiences of the last one while at the same time returning to the powerful insights of Marx and Engels on cities and rural areas, and recovers the powerful tools of dialectical and historical materialism.

Chapter 7

The Free-Market Metropolis and Enclave Urbanism

The persistence of orientalist ideas and practices in metropolitan development and planning around the world coincides with the growing influence of the approach that was made in the United States of America. Even as the relative role of the U.S. in the global economy declines, and its ability to exercise its military supremacy wanes, U.S. dominance in global communications, finance and real estate has placed it in a position to liberally market its model of metropolitan growth around the world. It is also copied, emulated, and independently adapted by the army of architects and planners trained under orientalist masters.

What then is the U.S. approach?[1] The U.S. model of metropolitan development is founded on a unique, orthodox free-market ideology. The free-market metropolis is not a coherent or readily identifiable form of human settlement but rather a collection of ideas and practices that lead to the formation of separate and unequal enclaves, what we call *enclave urbanism*. Backed by a powerful global Finance, Insurance and Real Estate (FIRE) sector, and facing weakened states and pliable governments, the U.S. model is appearing in every metropolis where resistance from national elites and residents is unable to stop it. It is different from traditional market-driven approaches but often there is a good deal of interpenetration of both. The unique aspect of the U.S. model, however, is that it is driven by a liberal (and neoliberal) belief in the value of an unrestrained global marketplace for real estate and finance, a hallmark of the U.S. role in global capitalist development even if U.S. capital is joined in its speculative ventures by capital from throughout the world.

In the twenty-first century metropolis, *free-market ideology* is based on a belief in limited government intervention in the use and development of urban land, and is part of the larger model of neoliberal economic development requiring a state that faithfully serves the interests of global capital. Unlike some other regimes of global capital it is especially wedded to short-term thinking, short-term profit-making, and short-term planning.

The free-market model in the U.S. is producing a twenty-first century metropolis constructed around *enclaves*, individual investor-driven urban projects consciously separated from the surrounding urban environment. Following the *Merriam-Webster Dictionary*, an *enclave* is "a distinct territorial, cultural, or social unit enclosed within or as if within foreign territory."[2] *Enclave urbanism* in the twenty-first century is the pattern of metropolitan development produced by the globalized real estate and financial sectors, and codified in planning regulations, whereby metropolitan regions are becoming agglomerations of unequal urban districts, sharply divided by race, class and other social distinguishers, and often physically separated. Enclave urbanism is not random. It reflects the conscious adoption of policies that shape the physical and social life of the metropolis; it is not the absence of planning but the presence of a particular kind of planning, just as the self-built *favelas* and *barriadas* in cities throughout the world are built and maintained as a result of conscious human intervention and planning.

The U.S. free-market model of enclave urbanism builds on the traditions of *urban orientalism* (see Chapter Two). It is reified by orientalist thinking as an approach to cities representing universal principles. It requires objectification of "the other," both the vast majority of North American "others" displaced and segregated in the modern metropolis, and the invisible others around the world who are being displaced and segregated. Enclave urbanism is being exported around the world and the ideology of "free trade" is making it more difficult for governments to regulate it.

Enclave Urbanism in Planning

Enclaves were present in the earliest human settlements. At first there was simply a separation of functions: separate places were established for religious worship, commercial exchange, residences, the storage of food and wealth, and burial of the dead. This separation was an evolving product of the everyday lives and needs of urban dwellers. Many of the places were originally part of the commons, spaces that were accessible to all; but with the emergence of private property in land, some enclaves were appropriated by powerful individuals and clans and consciously separated from the commons. As class, ethnic and other differences emerged along with the growth of cities, enclaves became defined by difference.[3]

Enclave urbanism emerged in the earliest cities when the more powerful groups and individuals consciously created separate enclaves to reinforce and protect their power and control over resources and people. Separate urban districts housed elites and surplus from production, while many cities were fortified to protect them. European colonialism introduced new enclaves in the landscapes of its colonies. The British, Spanish, and other European powers planned their residential and commercial quarters in the colonies as enclaves, often fully enclosed and militarily protected (see Chapters Three, Four and Five on dependent urbanization, India and Palestine). Following the traditions of the medieval walled city and some of the practices used in colonial town planning, enclave urbanism expanded in Europe with the birth of modern town planning in the late nineteenth century. Separation by class (in particular) became a defining element in Haussmann's Paris, spurred by conscious efforts by the ruling elites to control the increasingly restless working class. In England, the planning schemes of Patrick Geddes and Ebenezer Howard sought to create extraordinary examples of integrated urban development, but always within newly founded, separate enclaves. Thus, the theory and practice of creating cities around the enclaves of the powerful, isolating the enclaves of the working population, evolved for centuries in Europe before it took hold in the Americas, where it was perfected and made an essential part of the modern metropolis. Spatial separation of urban populations within cities, by class and ethnicity, is as old as cities themselves, but the U.S. paradigm, today promoted by global investors and development companies around the world, has unique features.

The U.S. version of enclave urbanism differs in some important aspects from its European precursors. European urbanism has been constrained by the lingering effects of feudal relations, the power of the welfare state, and the role of organized labor. Even though there has been a convergence of the two systems in recent decades, deep historic differences account for the continuing differences in urban regimes, their spatial configurations and social functions. The U.S. was never feudal[4] and the expectation of the American settlers was that they, and not a prince or the government, would own, control and sell land. In the U.S. there was limited experience with the commons; instead, the indigenous people whose land was taken by settlers were banished from their commons and confined to giant enclaves run like colonial possessions, the Indian Reservations. The settlers had no strong historic ties to land, rural or urban, and equated the right to buy and sell land with individual freedom as guaranteed by the U.S. Constitution. In the vast territory of North America, European settlers slashed and burned the landscape, exhausted the nutrients in the soil, mined the minerals, and then moved on. In the nineteenth century, the frontier mentality equated this mobility and exploitation of land with the accumulation of wealth. In Europe, however, remnants of feudal relations and the persistence of national and language barriers limited the mobility of both capital and labor, and led to a relative durability of existing urban enclaves. The formation of the European Union and the Eurozone has broken many of these barriers and the U.S. and European regimes may be converging, but there are still enormous gaps between the two regimes.

Unlike most of Europe, the U.S. never had a powerful welfare state. The U.S. government still does not guarantee universal health care and education. This reinforces class and social differences and makes the working population more vulnerable to displacement by the movement of private capital. U.S. labor and socialist movements never achieved the power they did in Europe, so there has been less of a counterbalance to the unfettered movement of capital and the expansion of free-market capitalism. The U.S. does indeed have a powerful state, arguably one of the most powerful in the world, but it is more of a warfare state than a welfare state.[5]

While U.S. enclave urbanism is historically and physically distinct from its European counterparts, it has become a real and powerful force, one of the most powerful in the world, even in today's Europe. What are its main characteristics? One of the unique characteristics is that the walls around enclaves are often imagined instead of real. For example, segregated black and white neighborhoods are not usually walled off or fortified enclaves. They are presumed to be part of an open city where freedom, diversity and equality reign. This apparent freedom is constrained and rationed by the economic laws that shape society and the state. The promise of free choice, that one may choose a place to live and shop, is constrained by the market, and subject to structural inequalities that limit what any one may buy in the market. It is subject to racial, ethnic and other structural imbalances, caused by historical injustices and perpetuated through legal, social and market-based institutions. With the growth of the internet, satellite technology and the global communications market, virtual firewalls and controlled access have now dashed expectations that cyberspace would become a new commons. The contemporary enclave city is all the more difficult to challenge because of its semblance of openness.

Freedom and the American Dream

The U.S. paradigm of enclave urbanism is founded on a series of planning myths. *Myths* are leading ideas that emerge from and govern practice, even if they do not exactly correspond with that practice. They are not simply ideologies but have a material base in the economic and political foundations of U.S. society; they both reflect the way people interpret reality and govern social action. In his discussion of Latin American indigenous social movements, Ronald Wright says that "Myth is an arrangement of the past, whether real or imagined, in patterns that reinforce a culture's deepest values and aspirations ... Myths are so fraught with meaning that we live and die by them. They are the maps by which cultures navigate through time."[6] Georges Sorel famously described myths as "not descriptions of things but expressions of a will to act ... A myth cannot be refuted since it is, at bottom, identical to the convictions of a group, being the expression of these convictions in the language of movement."[7]

Individual freedom and private property are essential elements of the myth of unregulated land development. The fifth amendment to the U.S. Constitution enshrines the right of individuals to own property, though indirectly, by stating that private property shall not be taken by government "for public use, without just compensation"; over the last century this, like all individual rights, has been extended to corporations.[8] The right to own property is often interpreted as a foundational economic principle that separates "free" people in the U.S. from the feudal societies that preceded the establishment of the U.S., twentieth century socialism, and those capitalist regimes that strictly regulate and tax property. The individual right to own property is not simply a narrow legal principle but a guiding myth informing public land use policy. It ignores indigenous traditions that understand land as a sacred living element, and historic traditions of the commons.

In North American mythology the attachment of freedom to the individual is paramount; in its national anthem America claims to be "the land of the free." The most serious challenges to this conception of individualized freedom have come from the civil rights movement, which has struggled to achieve freedoms for entire groups of people who are denied basic individual freedoms and rights. Movements seeking the right to city and the rights of nature also arose to challenge structural inequalities masked by the myths of individual freedom. More expansive notions of freedom have not held much sway in the U.S. These include the concept of positive freedoms—the ability to do something—and the concept of collective freedoms—the ability to form and express group identities and act collectively. For example, the right of labor to organize is not guaranteed and highly contested in the United States. Amartya Sen, for one, advances a more holistic understanding of freedom that includes development and social justice, as well as individual liberation.[9]

Individual free choice is therefore a powerful ideological prop, and it underlies government policies that promote free market urban development while at the same time obscuring limitations on freedoms due to institutional racism and class oppression. For example, the central focus of urban policy over the last two centuries has been the freedom to own the mythological single-family home; the central focus of transportation policy for the last century has been individual freedom to move from one place to another using the car; the central focus of communications is the personal phone, personal computer and a host of other electronic devices designed for personal use. These key elements of the urban built environment are all geared towards the promotion of individualized consumption and presumably maximize free choice. Community and urban environment are valued as places for individual consumption, not collective engagement. Indeed, individual consumer sovereignty is touted as the cornerstone of all development: consumers are said to choose individual homes, cars, phones and computers because they *prefer* them (not because of advertising!). The individual supposedly votes with her disposable income, and the result is the action of a free people who effectively construct their environment as a giant cumulative act of individual choice. As we will argue later on, this myth obscures the reality of corporate control over housing, transportation, and communication sectors, the power of advertising, and the limits they confer on individual rights and free choice. It forces us to forget about social needs and ignore the many practices of collective consumption (such as public theatres, museums, and sports) that continue to be produced and reproduced (although many of these are becoming commercialized, privatized and restricted).[10]

An essential element in the urban myth in the U.S. is "The American Dream" home—the single-family home on a separate plot of land, the title to which is held by the household that occupies the home. The Dream originated in the settler society created by European immigrants from the sixteenth century on. It guided settlement of America's vast interior during the nineteenth century, promoted and subsidized by huge land grants to railroads and the Homestead Act of 1862 which granted U.S. land to settlers. The Dream also helped to drive the most intensive suburban expansion in the U.S., after World War II. The suburban dream home was to be filled with the appliances and gadgets built for the individual homes (not neighborhoods or communities). The individual dream homes were served by individual (dream) cars and an array of products designed for consumption in each individual dream home. The mass markets for these consumer goods were said to be so huge not because corporations and the state created an environment that made them socially necessary but because individuals wanted them. The city built on the American Dream was supposed to be the product of individual choice and everyone could freely choose where to live and how to get around the city. The huge class and racial barriers in the segregated metropolis had to be explained as merely irrational distortions that could be corrected, or worse, the fault of minorities and poor people themselves because they made the "wrong" choices.

The American Dream today is unimaginable without the consumption goods that are marketed as fulfillments of the inexorable promise of progress. Thorstein Veblen astutely called it *conspicuous consumption*.[11] During the peak of suburban growth, the consumer society was a mostly suburban phenomenon.[12] Today, however, it characterizes most of metropolitan America, and though the material being consumed changes constantly the necessity of consumption remains constant. It feeds the mythology that growth is necessary for progress and social welfare—the myth of the growth machine that unifies the political bloc, in public and private sectors, that supports growth as by definition equivalent to progress.[13]

As the U.S. global empire expanded in the twentieth century, the American Dream also promised personal security; technological innovation from military research helped to create generations of new home security devices that thrived on racial fears. The institutional pillars of the American Dream were the homebuilders, the auto-petroleum-rubber industries, and giant retailers who benefited from suburban growth. Advertising developed as a powerful industry that promoted and reproduced the Dream while also profiting from it.

For most of U.S. history, the Dream was realizable only by a strictly male, European-descendent property owning class. Slaves, freed blacks, women, and immigrants from other parts of the world were excluded from the Dream. The U.S. was founded on legalized slavery, which lasted for some two centuries, followed by another century of Jim Crow (legalized segregation). Until the Civil Rights Act of 1968, the Dream was for white people only, as federal housing policy explicitly denied government-backed loans to Blacks. In the U.S. metropolis of the twenty-first century, race still defines the boundaries of urban space. While there has been a gradual spatial integration of diverse ethnicities in both central cities and suburbs, the overall pattern remains one of sharply divided residential enclaves.[14]

This spatial pattern characterizes a particularly North American form of enclave urbanism that flourished in the twentieth century metropolis. Its most prominent feature was the sprawled low-density suburb made up of separate subdivisions, each with detached single-family homes. Replacing the small town's main street—a row of small, independently owned shops—was the shopping mall, a commercial enclave occupied mostly by corporate-owned chain stores; the mall became a restricted commons on property owned by a landlord instead of a municipal authority. With little or no mass transit, the private automobile was usually the only way to get to the mall just as it was the only practical way to get to the Dream Home. Despite the lack of options, the auto industry and transportation planners nurtured the myth that people generally prefer the car over other modes of transportation.[15]

Since the earliest human settlements, the concentration of power and wealth has produced greater concentration in cities. The wealthy and powerful have occupied central locations and displaced those around them when their wealth and power, and the value of their land, grew. Those who lived and worked in the urban peripheries—usually the majority of the population—were left to their own resorts. They built their own housing, laid their own infrastructure, and pulled together whatever resources they could to develop and maintain their communities. In the twentieth century U.S. metropolis, where the commodification of everything proceeded with minimal restraint, most peripheral development was commodified. Banks and insurance companies, with government support, controlled the flow of capital, corporate developers managed the subdivisions, homebuilders did the construction, and the individual homeowners expected to own and live in a property they could eventually sell at a profit. Given the relative abundance of low-cost land, including operating farms, at the periphery of the metropolitan areas, it was more profitable to build horizontally and feed the American Dream. At its most absurd extreme, this low-density suburban sprawl spurred the proliferation of "McMansions"—giant single-family structures produced in large enough quantities to bring the price within range of middle-income buyers.[16]

Suburban Nation, White and Black Enclaves

At the beginning of the twenty-first century some 80 percent of the U.S. population lived in metropolitan regions, and two thirds of them lived in lower-density suburbs. This was made possible by federal government subsidies for construction of the interstate highway network and mortgage financing of suburban subdivisions, showing that the "free-market" model requires substantial government support. Most metropolitan growth in the twentieth century was in sprawling low-density suburbs. Even as many inner-ring suburbs in older metropolitan regions experienced gentrification and densification in the final decades of the twentieth century, new low-density suburbs continued to rise in fast-growing new metropolises such as Las Vegas and Phoenix (at least until the market crash of 2008).[17]

The suburban enclaves of the twentieth century were disproportionately white, wealthy, and middle class, while the central cities were disproportionately black, working class and lower-income. African Americans were excluded from the suburbs as a result of local and national government policy and the institutionalized structures of racism. Government mortgage financing was explicitly denied to African Americans and local zoning regulations and tax policies made the American Dream unreachable to people of color.[18] As African Americans, workers with limited incomes, and new immigrants were excluded from new suburbs, their neighborhoods in older central cities suffered disinvestment (by both public and private capital) and became "ghettoes"—that is, enclaves with a stigma instead of caché. In the ghettoes, banks, insurance companies and real estate played a key role in the creation and maintenance of the enclave. Banks and insurance companies redlined these neighborhoods (literally drawing a red line around them and refusing to finance new housing or home improvements there). "The market" moved to the higher returns available in new suburban development. At the extreme, in Detroit, Cleveland, Washington, DC, and New York City's South Bronx, vast stretches of land occupied by people of color with limited

Figure 7.1 Public Works Support Private Land Development: The U.S. Interstate Highway Network
Source: Image from the Metropolitan Design Center Image Bank. © Regents of the University of Minnesota. All rights reserved. Used with permission.

incomes were abandoned by capital and government, resulting in the demolition of entire blocks of housing and leaving huge patches of vacant land. Federal, state and local government consciously withdrew resources from central cities in accordance with a policy one local official called "planned shrinkage."[19]

The official response to the gutting of central cities was to re-launch the American Dream, attributing to the Dream almost magical powers. In the 1970s President Jimmy Carter went to the South Bronx, a neighborhood devastated by housing abandonment, to promote "Charlotte Gardens," a low-density housing prototype to be planted in the midst of what was once a high-density portion of the city. Today, there are many low-density enclaves like Charlotte Gardens, but in places such as Detroit and Cleveland, where industrial jobs that went to the suburbs were never replaced, huge tracts of vacant land remain.[20] On the other hand, the places like Manhattan that retained their financial/real estate cores have produced new up-scale enclaves in the form of business towers, luxury apartment blocks, and exclusive urban shopping malls—luxury enclaves that look nothing like the traditional American Dream.

In the last half of the twentieth century many older sprawled metropolises began to densify, particularly their inner suburbs, and new, more dense forms of suburban enclaves emerged, often as private spaces with limited public access. This was not mainly the result of conscious public policy to counter sprawl but followed the pattern of market-driven land value increases. These incremental changes in land value followed a ripple effect, from the central business districts outward. The new higher-density enclaves were a far cry from the ideal of the nineteenth century homestead but were nonetheless promoted as bastions of security and personal freedom consistent with the American Dream.[21]

The new urban enclaves of the late twentieth century included mixed-use residential–commercial parks, gated residential communities, and high-rise apartment complexes. Specialized enclaves for leisure time flourished. These included amusement parks, casinos, stadiums, health clubs, resorts, golf courses and private beaches. With the onset of neoliberal urban policy and the fiscal crises of the 1970s, parks and playgrounds once open to the general public were subdivided into private concessions wherever profitable. Neoliberalism in the U.S. was not really "new" but mostly a return to free-market roots to open up new opportunities for profitable development; this was facilitated by the more generalized attack on the welfare state and commons.[22]

Even as the reality of the single-family home on a separate lot began to erode in many places, the American Dream was promoted as the centerpiece of national housing policy. For the last 50 years, every president, Republican and Democrat, has made "home ownership" their chief urban policy objective. This produced a gradual increase in the homeownership rate to a high of 69 percent, but clearly some of this growth was attributable to the sale of homes at inflated prices to households that could not afford to pay for them. The housing bubble and sub-prime mortgage crisis of 2008 popped a giant hole in the inflated Dream, but it continues to dominate discussions on housing policy.[23]

Real Estate and Market-Driven Development

The real estate market in the U.S. is the driving force of market-driven metropolitan development, freed from local regulations, restrictions and the constraints of tradition and heritage. Within monopoly capital, the FIRE sector is the leading and most mobile sector, although real estate was the last major sector of the capitalist economy to become globalized. While land and buildings are stationary, new vehicles for real estate investment such as Real Estate Investment Trusts (REITs) and global equity funds seek maximum flexibility for investment capital, allowing individual and institutional investors from throughout the world to pour money into hot real estate markets and remove it quickly when the markets cool. In the U.S. and increasingly around the world, global real estate firms buy, sell and rent urban land, and speculate on land value increases. Their investments can create and displace entire urban districts and affect the daily lives of millions of urban dwellers.

In New York City, for example, Forest City Ratner, a prominent REIT, has been converting a large portion of densely populated land in Brooklyn into a series of suburban-style enclaves. Its Metrotech office complex and Atlantic Mall are joined by a new sports arena and a proposed residential complex. These megaprojects have been heavily subsidized and facilitated by government powers of condemnation, an example of how public/private partnerships usually favor the private investors and neutralize government powers to protect displaced residents and businesses.[24] Simon Property Group, the largest U.S.-based REIT, is building enormous mall enclaves all over the world, with properties in almost every U.S. state (and Puerto Rico), as well as 51 malls in Europe, eight in Japan, and one each in South Korea and Mexico.[25] Another global REIT, Hines Real Estate Investments, is responsible for 920 high profile commercial and residential developments around the world.[26] One firm, ProLogis, controls 3,500 industrial parks with over 600 million square feet in more than 22 countries in North America, Europe and Asia.[27] All of these REITs are building enormous, largely single-use enclaves meant to derive profits for the global investor class.

The growing power of global real estate means that the metropolis is increasingly shaped by the capital and land markets and secondarily responsive to the needs of the people who live and work there. In other words, the exchange value of urban land is more important than its use value. *Land* is a commodity first of all and secondarily a *place* where people and other species visit or reside. What happens on, above or below the surface is subject to the land market. Land is first of all a thing, a physical object, and any value it once may have had as a common space or an animate and living subject is subordinated to its value as a commodity. Enclave urbanism in the age of the global land market is especially necessary because enclaves can be more readily marketed to global investors, who see them as more secure investments. Every urban enclave now has its price; in the modern metropolis all enclaves are drawn into the vortex of the increasingly globalized marketplace.

Enclaves and Urban Inequality

Enclaves do not necessarily have to be unequal. Physical and social separation does not necessarily result in unequal access to material wealth, better living conditions or freedom. However, when enclaves become the main building block of the metropolis, and when enclave developers dictate urban policy, enclave urbanism produces and reproduces the inequalities in the marketplace. Without a strong public sector, private enclaves will rule and expand the spatial dimensions of inequality.

Urban growth in the twenty-first century metropolis will not necessarily produce inequalities by itself. However, when the physical separation promoted by enclave urbanism is defined by income and class differences, mediated by structures of racism and ethnic discrimination, it becomes a form of *spatial apartheid*. According to Peter Marcuse and Ronald van Kampen:

> There is a new spatial order of cities, commencing somewhere in the 1970s, in a period often described as one of a globalizing economy. While cities have always been divided along lines of culture, function, and status, the pattern today is a new, and in many ways deeper-going, combination of these divisions ... They include a spatial concentration within cities of a new urban poverty on the one hand, and of specialized "high-level" internationally connected business activities on the other, with increasing spatial divisions not only between each of them but also among segments of the "middle class" in between.[28]

Spatial apartheid is but the latest and most dramatic example of *unequal urban development* based on differences in income, education, personal health and access to basic services; it is structural and deeply imbedded in regimes of unequal economic development. This is not to be confused with *uneven development*, however, which signals differences and diversity that invariably characterize all human settlements. Thus, the city with sharp divisions of class and race is not the same as the city with multiple ethnicities, identities and lifestyles, or the city with strikingly contrasting high-rise and low-rise buildings (see Chapter Three for further discussion of unequal development).

A persistent characteristic of market-driven development is *displacement*—of individual households and entire neighborhoods. In its search for greater returns, real estate destabilizes places and leads to displacement. Real estate investors seek to buy land in areas where the potential future value of the land far exceeds its current value. If people with limited incomes happen to be living on this land and can no longer afford to stay, they are forced to move. Whether the landowner decides to demolish and rebuild, or simply renovate the building, the current tenants are unlikely to afford the new, higher-rent housing.

Displacement occurs through either one of two mechanisms: gentrification or urban renewal. *Gentrification* is the more or less gradual displacement of people, without resulting in the replacement of existing buildings. Gentrification is not a new phenomenon but simply a term that describes the "normal" functioning of market-driven development. *Urban renewal*, on the other hand, creates relatively sudden and catastrophic events that result in the eviction of residents and businesses, demolition of structures and new construction, all of which increases the value of land on the market. It is often the work of private investors but when they are unable to assemble individual properties they rely on the state to use their condemnation powers, as in the case of Atlantic Yards mentioned above. The federal urban renewal program in the U.S. resulted in the displacement of millions of central city residents, disproportionately African American (and was dubbed "Negro Removal" by civil rights activists).[29]

Market-driven enclave urbanism fragments urban space and forces sharp divisions between public and private spaces. It also reduces the most active and exciting zone for urban life in cities—the gray area connecting public and private functions. Stoops, sidewalks and streets are gray areas where public and private activities intersect. They are the places that make city spaces lively and dynamic. In the days before TV, private cars and air conditioning, the older cities in the U.S. had a lively street life, amply described by Jane Jacobs in *The Death and Life of Great American Cities*. As front doors shut, they closed off the private enclaves. When the streets became dominated by cars, they also became unsafe for people on foot and on bike. This was not strictly "privatization" of public space but it has had the same effect. In the gray area dividing public and private functions ownership of the land is less important than control over space, which evolves through the everyday practices of people as they are shaped by social, economic and political factors often beyond their control. Therefore, in the neoliberal U.S. city where public spaces are being privatized the gray areas between public and private spaces are also disappearing, further reinforcing the transformation of the metropolis into a giant collection of enclaves.

The Iconic U.S. Enclaves: CBD, Mall, Entertainment Complex

The original and iconic enclave in the U.S. is the *Central Business District* (CBD). It is the classical urban neighborhood of the FIRE sector, capital's very own enclave. In common discourse the CBD *is* the city; for example, Manhattan's Times Square and Wall Street areas are what visitors call New York City. The emblem of the CBD is the modern skyscraper and office complex, the supreme vertical enclave. It is separate and

Figure 7.2 New York, New York in Las Vegas

unequal in both space and time: during the work day it is an executive enclave and at the close of business each day it is abandoned by all except the low-paid cleaning workers. Average wage levels vary in both space and time. By the end of the twentieth century most metropolitan regions in North America had several CBDs, each with specialized financial, cultural and service functions. For example New York's Regional Plan Association counts some 12 CBDs. Los Angeles has seven and Chicago has four. Even though some of the oldest CBDs, such as lower Manhattan in New York, tend to have higher densities and dominate economically, that is not necessarily the case in all areas.[30]

In the late twentieth century CBDs in the U.S. gradually changed from single-function daytime business enclaves to mixed-use, commercial–residential 24-hour communities. The growth of luxury residential towers in the midst of downtown reduced commuting times for employees, particularly those in the upper income brackets who often lived in suburban mansions. Luxury residential enclaves in and around the CBD guarantee and emulate the tight security of Wall Street's towers; "human capital" is protected so that it can reproduce financial capital. Ubiquitous doormen, electronic surveillance, and intercoms gate the apartment towers. This has generated talk about the value of "the luxury city," a term used by New York City's billionaire mayor Michael Bloomberg to rationalize his priority focus on attracting more of the wealthy.[31] New tax and regulatory mechanisms have been devised to make the luxury city a relatively independent enclave whose excess wealth will not be available to finance services in other, needier parts of the city. These include the use of Tax Increment Financing (TIF), Payments in Lieu of Taxes (PILOT), and a host of other neoliberal devices to insulate the excessively wealthy from any possibility that the state might appropriate it.[32]

One of the indispensable functions of CBDs is now tourism. It is part of the global competition to recapture the disposable income of elites and the middle class. In the neoliberal model of urban planning, financial capitals of the world compete with one another for financial sector jobs, upscale housing for financial sector workers, and tourists. The tourist "destination" attracts high-value spectacles including sports (including the Olympics), entertainment, and leisure activities.[33] The top urban tourist destinations in the U.S.—including New York, Las Vegas, Washington, D.C., Boston, San Francisco, and Los Angeles—have adopted this competitive neoliberal model, and work hard to promote themselves as capitals of leisure.[34]

Another iconic enclave made in the U.S. is the *shopping mall*. The first generation of post-World War II malls were designed exclusively for shoppers and shopping in lower-density suburbs. The second generation of malls, however, entered older cities and began to mimic their street life. These malls were planned with benches, spaces for public events, and other amenities. Today many malls have become entertainment and leisure centers with movies, video arcades and theme park attractions. However, they are still private spaces with public functions that are subject to control by the mall owner. On the inside they may look more like Main Street but they still function as enclosed malls surrounded by acres of parking and protected by private security systems. Today, older suburbs continue to face the chronic problem of mall obsolescence and abandonment, as overbuilding driven by land speculation takes its toll. At the same time, new malls flourish within the CBDs as corporate retailers like Wal-Mart (the largest corporation in the world), having saturated the suburbs, seek to squeeze into higher-density areas, edging out the last remnants of locally-owned businesses with a combination of price-gouging and tax exemptions.[35] This latest trend in the monopolization of the retail sector has contributed to the transformation of many older industrial downtowns into collections of suburban-style malls. For example, auto-dependent cities like Columbus, Ohio and Atlanta, Georgia have malls all over their CBDs, and Wal-Mart is lobbying to open its first store in New York City. When these malls fail they create a spatial void in a potentially vibrant area, and attract local and federal aid to sustain the CBD. As a part of the post-2008 federal bailout program, the Federal Reserve purchased a failing mega-mall in Oklahoma City from Bear Stearns, socializing the risk from this urban disaster.[36]

In addition to the CBD and the mall, the U.S. also gave birth to the corporate *entertainment enclave*. Coney Island was the ruling model in the early twentieth century and Disneyworld dominated at the end of the century. These were iconic creations made possible by relatively lower land prices outside urban areas. Disneyworld created new standards for urban spectacle with its "World Showcase," a collection of down-scaled toy-like replicas of buildings and towns from around the world. Disneyworld's representations of both the architecture and culture of people around the world reflects an orientalist view that manufactures and reproduces stereotypes. It is Eurocentric as it portrays greater differences within Europe while using broad representations of Asian, African and Latin Amerian cultures. As with the shopping mall, Disneyworld is engineered to encourage (and carefully monitor) mass consumption, and helps redefine cities as commodities that have been reinterpreted by Disney designers using orientalist lenses.

In the twenty-first century, the central cities in the U.S. are becoming the locus of the most active entertainment complexes. Building on the historic role of the urban center as a place for elite cultural institutions, and following the decline of industrial activity, central cities now compete with one another for leading positions in music, theatre and dance. The U.S. entertainment industry has a powerful monopoly over the movie and music industries around the world, but its home base is the U.S. metropolis, the place where music is mixed and modulated to appeal to the vast global marketplace.[37] To urban experts like Richard Florida, attraction of "the creative class" is an indispensable part of urban revitalization. If we take a closer look, however, it is really the result of the commodification of culture and its concentration in the wealthiest metropolitan centers. As many critics of Florida have pointed out, it contributes to the gentrification of central cities, displacement of working class neighborhoods, and growing urban inequalities.[38]

The Fragmented Metropolis

The fragmented U.S. system of governance reinforces the powerful role of local and global real estate development. Fragmentation of the state serves the interests of the concentrated economic power of corporate finance and real estate. Unlike most European nations, the federal government in the U.S. has never had the power to develop and implement urban plans. Even though federal housing, transportation and infrastructure policies play a major and even decisive role in urban development, local decisions on land use remain one of the most important residual powers of the (now 50) states. State constitutions pass on these powers to individual municipalities, and there are about 50,000 of them in all. Local control over land use is certainly a powerful force in urban development but it also has a mythical quality to it because federal policies, free-market ideology and institutional racism play the determining role by limiting the real choices available to government at the local level. Federal funding for urban infrastructure and services comes with mandated regulations. Constitutional protections for private property limit local planning and zoning powers and are necessary for the preservation of enclave urbanism, particularly in the suburbs.

Exclusion of people based on race and class has been one of the consistent if unwritten elements in local zoning power and relatively resistant to civil rights court challenges. Municipal governments use zoning to keep low-income people of color out of upscale neighborhoods and entire municipal jurisdictions. Zoning is the most widely used means of land use regulation; it is chronically exclusionary, making lower-cost housing and jobs unavailable to low-income people of color. Suburban subdivisions, approved one at a time by local planning authorities, tend to be separately-owned enclaves physically divided from other subdivisions. They are planned and designed to reinforce a local real estate industry that makes it difficult or impossible for people of color to buy or rent homes in pursuit of the American Dream.[39] Exclusionary zoning includes regulations such as minimum lot size, maximum building height, and yard and amenity requirements that increase housing costs and place housing beyond the reach of low-income households. Though exclusionary zoning has been challenged in many places with some success, it is thoroughly commonplace across the U.S., and is frequently used around the world.[40]

"Fiscal zoning" refers to the practice of using zoning to attract wealthier residents who can pay higher property taxes to support local services including schools, roads and police. Wealthier newcomers are also less likely to depend on social services like public housing and mass transit, thus reducing the relative tax burden on higher-income residents. Fiscal zoning is a particularly powerful tool in the U.S. because many services such as education and health care are mostly local responsibilities in the absence of a strong national welfare state. Once people move into these fiscal enclaves, they reinforce already existing exclusionary tendencies to protect their property values and taxes. Fiscal zoning is not only legal in the U.S. but is legitimized in some planning and economic development circles.[41]

Fiscal and exclusionary zoning reinforce racial and income inequalities within metropolitan regions. With the development of the suburbs after World War II, central cities became home to working class and poor residents who were surrounded by wealthier suburbs. This model of spatial inequality led to a spatial mismatch between affordable housing in central cities and available jobs in suburbs.[42] Since few metropolitan regions have effective mass transit options, low-income people cannot usually afford long commutes to suburban jobs.[43] This leaves central cities with large needs for public services and limited tax bases to pay for them. The problem is especially visible in public schools, where dollars spent per pupil vary radically across municipal boundaries within metropolitan areas. This regional inequality has been criticized by policy analysts including Myron Orfield and David Rusk, who propose to create regional governance structures that provide services across city-suburban boundaries, minimizing the inequalities between them. These and other proposals for regional equity have met with fierce resistance based on racial and class animosities, highlighting the depth of the political, social and economic barriers to regional integration.[44]

Another advocate of metropolitan reform and "the New Regionalism," Bruce Katz of the Brookings Institution, became an advisor to President Barack Obama.[45] Building on the regionalist ideal promoted by the works of Patrick Geddes, Lewis Mumford, Clarence Stein and Benton Mackaye, new regionalists argue for planning on more than the local scale. They advocate for stronger urban cores, consolidation of public services and regulations across metropolitan areas, and cross-border environmental management.[46] However, facing significant opposition from state and local governments and officials, the new regionalism has so far been unable to make much headway. As local governments now face serious fiscal problems, the poorest among them are under pressure to consolidate, but wealthier municipalities and local authorities are closing ranks and turning away from any consolidation of governments and services that would include people and jurisdictions with low incomes and limited financial prospects.

In recent years, the spatial formation of metropolitan inequality has surely shifted, with some central cities becoming elite enclaves, and inner-ring suburbs increasingly becoming home to new immigrants and working class people of color displaced by gentrification. This marks a shift in the internal spatial makeup of the metropolitan model, but only changes the spatial configuration of class and racial inequalities.

Smart Growth and the End of Sprawl?

The urban planning establishment in the U.S. is solidly behind the concept of Smart Growth as a solution to the inefficiencies and inequalities of low-density suburban sprawl. Indeed the American Planning Association embraced the term, turning away from the sad history of its predecessor, the American Institute of Planners, which supported the federal interstate highway, mortgage subsidy programs and local planning and zoning powers that helped to create the sprawled metropolis.

The basic idea behind Smart Growth is that conscious planning can concentrate new urban development in more dense configurations. This is said to reduce the widespread dependency on auto use and the negative environmental and public health consequences of sprawl. Higher densities and compact development are to promote greater energy efficiency, and reduce heating, cooling, and other maintenance costs. They would conserve land and save on public infrastructure such as roads, water and sewer lines. Smart Growth could in theory be an answer to the game-changing problem of global climate change in the twenty-first century.

The American Planning Association defines Smart Growth broadly as

> using comprehensive planning to guide, design, develop, revitalize and build communities for all that: have a unique sense of community and place; preserve and enhance valuable natural and cultural resources; equitably distribute the costs and benefits of development; expand the range of transportation, employment and housing choices in a fiscally responsible manner; value long-range, regional considerations of sustainability over short term incremental geographically isolated actions; and promote public health and healthy communities.[47]

A similar concept—*compact cities*—has taken hold in Europe, where it is promoted to maximize transit use, public spaces, and pedestrian and bicycle infrastructure.[48] Fifteen of the 50 states in the U.S. now have legislation that sets priorities and provides incentives for a more concentrated form of growth.[49] None of the Smart Growth initiatives, however, prohibit sprawl or mandate more efficient forms of urban development.[50]

As a focus for urban planners in the U.S., Smart Growth raises many questions. First, it assumes that growth itself is necessary and a priority. It does not question the overwhelming bias in the public sector in favor of stimulating and subsidizing new construction. It does not question and encourages the functioning of "the growth machine."[51] Smart Growth also does not address questions of economic and social inequality even though many of its advocates are quick to include in their remedies some inclusionary housing schemes with subsidized low-cost housing. And the adjective "smart" implies that the problem with growth has been a lack of intelligence—a subtle way of validating the "smart" technocrats and planners who are trained as rational–comprehensive planners. Finally, by suggesting that the solution to all the problems associated with low-density sprawl—inefficiencies in the use of land, energy, and public infrastructure and the public health impacts including traffic injuries and fatalities, obesity, and stress—can be resolved by increased density is to fall into the trap of physical determinism. True to the technocratic heritage of orientalist planning, it overemphasizes the questions of efficiency and underemphasizes issues of equity and human well-being.[52]

A more recent part of this trend in the U.S. is Transit Oriented Development (TOD). Originally developed to address the inefficiencies of mass transit systems on the West Coast,[53] TOD was designed to encourage high-density growth around existing and future transit hubs. This is aimed at expanding transit use and counteracting the inefficiencies of sprawl. However, TOD is so far a palliative having no significant effect on region-wide auto dependence and in many cases has been used to legitimize high-value real estate deals around transit hubs.[54] In New York City, for example, TOD has become a tool for selling giant luxury complexes over transit hubs by dressing them up as "sustainable" and green while they encourage auto use and do nothing to stem the decline in mass transit service.[55]

The New Urbanism

Another trend, The New Urbanism (TNU), has been vigorously promoted by architects, planners, design professionals and preservationists. It calls for more dense, walkable communities and frequently uses as a model the late nineteenth century small town in North America. TNU advocates are a diverse group; some start from a critique of modernism and rational–comprehensive planning, embracing the work of Jane Jacobs. Many focus mostly on small-scale, local planning. In their charter, the Congress for a New Urbanism, the umbrella group that organizes new urbanist planners and architects, defines their priorities as "the restoration of existing urban centers and towns within a coherent metropolitan region, the reconfiguration of sprawling suburbs into communities of real neighborhoods and diverse districts, the conservation of natural environments, and the preservation of our built legacy."[56] Critics of the New Urbanism, including radical geographers Neil Smith and David Harvey, have referred to their mission as "gentrification as global urban strategy"[57] and a "communitarian trap."[58]

So far the "neo-traditional communities" inspired by TNU, such as Seaside and Celebration in Florida (the latter notably located at the edge of Disneyworld) have become exclusive suburban enclaves. Many of them fit into and continue the pattern of low-rise, low-density development. Since they are often inserted in sprawled suburbia, they only marginally reduce dependency on automobiles and encourage walking. Design details like balconies and porches facing the streets may be marketable gimmicks more than integral parts of a change in lifestyle or transformation from enclave urbanism to integrated urbanism (or integrated diversity, to use Jane Jacobs' term).[59]

Smart Growth, TOD, and TNU do not break with but instead are reinforcing the long historical trends of unequal enclave urbanism in the U.S. metropolis. They may modestly reduce suburban sprawl but they do not significantly challenge it. National and state transportation and housing policies continue to subsidize sprawl as highways get widened and new roads are built. More importantly, they help to rationalize the trend of in-fill development that comes out of and does not challenge the evolving market-driven system of enclave urbanism.

Profitable in-fill development, often sold as environmentally correct because it encourages higher density, is the product of land value increases in central areas that increase the potential future value of land. No longer are the detached single family homes of the American Dream the most profitable in terms of return on capital per square foot of land. This change is also driven by the decline in average household size. The idyllic nuclear family of husband, wife and children now represents a minority of households.[60] Thus, real estate developers seek out places for more intense residential development and propose to build town houses and small apartment complexes on available land, re-branding the American Dream in the twenty-first century as part of a multi-family enclave. New clusters of dense development are having ripple effects within sprawled suburbia, encouraging further speculation, land development and the conversion of other low-density areas to higher-density enclaves.

In-fill development is not the result of "smart" policies. It came about because of the dramatic expansion of metropolitan regions in the twentieth century. New employers emerged in the suburbs and created new demand for housing nearby, reducing their employees' transportation costs and, in the long run, helping to reduce pressures for rising wages. Commuting distances to the central cities had grown and the costs were unsustainable as the metropolis extended its reach. This was exacerbated by the lack of public mass transit, which increased congestion and driving time to central cities.

In-fill development does not necessarily stitch together disparate, sprawled parts of the metropolitan region. In fact, it is spawning new forms of unequal enclave urbanism. Existing suburban residents often oppose in-fill for a variety of reasons—including concerns about their quality of life and the environmental impacts of new development, but also rejection of the new economic and racial diversity. Often deeply-imbedded racial and xenophobic fears in white communities take the form of arguments about declining personal security or environmental quality. While the image of the sprawled suburb was imbedded in 'the American Dream,' it was also an exclusive white dream. As a result, new higher-density development can be associated with the entrance of new minorities, people of color, and new immigrants—"the other." This can be followed by a backlash and cries for "preservation" of the community. For example, in Yonkers, New York, city officials and planners sited 7,000 federally-mandated public housing units in a single segregated enclave, covering one square mile of the city's west side, leaving the much larger east side predominantly white and middle class. Though declared illegal after 27 years of litigation, the case of housing segregation in Yonkers was merely an egregious example of a phenomenon occurring all over the U.S., in which middle and upper class white communities defend their communities by using the language of neighborhood preservation, private property rights and freedom.[61]

These continuing tensions over race and in-fill development encourage the proliferation of many physically separate urban enclaves. However, physical separation is not the only distinguishing feature of enclave urbanism and many enclaves are not protected by physical barriers. "Gated communities" are an important and controversial trend in the United States. However, the gating of communities may serve multiple functions and is not necessarily or only motivated by economic and racial separation. These communities include age-segregated retirement communities, large suburban apartment complexes, and subdivisions of single-family homes. They are part of the free-market metropolis and the American Dream, with or without the gates.[62]

Nature and Metropolitan Enclaves

Throughout the U.S. today, there is deep concern among both urbanites and suburbanites about environmental quality. This stems from growing public health risks associated with urban growth and suburban sprawl, including epidemics of obesity and diabetes and exposures to toxic waste and contaminants. Environmental quality is beginning to vie for a privileged spot next to the American Dream as a driving myth. Since the passage of major legislation governing air and water pollution in the 1970s, and the institution of environmental impact statements, the notion that the metropolis should meet standards for environmental quality and public health has been accepted in public discourse. In the last decade, even while a large portion of the U.S. population does not believe that global climate change is a problem, there is also an emerging concern among the larger local governments, including New York City, Los Angeles and Chicago, that one of the greatest challenges in long-term planning is to confront the risks of climate change. Nevertheless, local planning generally reinforces local growth machines and favors environmental improvements mainly to encourage and benefit new real estate development.[63]

Despite the heightened concern about the environment, little has been done to get at the roots of the inefficient, wasteful regime of low-density suburban sprawl and reliance on the private automobile. The detached single-family house, a huge consumer of energy, is still the American Dream. The personal car, computer, cell phone, iPad and iPod, remain essential elements of conspicuous consumption in the twenty-first century and perpetual generators of waste. Greenwashing has proven to be a powerful palliative by giving people concerned about the long-term consequences of the consumer society a way to feel better about their behavior. Products labeled "natural" and "green" help to assuage the conscience of a society gone mad over consumption. The fundamental underpinnings of the U.S. model of wasteful, sprawled market-driven urbanization are not under threat in the U.S. political arena where there is widespread consensus about the need to preserve the American Dream.

The final, and most decisive, indication of how far the U.S. metropolis is from becoming a model of environmental health is the way it has completely purged nature from within. Other living species, both flora and fauna, are maintained in segregated enclaves, under strict control by humans. Flora is consigned to rationally-organized gardens, both public and private. Fauna is strictly controlled by reducing the footprints of its natural habitats, fumigating and poisoning it, placing it in zoos and wildlife refuges, and enslaving it as pets. The U.S. metropolis is above all the exclusive domain of the all-powerful and presumably rational being, the humanoid—also a species that could be responsible for the continuing extinction of other species and its own extinction as well.

Chapter 8

Latin America
Enclaves, Orientalism and Alternatives[1]

Latin America is the most urbanized of the world's former colonial regions in the world. By 2010, 80 percent of Latin America's population lived in cities with more than 750,000 people.[2] It is highly urbanized because most nations in Latin America achieved formal independence from Spain and Portugal in the early nineteenth century, long before most colonial nations in Asia and Africa. It is also highly urbanized because its elites and oligarchies, freed from direct colonial rule, developed their own urban real estate interests. While strong neocolonial cultures and practices were sustained, Latin American cities are outgrowths of many national projects striving to achieve economic and political independence while at the same time never breaking with their dependence on Europe and North America. Latin America's metropolitan regions are therefore products of the accumulation of both global and local capital.

Despite the relative maturity of Latin America's native capitalists, urbanization in Latin America continues to reflect persistent economic and political dependencies and orientalist planning. But as an outgrowth of its long experience with dependent development and urbanization, Latin America has generated powerful, mature urban social movements that have struggled against urban and rural displacement linked to both global capitalism and national property-owning oligarchies. These urban and rural movements are many and diverse, and represent the best hope for progressive alternatives to oriental urbanism. However, the movements are also tenuous and contradictory and the pull of global capital remains powerful and dominant. In the last part of this chapter we discuss some of these movements.[3]

The efforts to consolidate national centers of power in Latin America since formal independence from Spain and Portugal in the nineteenth century have been constrained, often with violence, by powerful economic interests in the North and the political and military intervention of the United States. According to Greg Grandin,

> by 1930, Washington had sent gunboats into Latin American ports over six thousand times, invaded Cuba, Mexico (again), Guatemala, and Honduras, fought protracted guerilla wars in the Dominican Republic, Nicaragua, and Haiti, annexed Puerto Rico, and taken a piece of Colombia to create both the Panamanian nation and the Panama Canal.[4]

This was followed by 80 years of support for military regimes (Argentina, Brazil, Paraguay, Dominican Republic, and Cuba, to name a few), counterinsurgencies (the Contra War in Nicaragua), dirty civil wars (El Salvador) and coups (Guatemala, Chile). Although it is losing ground, the U.S. remains the most powerful military and economic player in the region and when it comes to models for urban development it still manages to compete with the more established traditions of European city planning, deeply imbedded indigenous practices, and powerful forces of resistance.

Enclave Urbanism and Inequality

In recent decades gated communities and households, shopping malls, central business districts, and other new forms of segregated urban development began to proliferate in Latin American cities. They are now prominent features of large metropolitan regions such as Buenos Aires, São Paulo, Lima and Mexico City and many smaller cities throughout the hemisphere. Spurred by the latest wave of capitalist globalization and neoliberal urban policies, the Latin American metropolis is now more open to these new urban forms and as a result more spatially fragmented and unequal.

However, while many architects and planners focus on these new gated communities as a serious urban problem, unless they are placed in the context of Latin America's long history of enclave urbanism and dependent capitalism we will fail to understand the social and economic roots of the problem. The problem is not gated communities; it is urban inequalities. The fracturing of the urban landscape into enclaves is not at all new. Social and economic segregation characterized Latin American cities in the empires preceding the Europeans, the earliest Spanish and Portuguese settlements

Figure 8.1 Caracas, Venezuela

and the cities that flourished after the end of colonial rule. Similarly, dualism and orientalism in urban planning have been constants throughout Latin American history since the colonial era, reinforcing and reproducing segregation and inequalities. Latin America's urban enclaves therefore reflect a unique synthesis of global and local economic, social and spatial inequalities.[5] Neoliberal policies since the 1980s, including the privatization of public space, have reinforced inequalities; but in reality cities are not necessarily more private than they have been since the first colonial settlements. Urban social movements are confronting enclave urbanism in new and creative ways; however, urban policies in most countries continue to support the fracturing of the metropolis through both traditional (colonial) and new forms of urban enclave development.

In Chapter Seven we showed how the U.S. model of enclave urbanism, now emulated on a global scale, results in the fragmentation of the metropolis into enclaves that are physically, socially and economically segregated. The U.S. model includes the single-family "American Dream" home,[6] the gated residential community,[7] the shopping mall,[8] and the financial district, or central business district that towers over the central city.[9] Throughout Latin America there are signs that this model of enclave urbanism has gained some ground, particularly since the latest wave of globalization and the neoliberal shift of the 1980s.[10] North American-style shopping malls with privately-controlled spaces are appearing in cities typically dominated by busy shopping streets and street vendors. One mall that claims to be the largest in Latin America, Parque D. Pedro Shopping near Campinas in Brazil, has 368 stores, a match for the giant North American malls in size and business success. Another is Shopping Aricanduva, which boasts over 500 stores and dozens of anchor tenants including Wal-Mart and leading auto dealerships. As an indication of the scale of investor ambition, in 2006 plans were announced to build Aeromall, a 620,000 square meter megaproject in Caracas, claiming it would be the largest in Latin America. It would have included eight roller coasters, a 4,500 seat auditorium, ice skating rink and 12,500 parking spaces, but has not been built.

Malls are growing in Mexico City, the largest metropolitan area in Latin America. This is a result of the expansion of the service sectors of the economy and a growing consumer society, themselves brought about by the latest wave of capitalist globalization and the North American Free Trade Agreement (NAFTA).[11] However, while Latin American investors actively participate in these mall projects, the leading developers of many of the largest projects are from North America. Megamalls in Brazil and Colombia are the products of a Canadian multinational, Designcorp. After it saturated the Canadian market this company is now focusing its investments in Latin American cities.[12] Thus, what might appear to be an autonomous Latin American trend is in large part the latest reflection of dependent urbanization, heavily reliant on the service sector of the economy instead of the export of primary and manufactured goods as it had been in the past.

Gated residential communities are also growing. These are often designed and built separately from the urban grids of cities that were once physically integrated by unified road networks. One observer suggests that there is a "gating machine" much like the familiar urban "growth machines" of North America.[13] Brazil and Argentina, two of the most urbanized nations in Latin America, are the leading consumers of gated residential communities.[14] Some gated communities in Brazil play on fears of crime and reinforce social segregation.[15] Racial segregation is also a factor, although it takes a very different form than in the U.S.; in one *favela*[16] where a gated community was proposed, a struggle emerged in which race and racism were central issues.[17] However, the spatial implications of racism in Brazil and other Latin American countries are not as starkly evident as in the U.S.[18]

Gated residential communities are in both large metropolitan regions and smaller cities. They have emerged in Mendoza, Argentina[19] and define the new elite enclaves of Ecoville and Alphaville in Curitiba, Brazil,[20] underlining the strong elite bias that is often obscured by Curitiba's attempt to present itself as a global model for sustainable urban planning.[21] In Trinidad, gated communities arose along with increasing inequalities resulting from neoliberal policies and a structural adjustment program imposed by international lenders.[22]

The skylines of financial districts in Latin America's largest metropolitan regions often look like the iconic CBD from the North. These CBDs are replacing multifunctional urban cores and, where conditions allow, miniature Manhattan skylines are emerging, dominated by modern high-tech office space leased to multinational financial corporations. However, specialized downtown districts are relative newcomers. For decades, manufacturing districts, including everything from electronic components to textiles, were established by foreign investors in downtown and outlying areas, often in participation with local oligarchs. These investments from the north, and increasingly from other parts of the world, produce local *enclave economies* dependent on the flow of capital and labor generated by foreign capital.[23] They may

Figure 8.2 Gated Community in Dominican Republic

follow the pattern established by the duty-free manufacturing zones, *maquiladoras*, located at the U.S.–Mexico border to facilitate the flow of capital and labor across national borders with minimal regulation. There are also new mixed-use districts with exclusive residential buildings built on redeveloped land. The waterfront district of Puerto Madero in Buenos Aires is a leading example. It was redeveloped as a mixed-use showcase for "sustainable" growth around an upscale commercial, residential and tourist enclave strategically located near the city's downtown.[24]

While enclave urbanism may be on the rise and growing in Latin America, there are counter-indications. General Growth Properties, the Chicago-based multinational and second largest mall owner in the United States and a major investor in Latin American malls, has filed for bankruptcy. The recent burst of the North American real estate bubble will reduce the availability of excess capital, although replacements from Europe, Asia and from within Latin America are making up for some of that loss. British real estate developer Squarestone recently announced plans to expand and complete its Golden Square shopping mall development, a 330,000 square foot high end retail center in the suburbs of São Paulo, Brazil.[25] China's Export-Import bank has invested over $40 billion in Latin America, with $24 billion spent between 2003 and 2009 and a new $1 billion sovereign fund created in 2011.[26]

Gated communities everywhere are fairly diverse in character. Some are for the wealthiest social strata and others are for the middle and working classes; the mixtures of local and global capital vary. But even if they look the same, they may function quite differently due to diverse social histories.[27] For example, one study found that Brazilians tend to socialize more in malls than North Americans.[28] Another found a diversity of approaches to malls in Chile.[29] In Buenos Aires, less affluent municipalities have embraced gated communities not as a form of social exclusion but to encourage private provision of public services. This is related to the limited capacity of local governments to generate local revenue as well as the neoliberal fashion of seeking private financing for public services.[30]

> *Thus while gated communities may be encouraged by and fit in with elite philosophies of exclusion and neoliberal policies of reducing public expenditures, this may not always be the case in practice. They are not necessarily the exclusive products of multinational investors or powerful national investors. Nor are they designed as automatic reproductions of the North American dream. There are deeper roots of enclave urbanism in Latin America's colonial and neocolonial history, and Latin American capital is deeply involved in shaping its own particular version of the fractured metropolis that has emerged from deep colonial and neocolonial roots.*[31] (emphasis added)

Finally, one of the critically important elements in Latin America's enclave urbanism is the epidemic of violence connected to deep inequalities. In *Upside Down*, Eduardo Galeano describes how fears of violence imbedded in deeper social fractures isolate both elites and masses in the Latin American metropolis. He describes the sad consequences of this fractured metropolis for the children of the elite:

> In the ocean of desperation, there are islands of privilege, luxurious concentration camps where the powerful meet only the powerful and never, for even a moment,

forget how powerful they are. In some Latin American cities where kidnappings have become commonplace, rich kids grow up sealed inside bubbles of fear. They live in fortresslike mansions or groups of homes ringed by electrified fences and guardhouses, watched day and night by bodyguards and closed-circuit security cameras. They travel like money in armored cars. They don't know their own city except by sight....They grow up rootless, stripped of cultural identity, aware of society only as a threat.... In cities around the globe, children of privilege are alike in their habits and beliefs, like shopping malls and airports, which lie outside the realms of time and space.[32]

Throughout the metropolis, and not just in new gated communities, luxury buildings are enclosed by gates and electrified security fences; upscale residents enter and leave by car and never have to transit public places or encounter "the others." Thus, public places tend to be more crowded and dangerous and subject to disinvestment and privatization. In some neighborhoods residents close off public streets, erect barriers and set up their own private security systems that separate themselves from the rest of the city. This is a metropolis of enclaves segregated by class and race. This is not new but an evolution from the long colonial and post-colonial history.

Colonial Roots

The roots of gating and enclave development are strongly imbedded in colonial history. The Spanish Crown issued the Laws of the Indies as a prescription for the development of urban settlements in their American colonies.[33] These were a set of prescriptions for the organization of physical space in a way that reflected and served the economic, political and military dominance of the Spanish. The center of the colonial city was the *plaza*, an open space that would be the center of everyday life for the colonists and, when needed, the place to muster their military force (thus, it was often called the *Plaza de Armas*). The church, political leadership and major businesses were located around the plaza. And the settlers resided in the blocks surrounding the plaza which were laid out in an orthogonal grid pattern. At the same time the wealthiest households (in both urban and rural areas) built fences and gates around their large homes, creating an early version of the gated residential complex. The plaza has survived today and is reproduced even in squatter settlements by people whose social status is far removed from the elites, and sometimes indigenous populations from rural settlements with entirely different traditions of public space. However, though colonial icons may be reproduced in today's metropolis their meanings and social functions in everyday life may vary; for example, many plazas have become dense commercial hubs saturated with street vendors, something the Spanish would not tolerate.

As shown in Chapter Two, colonial powers throughout history established dualist planning paradigms that separated settler and indigenous neighborhoods.[34] The most significant thing about the Laws of the Indies is not what was to be included in the colonial town but what was excluded—the large indigenous populations. They were the majority of the population and were left to fend for themselves. They were outside the plan. They were marginal, in the periphery. Thus was born the most primitive form of enclave urbanism and the dualist pattern of urban development and planning that dominated in Latin America. The powerful elite enjoyed the benefits of the "planned" or "formal" city while the urban and rural masses were left to their own resorts in the supposedly "unplanned" or "informal" city. As shown in Chapter Two, this false dichotomy ignores the planning that inevitably goes on throughout the city—since planning is really conscious human intervention in the urban environment, whether it is by a trained professional or not.

Another historical practice of great significance for planning was the destruction by the colonizers of indigenous settlements whenever they happened to be in the way of the colonial plans. The new Spanish cities were located in places that were economically strategic (usually on coastlines to facilitate the export of raw materials) and politically strategic (to insure military control over territory). Resistance from the indigenous populations, whether real or potential, resulted in the forced displacement of people from their communities and often led to mass murder. Thus was born a profound disregard for the communities of the oppressed that continues in today's urban planning practice when it results in the massive displacement of residents by both public and private institutions.

Post-Colonial Urbanism

After the victory of the independence movements of the early nineteenth century, colonial governments were replaced by new republics mostly dominated by elite settlers who were committed to sustaining the policies of dualism and displacement. Even after the elimination of slavery and establishment of formally democratic

Figure 8.3 A Barrio in Caracas, Venezuela

republics, discrimination in housing against indigenous and African-descendent people reinforced existing patterns of residential segregation. This segregation continued in new and more complex forms with the emergence of large metropolitan regions in the twentieth century. Massive migration to cities encouraged by disinvestment in agriculture, large-scale rural infrastructure projects facilitating resource extraction, and the disproportionate concentration of capital in cities produced a Latin America that is now one of the most urbanized (and unequal) regions of the world.

In the twentieth century, the large metropolitan regions of Latin America became increasingly complex and divided into bewildering collections of separate enclaves. The excluded masses were no longer solely at the physical periphery of cities but also in the very cores, living and often working at the very feet of the masters. The elite strata were increasingly separated in residential enclaves, but drawn together by transportation networks designed for motorized vehicles that granted greater mobility to those who could afford it.

Orientalist Urban Planning

Urban planning in Latin America came out of the professions of architecture and engineering as a specialized discipline that would ostensibly apply the principles of scientific management to urban development. It incorporated the philosophical premises of positivism and rationality, and a strong tendency towards *physical determinism* (see Chapter Two). The first generations of urban planners were from the elite classes and often trained in European and North American universities where modernist principles and prejudices prevailed. The urban theories of the North were often seen as new, more attractive and more sophisticated versions of urban dualism than those inherited from the colonial period.

In the late nineteenth and early twentieth centuries, examples of Baroque architecture and planning from Europe, particularly France, were applied in Latin American cities, notably Mexico City, Buenos Aires, and Caracas.[35] The modernist theories and practices of the Bauhaus and Le Corbusier also left their imprints on the central areas of many Latin American cities throughout the twentieth century. These were applied by European planners and, as time went on, most frequently by Latin American architects who had assimilated and adapted the dominant ideas and practices from the North, often providing dramatic innovations in execution if not conception of urban projects.

Part of the elite solution of modern urban planning in Latin America has been to replace the "slums" with modern, planned districts, so a fundamental premise of urban planning has been that the slums themselves are the source of urban problems. Following the tradition of Haussmann, the City Beautiful and the U.S. urban renewal program, eliminating slums was supposed to improve living conditions for the poor and reduce urban inequalities. It required a *tabula rasa* by leveling the slums and moving the inhabitants to better housing. Thus through rational–comprehensive planning the "informal city" was to be replaced by the "formal city." The new "planned" communities were supposed to have modern infrastructure, including sewage and water supply, a modern road network, and sanitation. Unlike the "slums," they would be built and maintained in accordance with "proper standards" that had been tested and proven true in European and North American cities.

Schemes claiming to solve the problems of "slums" promote images of these communities as relatively homogenous nests of desperation, crime, violence, and unmanageable dysfunction. The mirror opposite is the new, sanitized, secure and planned community, a paradise of social harmony. This paradigm fits well with the orthodox dualism of conservative Catholicism: the "slums" breed Evil, the new city is Good.

The dualism of modern urban planning, however, is not problematic only for its simplistic epistemology. It is most damaging because it rationalizes greater segregation and inequality in cities. As a strategy for solving urban problems it has been a historic failure. It gives all the power to the elite professional planners and leaves out any agency for the people who live and work in the "slums." As a result, powerful resistance to displacement has stopped the urban bulldozers more often than not. For example, in Brazil, large urban social movements effectively forced a reversal of the national urban policy of slum clearance and became one of the building blocks in the electoral success of the Brazilian Workers Party. Large and militant urban movements in Mexico City, Caracas, Buenos Aires, and Lima, to name only a few, also expanded the political power of those neighborhoods that had been targeted for removal and contributed to shifts in public policy and the success of progressive and left governments. While these changes are always vulnerable to pressures from real estate interests anxious to capture the potential land value of "slum" neighborhoods, and the influence of many urban movements may have now diminished, the overall result of a century of urban land struggles is that few can now argue with the view that the "slums" are here to stay.

The "slums," in fact, have turned out to be quite viable and complex communities, not the homogenous repositories of poverty as depicted in the orientalist imaginary. In fact, it is the elite who tend to live in exclusive and relatively homogenous enclaves for the wealthy and powerful. The "slums" are usually multi-class and multi-ethnic and often have an assortment of economic activity spanning multiple sectors. They are complex mixed-use communities where economic and residential functions often share space and interact. In 1976, Janice Perlman demonstrated in her research that urban marginality in Brazil was indeed a myth.[36] This reinforced the work of Brazilian experts, and it has helped urban researchers from around the world to understand that what had been designated as informal, marginal and unplanned was in fact the way of life for the vast majority of the world's urban population, incorporated a good deal of conscious planning, and was valued by its inhabitants and workers.

Dualist paradigms force us to make invisible the extensive planning and development that actually goes on within the "unplanned" city. In 1972, John Turner was one of the first in the global North to understand the way that most communities in Latin American cities are built by occupants without government support or financing by private institutions.[37] In fact, what looks like an "unplanned city" is a city that is planned in a different way, a different kind of urbanism. Planning is usually incremental and limited, not the result of large-scale interventions. This is not a new phenomenon but has been standard practice since the beginning of urban history. Unfortunately, Turner's insights were often used to justify the failure of governments to intervene and increase expenditures on infrastructure and services. Hernando de Soto's later glorification of individual, private initiative over public action carried this to an extreme and supported neoliberal programs to expand the role of private property and lending institutions, potentially displacing residents and businesses with modest incomes.[38]

The dualist myth also leads to a view of modern planning as a logical, rational process relatively free from contradiction and social conflict, guided by a coterie of trained professionals. According to the myth, the "slums" breed only chaos and its residents are incapable of rationally managing their communities or projecting visions for a better future. This mythology forces us to ignore the myriad ways in which communities have always managed their own problems and shaped their own futures, both in the physical city and its social and economic livelihood.

In the last century, the majority of people living in urban Latin America have built and managed their own communities without the "benefit" of urban planning. Urban social movements have waged many struggles to protect themselves from displacement by grand plans imposed on their communities, and generated their own alternative future visions. Nevertheless, violence and extreme poverty continue to plague urban neighborhoods throughout Latin America and structural inequalities prevent any long-term improvements for most urban residents. However, the newest generation of social movements in Latin America is beginning to advocate for different kinds of changes that include new relationships between urban and rural areas, and between people and land, and new approaches to the metropolis that address environmental and social injustice. Let us now turn to some examples.

Latin America's Hopes for Greater Equality in this Century

Until now we have presented a critical and historical analysis of orientalist planning and development in Latin America. We have not emphasized the importance of the urban social movements that have arisen especially over the last century as the "invisible" objects of urban development schemes have become the authors of new ideas, practices and utopias that suggest alternative urban scenarios in the new century. If we scan the globe in search of hopeful signs for the twenty-first century, Latin America has many to offer. The wealthier nations of the world seem to be wedded to regimes of resource consumption and accumulation that will be difficult to breach without substantial internal disruptions. The "developed" nations as a whole have built their cities by alienating land and expelling nature, and it will be difficult for them to reverse course. Many of the "newly developing nations," particularly in Asia but also in Latin America, are busy trying to catch up with them. The greatest hope lies instead at the margins of the urban world, with the social movements seeking to reclaim the rights of land and nature, in Latin America, Asia and Africa. They are part of a new phenomenon—movements that straddle both rural and urban places and link the struggles for the right to agrarian land with the struggles for the right to the city. These movements often project alternative sustainable futures based on long-term visions extending many generations into the future; indeed, they avoid the fragmentation of time as much as they condemn the fragmentation of space. They challenge the system of enclave urbanism.

Thus in the new century *the greatest hope for the center lies at the periphery* (including the peripheries within the urban centers). The metropolis can be salvaged by its hinterland and the natural world and people that have been historically excluded from its fragmented enclaves. Those who have been displaced from the land and those who seek to reclaim the land are posing new ways that the human species can sustain a more stable and lasting relationship with the land. They are in the movements of displaced rural producers and urban inhabitants who are seeking to reclaim land (and water) and establish new relationships between people and the environment. Although they are called "primitive" and "uncivilized" they may well harbor the answers to the systemic problems of global economic inequality, environmental injustice and climate change that threaten many civilizations.

Let us look at only three examples from Latin America (there are many more) that raise our hopes: the groundbreaking 2010 World People's Conference on Climate Change and the Rights of Mother Earth in Cochabamba, Bolivia; the Brazilian *Movimento Sem Terra* (MST, the Landless People's Movement), an organization of farmers and rural workers that aims to change the urban world; and Cuba's pioneering urban agriculture and progressive approach to human development. A more in-depth look at each of them will show that not all is hopeful, but those who are committed to finding alternatives in this century must search for those threads of hope that can be woven into new pieces of cloth.

In these cases, the prevailing paradigm for urban development remains imbedded in the traditional orientalist models from urban Europe and North America. The four wealthiest and most powerful nations in Latin America—Brazil, Argentina, Mexico, and Venezuela—are highly urbanized and, like the U.S., strapped with existing urban infrastructures—physical and political—that will be difficult to change. Their economies have powerful structural ties with global capitalism and their cities have undergone centuries of dependent urbanization and have large carbon footprints. These nations also have their own powerful bourgeoisies that are heavily invested in urban land, have formed partnerships with global capital, and are locked into the energy-intensive consumer society. While all with the exception of Mexico have governments that disavow neoliberal and imperialist politics, it remains to be seen whether they will seriously overturn free-market and orientalist planning and institute structural reforms that confront enclave urbanism.

Bolivia and the Rights of Nature

Bolivia is one of the smallest nations in Latin America and in terms of the traditional measures of development, it is one of the poorest nations: its Gross Domestic Product and per capita income are ranked 16th and 28th (with only Haiti and Nicaragua below) in Latin America and the Caribbean.[39] Lacking access to a port, Bolivia's main value to the Spanish crown was the extraction of valuable ores for export via ports in neighboring Peru and Chile. Bolivia's rich tin mines, once the largest revenue producer in the nation, thrived due to extremely low wages and oppressive working conditions for miners; this situation has been sustained by the lack of viable alternatives for labor in the cities. Today natural gas is the chief export and under state control but Bolivia remains dependent on a global marketplace dominated by powerful transnationals.[40]

A third of Bolivia's population of ten million lives in two large metropolises, La Paz and Santa Cruz. The largest part of these sprawled metropolises is a collection of lower-density communities with relatively limited ties to the rest of the urban region. Thus the cultures, languages and practices of rural Bolivia remain important elements in the everyday lives of Bolivia's cities.

The majority of Bolivia's population is indigenous people not descended from the Spanish. From the time of the conquest they were excluded or marginalized from political power. A revolution in 1952 opened up space for change but ruling groups and parties continued to be dominated by leaders with stronger political and cultural ties to Europe and North America. In 2005, indigenous leader Evo Morales became President. Significantly, Morales had entered the political scene as an organizer of the nation's coca growers, indigenous farmers whose production was caught between the U.S.-financed campaign for coca eradication and against the global trade in cocaine. Traditionally Bolivians have produced coca for local consumption—it is chewed and used to make tea—and had nothing to do with industrial cocaine or its export to meet the demand for consumption in the United States. Bolivia's revolutionary process— much like Cuba's in 1959—has brought together urban and rural populations around issues that linked city and countryside, and in Bolivia the campaign against coca eradication was critical.

Another major trigger of change in Bolivia was the water war—a struggle over natural resources spanning urban and rural areas. The most intense water war was in Cochabamba, a large mostly indigenous settlement at the periphery of La Paz. In 1999, the government sold Cochabamba's water system to a consortium controlled by Italian and North American corporations. This led to years of popular resistance, reversal of the privatization and collapse of the government, opening up the way for new elections that brought Evo Morales to the presidency.[41]

Evo Morales was the public face symbolizing the historic rise of the indigenous majority and social movements after centuries of minority rule and struggles for democracy and social justice. This has not been without contradictions and some voices from within the indigenous communities consider Morales to be an undependable ally. His government drafted a new constitution codifying indigenous rights, which was approved by a majority of voters. Since it was also a product of a powerful class conflict—including decades of militant struggles by tin miners—a major thrust was for public control over land and resources that had been appropriated by global capital for export.[42] In their analysis of Bolivia's transformation, Benjamin Kohl and Linda Farthing quote a leader of the coca growers in a 1997 interview:

> The root problem that concerns everyone is land. In Bolivia, the 1953 Agrarian Reform mostly benefited landowners, logging companies, cattle ranchers, and transnational companies. Of 88 million acres of productive land in Bolivia, *campesinos* only control about ten million. We are beginning to recognize our identity. We are neither peasants nor colonizers: we are the original owners of the country.[43]

Bolivia's new constitution, ratified in 2009, established an approach to land distinct from the many post-colonial constitutions of Latin America that sanctified private ownership and retained a powerful state to guarantee it. Although it built on many previous constitutional reforms that progressively eliminated discriminatory structures excluding the "others," the new constitution explicitly defines the Bolivian state as *plurinational* and *communitarian*—a state that guarantees broad rights for people of multiple ethnicities to govern themselves and achieve self-determination (the constitution establishes 36 official indigenous languages).[44] It opens more space for the *ayllu* (a form of cooperative labor) and other indigenous forms of self-organization while turning away from reliance on traditional approaches to land reform that granted land titles to individuals, an approach that was consistent with and encouraged the growth of a conservative and relatively well-to-do *mestizo* (non-indigenous) landowning class in southern Bolivia that is now the most powerful social base for opposition to the Morales regime.

In the six years under Morales, key extractive industries, such as oil and gas, have been nationalized, and there is movement towards nationalizing the mines as well. The country no longer cooperates with U.S. counter-narcotics and coca-eradication programs, and has expelled several U.S. narcotics agents. The welfare state has been significantly built up, with special attention paid to pensions for the elderly and food for students. Most of the country's debt to the International Monetary Fund has been paid off or canceled, greatly increasing the country's political autonomy and fiscal resources. And after years of militant mobilizations against water privatization, water resources have been safeguarded as public goods and protected by the state. However, while the Morales reforms stress collective ownership of industries and access to land, they also depend on environmentally harmful extractive industries, creating a tension between Morales' goals, programs and indigenous political base.

While the efforts of Evo Morales and his MAS (Movement Towards Socialism) to chart a new path for development in Bolivia are filled with internal contradictions, paradoxes and difficulties, perhaps one of the most important aspects of the new Bolivia is the role it aspires to play more broadly in Latin America and the world. Indigenous populations in other Latin American nations—Guatemala, Peru and Ecuador in particular—are also expanding their political strength through protest and organizing. Bolivia joined with Cuba, Ecuador, Nicaragua, Venezuela and several small nations in a new regional alliance (ALBA, Alianza Bolivariana para los Pueblos de Nuestra América) emphasizing cooperation and independence from the U.S. But one of the most important initiatives of Bolivia was the 2010 World People's Conference on Climate Change and the Rights of Mother Earth, held in Cochabamba.

The 2010 conference brought together more than 32,000 people from all over the world, including representatives of the smaller and less powerful nations that had walked away from the Copenhagen and Cancún debacles in previous years, and representatives of indigenous people and environmental movements. The conference approved "The Universal Declaration of the Rights of Mother Earth."[45] Though summarily discounted by the more powerful as "quaint" and "romantic," the Declaration introduces an entirely new concept into the global debates on sustainability, the environment and urbanization—the *rights of the earth*. The Declaration attributes to the earth rights that are comparable to and complement human rights, housing rights, the right to the city and other rights. It implicitly turns away from the conceits of modernist urban planning in which rights and privileges, such as the right to own land, are reserved for the human species alone:

> The Declaration recognizes that all natural entities which exist as part of Mother Earth, including plants, animals, rivers and ecosystems, are subjects that have the inherent and inalienable right to exist and to play their role within the community of beings.[46]

The Declaration says there is an imbalance in the relationship between humans and other beings and calls for correcting that imbalance, restoring ecosystems and addressing climate change. It acknowledges a role for many "wisdom traditions and faiths" as well as contemporary science.

> However, it is incompatible with the belief that human wellbeing should be achieved by rapidly exploiting "natural resources" in order to maximize economic growth indefinitely, which is the foundation for most contemporary legal, political and economic systems.[47]

From the margins of urban Latin America, Bolivia is part of a fundamentally new and alternative political current that could build an alternative future free from orientalist theory and practice and the fragmentation of enclave urbanism. The process of transformation within Bolivia, and in the other nations in ALBA, is contradictory and complex, and may not succeed, but the Declaration from Cochabamba offers an alternative paradigm as a way to forge new relations between land, people and the environment.[48]

Reclaiming the Land, Reuniting City and Countryside: the MST in Brazil

Brazil and Mexico are the largest, most urbanized nations in Latin America and well on their way towards greater integration with global capitalism. Two of the ten largest metropolises in the world are in Brazil (São Paulo and Rio de Janeiro) and another (Mexico City) is in Mexico. These metropolitan regions are powerful economic engines with strong sectors in finance capital, manufacturing and services. The commodification of land and expansion of global real estate are part of the process. However, in these nations there are also powerful countercurrents resulting from significant levels of social inequality and the devastation visited on rural areas by neoliberal reforms. In Mexico, small- and medium-sized agricultural producers, including the *ejidatarios* granted land during the 1910 Mexican Revolution, were hit hard by years of neoliberal policies and the North American Free Trade Agreement, which opened up the nation to food exports from the U.S. and led to a massive migration of labor to northern metropolises.[49]

In Brazil, which has one of the highest levels of social inequality in the hemisphere, the process of rural devastation is instead driven by state concessions of land in previously undeveloped rural areas for capital-intensive, industrialized agriculture, which promises to have significant long-term environmental impacts. The opening up of new land for speculative development in Brazil's interior creates some new jobs but fails to address the structural unemployment among farm laborers. This has opened up a political space for a countercurrent led by the MST, founded in 1984. Building on a long tradition of organizing by rural workers, the MST came together in the final years of a military regime whose statist and nationalist policies favored industrialized agriculture and urban growth. Peasants and farmworkers who were displaced organized to fight for their right to the land. The MST opposes *latifundio* (large rural estates) and advocates for agrarian reform, sometimes taking direct action to occupy abandoned or underused rural land. It has also become a voice against deforestation in the

Amazon basin, Latin America's largest carbon sink; for sustainable land and water management; and democratic control of land. With some 1.5 million members it is the largest organized social movement in Latin America in a nation with Latin America's largest population and land mass, and the largest urban population.[50]

What makes the MST interesting from the perspective of alternatives to dependent urbanization and orientalism is that this rural movement has strong ties to urban Brazil. Unlike many other peasant movements, MST politics were formed in a national democratic struggle through a strong alliance with urban movements, including labor unions and left political parties. Many of the landless peasants in the MST lived for years in cities and have sustained their struggles so they could return to the land. Most of the MST's campaigns and mobilizations, including their massive 1997 National March for Employment Justice and Agrarian Reform, bring together the demands of rural farmers, urban workers and indigenous peoples.

MST demands and proposals are comprehensive and, taken together, call for a revolutionary change in the organization of the economy, land use and land ownership. They call for an end to the leasing and renting of farmlands, a cap on the size of farms, and access to farmland for any family that is willing to work it. In turn, they demand that farmland never be owned by any entity that will not themselves cultivate the earth, including foreign corporations, banks and churches. Any land owners violating the social contract—either on labor or environmental grounds—should face expropriation, and farmers underutilizing their land must be taxed progressively to extract social value. The MST proposes that the business of agriculture be run by farm workers in locations near the sites of production. They would ban monocultures and mandate organic, non-GMO farming, and prioritize land reforms near urban centers. They demand public ownership of water and the use of water conservation technologies. The MST calls for universal free public education and full employment based on infrastructure and development needs of both urban and rural Brazilians. Significantly for our discussion here, the MST's stated goal is the elimination of differences between life in the city and countryside, but not the elimination of the city or the domination of the rural over the urban, which is consistent with the major themes of this book.[51]

The MST is a leading participant in *Via Campesina*, a global coalition of like-minded groups focused on the rights of small- and medium-sized farmers and food sovereignty. Via Campesina has 150 member organizations in 70 nations, comprising 200 million farmers.[52] This is still a fraction of all farmers in the world and the global coalition faces powerful economic interests advocating free trade, industrial agriculture, monocultures, and GMOs.

Cuba's Urban Agriculture and Approach to Human Development

Another daring initiative from Latin America's periphery is Cuba's foray into urban agriculture. This is not simply a story of upscaled community gardens, or the kind of peri-urban agriculture that has been an integral part of many African, European and Asian cities that developed in regions with deep rural traditions. Cuba's urban agriculture emerged from within the urban fabric and is entirely organic—that is, it does not use synthetic fertilizers, pesticides or herbicides. Urban agriculture in Cuba is not what it may first appear to be at the ideological extremes: either a showcase of the Cuban Revolution or its opposite, a sign of the Revolution's failures. The story of urban agriculture in Cuba shows the tremendous potential for a revolutionary approach to urban rebirth, the contradictory aspects of the Revolution, a lesson in how cities can be resilient in a period of crisis, and a hint at the ways that the countryside can be reintegrated in the twenty-first century metropolis. We will devote more attention to this example because of its great importance for our exploration of urban planning in the new century.

Cuba's urban agriculture emerged abruptly in the 1990s, but to understand why, we need to first look at Cuba's history. While the Spanish were forced to give up most of their colonies in the Americas before the mid-nineteenth century, they frustrated Cuba's liberation forces and by the end of the century when their grip loosened, the U.S. invaded Cuba in 1898. This ushered in a period of domination by the U.S., including a period of occupation and direct rule. In the twentieth century various regimes backed by the U.S. supported a Cuban economy that continued to depend on sugar cane exports. Most sugar was exported via the port in Havana, the capital city, and it was there that the growing tourist industry was also concentrated. By the mid-twentieth century, tourism, gambling and prostitution made Havana the largest and wealthiest city in the nation. Havana's elites had strong economic and cultural ties with the U.S. and Europe, visible by the 1950s in the city's high rise skyline and sprawling new suburbs built to emulate the urban ideals from the North. Typical of dependent urbanization around the world, capital was concentrated in the urban centers of power and rural areas were left to serve as reserves for cheap labor in plantation agriculture. Sugar cane, gambling and prostitution were Cuba's "comparative advantage."[53] (On comparative advantage, see Chapter Three.)

The Cuban Revolution in 1959 ended the monopoly of foreign-owned sugar producers; the plantations were nationalized and operated by a state-owned enterprise. While the expropriation of the *latifundia* was denounced by the U.S. and used as a rationale for the failed CIA-backed invasion of Cuba's Playa Girón (Bay of Pigs) in 1961, the new Cuban government let the small farmers in the interior retain their farms (except for lands abandoned by those who fled to Miami). This retention of small farms in Cuba's interior was the result of a revolution that had closely linked the urban and rural resistance to oppose the U.S.-backed regime of Fulgencio Batista. Fidel Castro had formed a ragtag army that expanded and gained strength in the rugged eastern mountains far from the capital city, with support from peasants and small landowners. In this sense it was a truly national revolution, and after the victory on January 1, 1959 rural Cuba began to benefit from the reforms instituted by the new government. These included the widespread construction of schools and clinics in the countryside and extension of the right to education and health care throughout the island. This was a foundation for a social policy that aimed to equally serve both urban and rural needs.[54]

During the 50 years since the Cuban Revolution, Havana's population remained relatively stable as a proportion of the total Cuban population while other cities grew. As noted in Chapter Three, this was not related to any national urban policy (in fact, Havana's urban planners had grand visions for that city's growth that were never realized) but a national economic policy aimed at correcting the sharp inequalities between urban and rural areas and among workers and peasants. A perverse effect of this policy, however, was the serious decline in the quality of Havana's built environment. As a result the city today is filled with buildings that require substantial renovation, local governments with limited resources, and owners lacking access to materials and funds for improvements. Today Havana is a unique historic gem that mostly evaded, for better and for worse, the ravages of a real estate market fed by global and local capital seeking profits and displacing residents without mercy.[55]

Until the collapse of the Soviet Union in 1991, farm policy in Cuba depended heavily on the export of sugar and imports of some basic staples. In the wake of the 1961 confrontation with the U.S., Cuba had developed a close alliance with the Soviet Union and the socialist bloc nations. Although Cuba is a small island nation it is located a mere 90 miles from the U.S. mainland, and despite widespread sympathy for the Revolution throughout Latin America most governments at that time were pressured into breaking relations with Cuba by an aggressive U.S. fearful that other revolutions would follow and threaten U.S. interests throughout the hemisphere. Cuba's trade with the socialist bloc was dominated by sugar, which was bartered at relatively favorable prices for petroleum, manufactured goods and foodstuffs. Tobacco exports also retained a strong position among exports. Tourism declined drastically, though years later it expanded with the participation of European capital. Cuba also developed a modern biotechnology industry and became a major center in Latin America for (substantially undercapitalized) arts, music, and movie industries.

After the Cuban Revolution, the agriculture sector beyond sugar and tobacco was small, and imports of basic staples such as rice, beans and beef remained relatively high. In sum, Cuba was anything but a model of urban–rural integration or food sovereignty. While the terms of trade had improved with the socialist bloc, Cuba was still dependent on producing sugar for export as a "comparative advantage." This differed from the typical capitalist dependency because the terms of barter were actually favorable to Cuba, but structurally it was really no different than the classic post-colonial model of dependency. Cuba's monoculture increased the nation's dependence on the more "developed" nations of the socialist bloc, but even more importantly reduced its capacity for resilience in the face of crisis. It also masked the high energy and environmental costs of importing basic foodstuffs from thousands of miles away and burning cheap petroleum.

Collapse and Rebirth

This all changed with the collapse of the Soviet Union. Cuba lost its privileged customer for sugar at a time when the global market for sugar cane collapsed due to the global monopoly of cheap corn derivatives. Many of the smaller Cuban farms producing food could no longer buy the inputs they needed to sustain production—fuel to run machinery, chemical fertilizers and pesticides. There were massive food shortages, especially in Havana, which did not have enough farms in its hinterland to meet local consumption needs. Havana and all Cuban cities were affected by the limited capacity to transport fresh food long distances due to the scarcity of fuel. So people started to grow their own food on available plots of land. This drew immediate support from people with experience and training in agricultural production and was backed by government institutions. Like many urban gardening initiatives up north in U.S. cities, Cuba's urban agriculture came from the bottom up, but in Cuba they also received strong support from the top down so that these initiatives could expand. Also, unlike some of the experiences in the North, Cuba's urban agriculture arose in response to a severe crisis and not as a movement of consumers seeking better choices.

In Havana today approximately 50 percent of all produce is farmed locally, and the proportion is larger in most other cities (over 75 percent of Cuba's population lives in urbanized areas).[56] About 370,000 people work in organic urban agriculture throughout Cuba.[57] Increased local production of fresh produce also led to the creation of produce markets—1,204 in the capital and 9,856 in the nation.[58] These markets are publicly owned and usually operated by private producers; the markets may be run by the associated retailers, who establish retail policies and may set standard prices for some basic products. In recent years, privately-owned restaurants have been permitted and many of these, especially those serving the tourist industry, buy local produce. The local producers and markets are slowly changing the Cuban diet which has been traditionally poor in vegetables; however, this is a difficult and complex process as long as imported foods are cheaper.[59]

The Alamar Organic Farm is an instructive case.[60] This is a producer's cooperative with 185 workers. It was started in 1997 on vacant land near the giant Alamar apartment complex, an array of apartment blocks built in the 1970s using models and technology from the European socialist bloc nations. Alamar's planning and design drew criticisms from residents and planners for its high energy use, distance from Havana's center, and lack of services. The farm takes advantage of the unused land around the apartment complex, and provides fresh food and jobs for residents. The farm sells its products to residents but also contributes food to a local school. While on public land, the Alamar Organic Farm is organized as a cooperative and

Figure 8.4 Organic Farm in Alamar, Havana

involves a form of limited private ownership. Workers are paid salaries but accumulate shares depending on the number of years they have worked; 70 percent of net profits are distributed to shareholders. However, there is a maximum number of shares available per worker.

The legacy of Cuba's sugar monoculture weighs heavily on efforts to achieve food sovereignty. Today most sugar plantations are abandoned. There are significant problems of soil depletion, salinity, deforestation and erosion. Only 30 percent of all land in Cuba is arable. Recent legal reforms call for the leasing of many former sugar farms to cooperatives and private farmers, and this will also require the creation of a better transportation, communications and distribution infrastructure. The legacy of a monoculture rooted in colonial exploitation also affects the prospects for sustaining a more diverse urban agriculture. In a nation where hard labor on sugar plantations was performed by slaves and descendants of slaves, many young people, especially Afro-descendent people, are not clamoring to work in agriculture, except perhaps as technical experts or managers.

Despite the many problems and constraints, urban agriculture in Cuba is now two decades old and continues to thrive. This by itself is a significant fact. Once the immediate crisis of hunger and food supply was overcome by the late 1990s, Cuban policy could have easily returned to the old export-driven model and a new monoculture (as happened with Victory Gardens in the U.S. after World War II). The fact that it did not is worth exploring to understand how such a move towards food sovereignty might become a long-term reality in other urbanized nations that may also face similar challenges due to global climate change or other catastrophic events.

First, the shift to urban agriculture was the outcome of contradictory tensions within Cuban government and society. There were agronomists and economists imbedded in the old system, out of touch with the immediate crisis and quite helpless in confronting it. They would see urban agriculture as at best an emergency measure that would never be able to achieve the scale economies of extensive, industrial agriculture. Most urban planners saw no lasting role for agriculture in cities and only after significant debate conceded a place for agriculture, but as part of the city's "open space." Then there were those who took action on the ground and in government, who saw an opportunity to change the paradigm. One of them was Fernando Funes Aguilar, a dynamic technical expert who speaks with the authority of a life-long Cuban revolutionary about the critical importance of linking national sovereignty with food sovereignty, resilience and social justice. Funes is a scientist who understood the long-term need to change the structure of agricultural production and its relationship to human development. Another was Caridad Cruz, a leader in the Fundación Antonio Núñez, a foundation created in 1994 that introduced the theory and practice of permaculture that was taken from Australia and given a distinctly Cuban interpretation.[61]

The old way of thinking persists among agronomists and urban planners, and continues to support arguments by pragmatically-minded economists who advocate an expansion of imports, particularly in periods of economic growth. According to a recent account from experts actively supporting Cuba's urban agriculture, there remains a paradox at the center of the nation's policies:

> It is in fact paradoxical that, to achieve food security in a period of economic growth, most of the resources are dedicated to importing foods or promoting

industrial agriculture schemes instead of stimulating local production by peasants. There is a cyclical return to support conventional agriculture by policy makers when the financial situation improves, while sustainable approaches and agroecology, considered as "alternatives," are only supported under scenarios of economic scarcity. This cyclical mindset strongly undermines the advances achieved with agroecology and organic farming since the economic collapse in 1990.[62]

The dramatic shift towards food sovereignty in Cuba could still be reversed. The vast majority of the Cuban population was not even born at the time of the 1959 revolution, and new interpretations of the Revolution and independence are evolving. These include greater opening to the rest of the world which could also mean opening the door to more food imports, fast food culture, and global marketing. Large cracks are appearing in the five-decade-long economic embargo and political assault on Cuba by the United States. For example, poultry producers in the U.S. successfully lobbied for an exception to the trade embargo and today most chickens are imported from the United States. Most other Latin American countries now have friendly relations with Cuba, a sign that the U.S. is losing its hegemonic role in the hemisphere and the embargo of Cuba has been a failure. While commercial relations based on solidarity with Venezuela and other ALBA nations may expand, Cuba's gradual integration with the global marketplace will surely be filled with enormous contradictions and paradoxes.[63]

Cuba's experience with organic urban agriculture can become a positive example for other nations with histories of dependent economies and dependent urbanization to follow as they face future food security crises. The lesson from Cuba is that resilience requires both top-down support from government—a progressive state—and bottom-up engagement by residents—participatory democracy. And that it is possible to reunite urban and rural areas through a new approach to urban land. Since socialist Cuba survived the collapse of the USSR and the socialist camp, there may also be implications for the prospects of a socialism in the twenty-first century that joins democratic participation with a more equitable social order. However, the continuing pressures facing nations and social movements attempting to put forth new models of urban and rural development—to the cases of Cuba, Brazil and Bolivia discussed here we might add Venezuela, Ecuador and Nicaragua—could be overwhelmed by a global marketplace ruled by the most powerful centers of financial capital unless there is a more powerful global alternative.

Part III

Looking Ahead

Chapter 9

New Century, New Ways of Planning

In this book we have emphasized the chronic problems with development and planning of cities in the twentieth century and until today. The chapters on India, Palestine, the U.S. and Latin America emphasize everything that is wrong with orientalist city planning, dependent urbanization, and enclave urbanism. But are there any alternatives? Is urban planning of any use and is there any constructive role for planners, architects, engineers and designers in the century ahead? If we look carefully at these chapters, they strongly suggest that there is a role for professionals who understand and can help shape the built environment, not as independent technocrats but as participants and collaborators with global community movements. We have mentioned some models that can be followed: the ideas and practices of Mahatma Gandhi and Vandana Shiva in India are foundations; the groups like Bimkom, ICAHD, Ir Amim and the Regional Council of Unrecognized Villages in the Negev, all in Israel/ Palestine; the makers of New York City's one hundred community-based plans; the MST in Brazil; and Cuba's urban organic farms. We would need at least another book to unearth the vast wealth of ideas, proposals and plans that have emerged from these and many other social movements and their leaders, not from the centers of the "enlightened" societies but from the peripheries of the world. They are setting out for us the premises for a more just way of organizing human life on earth in both cities and rural areas, and they should inspire all those who profess to become urban planners. They are helping us collectively invent new ways of planning in the new century of the metropolis. They will be the urban/rural planners of the twenty-first century and those of us fortunate enough to be professionally trained would be even more fortunate to have them as our collaborators, advisors and "clients."

Orientalist Planning is Dead! Long Live Planning!

If urban planning fails to give up its allegiance to orientalism it will continue to be an irrelevant poster child for free-market capitalism, global climate change, and the widening economic, social and environmental injustices in the world. It is already obvious that in a world dominated by large metropolitan areas, the old master plans and even the newer strategic plans are unable to alter the logic of land development driven by the needs of capital accumulation, or the incessant drive to produce and consume more commodities (and thus more waste). The grand visions of the good city springing from the rational minds of distinguished technocrats might have been implemented in Victorian England before the age of the metropolis but now if they have any relevance it is more likely to be as a blueprint for the reproduction of segregated enclaves to be sold in the vast metropolitan markets of the world.

Many planners will maintain that colonialism was laid to rest long ago and all that is left are traces that will eventually evaporate. However, colonialism as an all-encompassing system has ceded primacy to new forms of imperialism in the twenty-first century that have absorbed the ideas and practices of the old colonial regimes. Orientalist notions of the city and the orthodox rational–comprehensive paradigm are so thoroughly assimilated in the minds and practices of planners throughout the world, especially the educated elites of former colonial nations, that it is no longer a phenomenon visible only in the global centers of power. The orientalist prejudice that our urban problems reside in the "slums" is as widespread as the notion that rational and comprehensive solutions introduced from above are the solution.

Planners and design professionals need to be concerned that a minority of the world's population lives in urban areas that consume a disproportionate share of the world's resources and escape from the worst environmental and public health consequences. How we deal with this question of environmental justice will influence how our communities are designed.

As we demonstrated in the first chapter, the problem for this new century is not the metropolis and it is not population growth. The problem for urban planning is not how to concentrate or deconcentrate population but how to improve the quality of life of people wherever they live, whether in high-density urban cores or in low-density suburbs or rural areas. The problem is not to make us more or less urban in a century in which most people will already live in cities. The problem is not the "slums," especially if we recognize them as the diverse communities that they are. The problem is applying human consciousness in shaping and adapting to the environment, including both the built and natural environment. The twentieth century approach to planning relied primarily on the consciousness of the technocrat managing the market; however, the free-market approach requires very little consciousness. It discourages intervention in shaping the environment by warning that humans must stay out of the way of the mysterious, invisible hand. At most, it allows for short-term planning for the mall, the business center, the industrial park, or the resort. It leaves to succeeding generations the social and environmental consequences.

Urban planners will have to break with the neo-Malthusian myths that focus on reducing population growth in the former colonial world and instead advocate measures to reduce inequalities, improve access to health care and education for all—in short, planning must be based on the principles of environmental justice. The problem is not the "population bomb" that Paul Ehrlich warned of in 1968;[1] on the contrary, a better standard of living generally leads to lower population growth. While it is now true more than ever that a population of more than 10 billion on the earth by the end of the twenty-first century could face severe shortages of energy and resources and environmental catastrophes resulting from global climate change, the worst-case scenario is not inevitable. However, if capitalism as we know it continues to grow, as it must in order to survive, it may bring back serious discussions about limits to growth—the topic of a controversial 1972 book by Donnella H. Meadows and others[2] that was widely cited by conservatives anxious to rationalize social austerity measures. Today progressive planners and environmental justice advocates will need to appropriate the notion of *limits* and propose development policies that decrease inequalities, not ones that will expand them. In the end, the alienation of humans from nature and the environment is primarily an economic and not an environmental problem.

Growth in itself is not a problem. The problem is rooted in what is growing and who is benefiting. Under capitalism growth is usually measured by the amount of goods produced and consumed, or the total amount of capital that is accumulated. These quantitative measures do not necessarily go along with improvements in the quality of life or standard of living for most people, and often conceal growing inequalities. Growth doesn't happen automatically in successive stages following the models that describe growth in the "developed" countries; indeed this "natural" succession has eluded most of the world. Development isn't about finding your "comparative advantage" in the global marketplace. It is about living healthier and longer lives in harmony with our natural environment, engaging in meaningful labor (but not too much), and having access to education and diverse cultural opportunities. Development is about living in a society without gaping inequalities.

Since urban planning is still driven by the growth mentality emulating the "developed" world, it is orientalist to the core. The industrial model of urban development that relies on the serial reproduction of a limited set of urban systems, the establishment of exclusive residential and commercial enclaves, a public–private partnership for infrastructure, and the spread of a speculative system of private land ownership, is imposed on traditional local systems that have diverse histories, fragmented and incrementally developed infrastructures, and multiple models of land tenure with a history of greater stability. The "modern city" is proposed as a universal model even when it may be dressed up with design elements harking back to traditional notions from pre-capitalist cities.

Planning for Seven Generations

In the twenty-first century more than ever before, we humans need to learn how to plan for the next seven generations, following the Great Law of the Iroquois Confederacy: "In our every deliberation, we must consider the impact of our decisions on the next seven generations." This of course puts us well into the twenty-second century. With technological innovation proceeding at a lightning pace today, new products are introduced almost daily by corporations out to win the competition for customers. There is no process for assessing the long-term health and environmental impacts of most of these products. By the end of this century we may very well end up surrounded in our compact cities by a huge population of devices whose cumulative impact is to shorten our lives or guarantee the disappearance of other species, or our own. We could be facing mountains of "green" electronic waste, trapped in a "man-made" (as women had little to say about its creation) environment that is more vulnerable to disaster than the ones we live in today.

Planning for seven generations requires a deliberate process and precautionary approach to both physical changes in the environment and technological innovation. It means *the end of the technological fix*—the short-term solution to existing needs and problems. It means an end to green gimmicks that help to sell luxurious condos and make life healthier for a small minority of the population. It requires a systemic, ecological, holistic approach to human settlements linking production and consumption, land, water, energy, air and all elements of the human environment. Such an ambitious enterprise can no longer be left to small teams of experts contracted to file reports. It is an enormous task that will take many more people and much more time. Just as slow food is healthier, so also is *slow planning* and the *slow metropolis*.

From Land "Use" to Land

Twenty-first century urban planners will need to understand more deeply the one thing they have always claimed as their specialty—land. But they will need to stop trying to control "land use." This phrase, popular in the profession, implies that land is only a thing to be used, or not, and that "use" by and for humans is the most important thing. Instead, land must be understood as a set of relations that occur in space. It is not just "location, location, location"—the meme of the real estate industry, which is mainly concerned with its exchange value. It ought not be defined only by the way that humans relate to it—for housing, recreation, or transportation, for example. It should be understood as multidimensional, involving what goes on beneath the surface and far above it, its long histories, the stories people tell about it, and how other species relate to it. No individual piece of land should be treated any differently because some humans have a legal title that says they own it. For all pieces of land are parts of a larger territory; individual titles cannot alter this. Walls and gates, whether real or virtual, may change the way individual plots of land relate to the rest of the metropolis but they should not negate the metropolis.

We must also listen to those who have long believed that land is multidimensional and integrated with all life. The Universal Declaration on the Rights of Mother Earth, like the one proposed in Cochabamba, Bolivia in 2010 and mentioned in the previous chapter should be the foundation for all planning. Such concepts are alien to urban orientalism, which is founded on a narrow, reductionist science and rationality serving modern capitalist growth. This would take us far beyond expressed concern for "the environment," cumbersome environmental impact statements, and token greenwashing.

Water is another critical element for all urban life that is in our thinking and practice treated as an object, usually brought in from afar for our benefit, rather than one element in a complex ecosystem. The global water supply is being monopolized and privatized instead of dealt with as an essential element in the commons. Per capita consumption rates may be lower in some densely developed cities such as New York City but this is overshadowed by the very high consumption rates in the suburbs, which are after all the majority of the population in the New York metropolitan region, and the enormous amounts of water used for industrial agriculture which feeds the metropolis. The chronic inability to put an end to the contamination of urban surface waters exacerbates the scarcity of clean drinking water and increases dependence on commercial water suppliers, whose charges are a disproportionate burden on those who can afford them the least.

There are similar problems in the energy sector. Individual buildings filled with luxury condos having zero carbon footprints are not good enough. They may win prizes for the architects and planners, but at the pace we are going they will continue to be tiny energy-efficient enclaves in a sea of carbon consumption. The problem is not just power generation and energy efficiency as a quantitative goal, though that is part of it, the problem is planning for energy reduction on a broad scale. In an economy that relies on ever greater levels of consumption—indeed, conspicuous consumption—this is a systemic problem. In an economy chronically plagued with overproduction and underconsumption, it is inevitable that more resources will be used than are needed to reproduce life. This is not about peak oil (whose peak keeps getting higher) or peaking alternative fuels, it is about calling into question the very foundation of a wasteful economic system.

Learning from the village, we also need to rediscover *the commons*—land as a shared space with many stewards. Cities with lively public places are already moving in this direction, though many are also privatizing these spaces and limiting access to them. By expanding the commons we can enrich the social life of cities and build local communities. However, the commons should not be an exclusive playground for downtown elites. It needs to permeate the entire region and world and be accessible to all. When "the others" are excluded from the commons and deprived of their right to the city, the commons becomes nothing more than a segregated enclave and no longer the great democratic space in which local, regional and global communities are constructed.

Ruralizing the Cities and Renewing Food Systems

To reunite the urban and rural worlds, two broad strategies might be possible in the twenty-first century: bringing the countryside to the city and the city to the country-side. However, these strategies by themselves will never work unless they come to grips with the problem of urban orientalism. By themselves, they are merely physical or spatial changes and do not necessarily deal with inequalities and historical dependencies. Instead of simply bringing the countryside to the city, we need to create a new urban/rural landscape that incorporates knowledge and practices from the village and centuries of close human ties with land and nature. This is not to go back to village life, with all its deprivations and inequalities, but to reject the simplistic dualism of rural vs. urban life and take whatever positive lessons we can from our appreciation of this history. The urbanized world of the twenty-first century is the product of the domination by urban capital over rural areas, the urbanization of the countryside. It eliminated rural areas as we have known them, replacing them with empty spaces, preserves for the generation of resources to feed capitalist expansion, "ecological" reserves, and above all factories for food to sustain and reproduce the urban population. To create new urban landscapes we have to go beyond the limited, orientalist strategies such as the City Beautiful, which would bring only selected elements of the countryside to the city but fundamentally turn away from the countryside and nature (see critique in Chapter Two). To truly bring the countryside to the city we need to integrate throughout the metropolis some of the activities that characterized human reproduction in villages and towns. This includes, first of all, the production and circulation of food. We need to move far beyond experiments in community gardening as a pastime, or Slow Food as a cultural choice, or intensive commercial farming in cities, to the creation of metropolitan regions able to engage residents in the production and distribution of healthy, local food. This will help us reestablish our relationship to land and the earth, touching "dirt" and rejecting the Victorian fixation with "cleaning up" cities through urban planning. These new systems can reduce dependence on fossil fuels, help establish new relationships between people and the earth, and among people, conserve water, improve air quality and generally provide a better quality of life. It will help slow down the consumption of food—with all of the social, environmental and public health benefits that entails—and move us towards the *slow metropolis*. It will reduce our carbon footprint and the risks of catastrophic global climate change.

Along with the reinvention of our relationship to food, the twenty-first century metropolis can help reestablish our relationship with other species. This includes the other species that have been kind enough to offer their bodies to us so we could meet our omnivorous nutrient desires. But it should also include other species whose main role is to contribute to the re-creation of resilient local ecosystems. Without them we cannot preserve watersheds, aquifers, wetlands and forests. All of these things were buried, channelized, tamed and eliminated in the modern metropolis but will now need to be integrated in the urban fabric.

If bringing the countryside to the city is much more complicated than planting a garden, equally difficult will be bringing the city to the countryside. We can recapture the spirit of the Soviet "disurbanists" of the 1920s (see Chapter Six) who sought an alternative to capitalism's plunder of the countryside. We don't necessarily need to build new suburbs and Garden Cities. We have to go beyond the boundaries of the metropolis and find new ways of creating urban life integrated with natural systems, *learning from but not necessarily reproducing the village.* We are not talking about building exclusive ex-urban paradises, dream homes in the wilderness, or promoting gentleman farmers. We know that there can be enormous environmental and social benefits in medium-sized cities (as Timothy Beatley showed in his book, *Green Urbanism*[3]) and perhaps there should be more of them. But we also know that it takes a high-density metropolis for a cost-effective urban rail system and a rich and diverse economic and cultural life. We need to resurrect the notion of "optimal city size" as part of our efforts to plan human settlements, not as abstract exercises that search for ideal numbers but a real effort to place limits on inequalities. This means national and global planning—not as market-driven infrastructure planning (the example of twentieth-century capitalism) or the exclusive domain of an undemocratic state (the example of twentieth-century socialism), but as a participatory planning process engaging people—as subjects who can shape the future, not as objects of the market or state.

Local and Global: Why Scale Matters

If urban planners want to chart any sort of relevant pathway for themselves in the twenty-first century, they will need to leave behind all pretensions of being the experts of the local. They missed their chance of being relevant in the twentieth century by getting bogged down in the business of enclave urbanism—building and designing the new urban complex, community, or town. They turned away from national and global politics and did not address the accumulating problems of inequality and climate change. They used their isolated "best practices" to sell their local wares instead of promoting global transformations. Now, in the globalized world of metropolitan regions, the myth of isolated local communities (villages, enclaves, cities and metropolitan regions) can no longer be sustained without reproducing everything that is wrong in our cities. Enclave urbanism will continue to dominate as long as it serves the interests of short-term investors, both public and private, and parochial interests. It is really project development and not planning in the fullest sense of the term. Planners can and should think and act globally, for in the twenty-first century more than ever before there is less and less locally that is even partially detached from the global. Paradoxically, global capitalism has compressed time and distance, and suspension of a world view by those who would question capitalism is more problematic than ever.

But this does not mean that the local does not matter. On the contrary, the reification of globalization is now used to neutralize and defeat attempts at local change that could have global implications. Globalized financial capital, we are told, is so powerful that it is useless to do anything more than adapt to it. There Is No Alternative, to use Margaret Thatcher's dictum. This effectively tells everyone who lives and works in cities—the majority of the world's population—that they are powerless. It is a message especially meant for the millions of people resisting displacement and eviction due to public and private development schemes. It makes local governments only instruments for negotiating deals with the powerful.

This neoliberal gambit also tells us that national governments are not able to play any independent role in urban planning. These governments are only supposed to be the gatekeepers for global exchange. Those that were once powerful in shaping cities are now downloading their responsibilities to weak local authorities, limiting their regulatory powers, and starting "public–private partnerships" in which the public is always the junior partner. This is not a weakening of the state but a transformation of state power to more directly serve global capital. Indeed, local and national governments even in free-market havens like the U.S. continue to use their sovereign powers to assemble urban land for global investors, exempt them from local taxes and laws, and create partnerships with them.

The narrative of invincible global powers breaks down when we look at the evidence of resistance and struggle occurring in cities everywhere. Indeed, it appears that the stronger the intervening global power the more persistent the resistance movements. Not since the Paris Commune of 1871 have there been so many organized efforts to both oppose incursions by capital and propose alternative ways of organizing urban life. Whereas many early utopias were abstract visions of the good city dreamed up by elites, today popular utopias have sprung from the struggles to protect neighborhoods and cities. People are learning how to plan cities from the bottom up, by gaining control over land that is otherwise coveted by global capital and local oligarchies. The inspiring visions come from, for example, the MST in Brazil, the "slumdwellers" in Mumbai and the Zapatistas in Mexico. We need to learn from them and from their innovations and mistakes, and from each other. Alternative approaches to cities in the twenty-first century are all over the place; we have only to discover them.

Twenty-First Century Socialism?

We can envision and move towards a world oriented towards the satisfaction of human needs and not the eternal growth of capital; a world based on cooperation and not competition for resources; a world based on the welfare and survival of other species in complex ecological systems. But is this just bound to be a repeat of twentieth century socialism, with all its deprivations, environmental problems and undemocratic abuses? Are we just repeating the instrumentalist fallacy that once the state becomes "ours" in a single violent event, it will perform the dualist magic of going from "bad" to "good"?

Millions of activists all over the world, many in large social movements like Brazil's MST but many more only associated at the neighborhood or village level, are conscious of the need to build alternatives to the existing regimes and the serious challenges to getting there. As they fight against displacement by megaprojects, land speculators, and government agencies, they are developing powerful visions for the future of their communities and the world. They are calling for socially responsible policies on land, food security and food sovereignty, a right to live and work in a healthy environment and a right to the city and countryside. They are women demanding equal rights, indigenous people demanding that land and nature be respected and honored. If there is to be a comprehensive alternative to capitalism in this century, this is where it will come from. It will fill the largest gaping hole left by twentieth century socialism: participatory democracy.[4]

Today many people concerned about the future of the planet are wisely turning away from ideological battles divorced from political practice, and simplistic dualisms. The question is not the twentieth century binaries of capitalism or socialism, urban or rural, "slums" or "planned cities," but rather what kind of system will sustain a quality of life on the planet without destroying our own habitat and other living species along the way. No mythical free-market machine will do it, nor will any

Figure 9.1 The Multigenerational Olive Tree

abstract ideal of a socialist paradise. If capitalism has proven incapable of doing this, does it make much difference what we call the more socially and environmentally responsible system that will replace it?

The question is not whether the metropolis will be our doom or our salvation but whether we are able to guarantee productive and healthy lives for everyone no matter where they live. In other words, if we go back to the critique of the urban fallacy that we started with, it can lead us forward towards a more penetrating search for an alternative to capitalism in the twentieth century that will sustain life on the planet for at least the next seven generations, which is but a fraction of the lifespan for the olive tree.

Notes

1 The Metropolis in the Twenty-First Century

1 In this book we define the metropolis as a city with more than 750,000 people, following the usage of the UN-HABITAT and in most cases using their most recent data. Our use of the term "urban" follows this same criterion unless otherwise indicated. The threshold of 750,000 is a somewhat arbitrary one—in *Metropolis 2000*, I used the threshold of one million. T. Angotti, *Metropolis 2000: Planning, Poverty and Politics*, New York: Routledge, 1993.
2 Portions of this chapter are substantially revised and updated from T. Angotti, *Metropolis 2000: Planning, Poverty and Politics*.
3 J. Diamond, *Collapse: How Societies Choose to Fail or Succeed*, New York: Penguin, 2005.
4 E. Banfield, *The Unheavenly City: The Nature and Future of Our Urban Crises*, New York: Little Brown, 1970.
5 A. Gilbert, "The Return of the Slum: Does Language Matter?" *International Journal of Urban and Regional Research* 31 (4), 2007, pp. 697–713.
6 United Nations Human Settlements Programme (UN-HABITAT), *The Challenge of Slums*, New York: United Nations, 2003.
7 E. Eaves, "Two Billion Slum Dwellers," *Forbes*, June 11, 2007.
8 E. Glaeser, *Triumph of the City*, New York: Penguin, 2011.
9 J. Brash, *Bloomberg's New York: Class and Governance in the Luxury City*, Athens, GA: University of Georgia Press, 2011; M. Greenberg, *Branding New York: How a City in Crisis was Sold to the World*, New York: Routledge, 2008.
10 The term comes from M. Castells, *The Urban Question: A Marxist Approach*, Cambridge, MA: MIT Press, 1979.
11 H. Blumenfeld, *The Modern Metropolis*, Cambridge, MA: MIT Press, 1971, p. 61.
12 Ibid.: 64.
13 According to Peter Hall, "...twentieth-century city planning, as an intellectual and professional movement, essentially represents a reaction to the evils of the nineteenth-century city." P. Hall, *Cities of Tomorrow: An Intellectual History of Urban Planning Design in the Twentieth Century*, Malden, MA: Blackwell, 1988.
14 P. Smith, D. Martino, Z. Cai, D. Gwary, H. Janzen, P. Kumar, B. Mccarl, S. Ogle, F. Mara, C. Rice, B. Scholes, and O. Sirotenko, *Agriculture Climate Change (2007): Mitigation. Contribution of Working Group III to the Fourth Assessment Report of the Intergovernmental Panel on Climate Change, United Nations World Meteorological Association*, New York: United Nations, 2007.
15 J. Garreau, *Edge City: Life on the New Frontier*, New York: Doubleday, 1991.
16 M. Castells and P. Hall, *Technopoles of the World: The Making of Twenty-First-Century Industrial Complexes*, London: Routledge, 1994.
17 United Nations World Commission on Environment and Development, *Our Common Future*, 1987.
18 M. Castells, *The Urban Question: A Marxist Approach*; T. Angotti, *Metropolis 2000: Planning, Poverty and Politics*; M. Weber, *The City*, New York: Free Press, 1921; E. Burgess

and D. Bogue, *Contributions to Urban Sociology*, Chicago: University of Chicago Press, 1967.

19 L. Mumford, *The City in History: Its Origins, Its Transformations, and Its Prospects*, New York: Harcourt, Brace and World, 1961, p. 551.

20 M.T. Vázquez Castillo, *Land Privatization in Mexico: Urbanization, Formation of Regions and Globalization in Ejidos*, New York: Routledge, 2004; R. Mize and A. Swords, *Consuming Mexican Labor: From the Bracero Program to NAFTA*, Toronto: University of Toronto Press, 2010; J. Contreras, *In the Shadow of the Giant: The Americanization of Modern Mexico*, New Brunswick: Rutgers University Press, 2009; J. Audley, S. Polanski, D. Papademetriou, and S. Vaughan, "NAFTA's Promise and Reality: Lessons From Mexico for the Hemisphere," Carnegie Endowment Report, 2003.

21 L. Mumford, *The City in History: Its Origins, Its Transformations, and Its Prospects*, p. 553.

22 P.R. Ehrlich, *The Population Bomb*, New York: Ballantine Books, 1968.

23 D. Kleinman, *Human Adaptation and Population Growth: A Non-Malthusian Perspective*, Lanham, MD: Rowman & Littlefield, 1980, p. 252.

24 Ibid.: 248–58.

25 US Census 2010.

26 UN Statistics Division, "Demographic Yearbook 2008," http://unstats.un.org/unsd/demographic/products/dyb/dyb2008.htm, accessed June 3, 2011.

27 C. Fischer, M. Baldassare, and R. Ofshe, *Crowding Studies and Urban Life: A Critical Review*, Berkeley: Institute of Urban & Regional Development, University of California, 1974; F.J. Osborn, "Reflections on Density," *Town and Country Planning* 9 (35), 1941, pp. 121–6, 146.

28 United Nations Human Settlements Programme (UN-HABITAT), *State of the World's Cities 2010/2011*, New York: UN-HABITAT, 2010; C. Brennan, D. Hackler, and C. Hoene, "Demographic Change in Small Cities, 1990 to 2000," *Urban Affairs Review* 40 (3), 2005, pp. 342–61; Z. Xu and N. Zhu, "City Size Distribution in China: Are Large Cities Dominant?" *Urban Studies* 46 (10), 2009, pp. 2159–85.

29 S. Sassen, *The Mobility of Labor and Capital*, Cambridge, UK: Press Syndicate of the University of Cambridge, 1988; S. Sassen, *Globalization and its Discontents*, New York: New Press, 1999; D. Harvey, *A Brief History of Neoliberalism*, New York: Oxford University Press USA, 2007.

30 The 1987 United Nations Conference on the Environment defined sustainability as addressing current needs without sacrificing the needs of future generations. Today the term is widely equated with improving environmental quality. In this book I avoid using sustainability because of its multiple definitions and uses and use it mostly in its generic sense to signify continuation of something over time.

31 US Energy Information Administration, "International Energy Annual 2006," 2006, www.eia.gov/emeu/international/energyconsumption.html, accessed June 3, 2011.

32 Cited in T. Angotti, *New York for Sale*, Cambridge, MA: MIT Press, 2008.

33 J. Perlman, *The Myth of Marginality*, Berkeley: University of California Press, 1976; J. Perlman, *Favela: Four Decades of Living on the Edge in Rio de Janeiro*, New York: Oxford University Press USA, 2010; T. Angotti, "Apocalyptic Anti-Urbanism: Mike Davis and his Planet of Slums," *International Journal of Urban and Regional Research 2006*, 30 (4), pp. 961–7; A. Gilbert, "The Return of the Slum: Does Language Matter?".

34 UN-HABITAT, *The Challenge of Slums*.

35 M. Davis, *Planet of Slums*, New York: Verso, 2007.

36 E. Said, *Orientalism*, New York: Vintage, 1979, p. 1.

37 Balfour played an important role in the entry of Patrick Geddes, a noted planner from the U.K., into the British Mandate of Palestine, where Geddes developed one of the twentieth century's premiere examples of orientalist planning. See Chapter Six for details.

38 E. Said, *Orientalism*, pp. 32–3.

39 T. Williamson, "The 2016 Olympics in Rio: A Community Plays Against the Real Estate Game," *Progressive Planning*, 184, Summer 2010, pp. 9–12.

40 C. Hartman and G.D. Squires (eds.), *There Is No Such Thing as a Natural Disaster*, New York: Routledge, 2006.

41 A recent argument for denser urban living is D. Owen, *The Green Metropolis: Why Living Smaller, Living Closer, and Driving Less are the Keys to Sustainability*, New York: Riverhead, 2009.

42 R. York and B. Clark, "Stephen Jay Gould's Critique of Progress," *Monthly Review* 62 (9), 2011.

43 J. Diamond, *Collapse: How Societies Choose to Fail or Succeed*.

44 Metropolitan areas generally have measurable carbon footprints that extend far beyond their geographic boundaries; what this means is that they are dependent for their survival on using resources from a vast hinterland. This can make them more vulnerable and less resilient in times of crisis. One of the great challenges of urban planning in the twenty-first century is reducing the ecological footprints of urban areas. W. Rees and M. Wackernagel, *Our Ecological Footprint: Reducing Human Impact on the Earth*, Gabriola Island, BC: New Society Publishers, 1995; M.A. Brown, F. Southworth, and A. Savzynski, *Shrinking the Carbon Footprint of Metropolitan America*, Washington, DC: Brookings Institution, May 2008.

45 D. Owen, *Green Metropolis: Why Living Smaller, Living Closer, and Driving Less are the Keys to Sustainability*; D. Hendrickson and M. Roseland, "Green Buildings, Green Consumption: Do 'Green' Residential Developments Reduce Post-Occupancy Consumption Levels?" Centre for Sustainable Community Development, Burnaby, BC: Simon Fraser University, 2010.

46 U.S. Energy Information Administration, *Annual Energy Outlook 2011*.

47 D. Harvey, *Social Justice and the City*, Baltimore: Johns Hopkins University Press, 1973; P. Baran and P. Sweezy, *Monopoly Capitalism: An Essay on the American Economic and Social Order*, New York: Monthly Review Press, 1966.

48 C. Wheeler, "Evidence on Agglomeration Economies, Diseconomies, and Growth," *Journal of Applied Econometrics* 18 (1), 2003, pp. 79–104; L. Gabler, "Economies and Diseconomies of Scale in Urban Public Sectors," *Land Economics* 45 (4), 1969, pp. 425–34; K. Park, "The Impact of Special Districts on Local Expenditures in Metropolitan Areas: An Institutional Paradox," *State & Local Government Review* 27 (3), 1995, pp. 195–208.

49 UN Secretary-General's High-Level Task Force on the Global Food Security Crisis, "Progress Report of the High-Level Task Force on the Global Food Security Crisis, April 2008–October 2009," 2009; R. Patel, *Stuffed and Starved: The Hidden Battle for the World Food System*, Brooklyn, NY: Melville House, 2007; F. Magdoff, J.B. Foster, and F.H. Buttel (eds.), *Hungry for Profit: The Agribusiness Threat to Farmers, Food, and the Environment*, New York: Monthly Review Press, 2000; D.H. Boucher, (ed.), *The Paradox of Plenty: Hunger in a Bountiful World*, Oakland, CA: Food First, 1999.

50 US Energy Information Administration, "International Energy Annual 2006."

51 J. Olivier and J. Peters, "No Growth in Total Global CO_2 Emissions in 2009," Netherlands Environmental Assessment Agency (PBL), The Netherlands: Bilthoven, 2010.

52 H. Blumenfeld, *The Modern Metropolis*, pp. 171–5; D. Hayden, *Redesigning the American Dream: The Future of Housing, Work, and Family Life*, New York: W.W. Norton & Company, 1984, pp. 3–62.

53 Contrary to common belief, New York is not an exception. Although Manhattan and other cores in the region are relatively dense, the region is about as sprawled as Los Angeles. E. Eidlin, "What Density Doesn't Tell Us About Sprawl," *Access* 35, 2010, pp. 1–9.

54 K. Jackson, *Crabgrass Frontier: The Suburbanization of the United States*, New York: Oxford University Press USA, 1987.

55 D. Sperling and G. Deborah, *Two Billion Cars: Driving Toward Sustainability*, New York: Oxford University Press USA, 2009.

56 U.S. Department of Commerce, Bureau of Economic Analysis, *National Income and Product Accounts Tables*, 2008.

57 International Organization of Motor Vehicle Manufacturers, "World Motor Vehicle Production by Country and Type, 2009–2010," http://oica.net/wp-content/uploads/cars-2010-provisional.pdf, accessed June 3, 2011.

2 Urban Orientalism, Planning and the Metropolis of "The Others"

1 E. Said, *Orientalism*, New York: Vintage, 1979, p. 1.

2 F. Fanon, *Black Skin, White Masks*, New York: Grove Press, 1967.

3 K. Marx and F. Engels, *The German Ideology, Parts I & III*, New York: International Publishers, 1947.

4 These dichotomies stem from the philosophy of "Cartesian Dualism," named for René Descartes, which strictly separates the mind from the body. That dualism became the handmaiden of an Enlightenment rationalism also compromised by religious dogma.

5 S. Huntington, *The Clash of Civilizations and the Remaking of World Order*, New York: Simon and Schuster, 1998.

6 N.C. Nash, "Squalid Slums Grow as People Flood Latin America's Cities," *New York Times*, October 11, 1992, p. 1.

7 J. Yardley, "Where Growth and Dysfunction Have No Boundaries," *New York Times*, June 9, 2011, pp. A1, 12–13.

8 A.D. King, *Colonial Urban Development: Culture, Social Power and Environment*, New York: Routledge, 2007; A.D. King, *Urbanism, Colonialism, and the World-Economy: Cultural and Spatial Foundations of the World Urban System*, London: Routledge, 1990.

9 J.E. Hardoy, *Urban Planning in Pre-Columbian America*, New York: George Braziller, 1968; M.E. Smith, "Form and Meaning in the Earliest Cities: A New Approach to Ancient Urban Planning," *Journal of Planning History* 6 (1), pp. 3–47.

10 E. Howard, *Garden Cities of To-morrow*, London: Faber & Faber, 1946.

11 R.E. Foglesong, *Planning the Capitalist City: The Colonial Era to the 1920s*, Princeton, NJ: Princeton University Press, 1986.

12 C. Smith, *The Plan of Chicago: Daniel Burnham and the Remaking of the American City*, Chicago: University of Chicago Press, 2006.

13 Le Corbusier and F. Etchells, *The City of To-morrow and its Planning*, Mineola, NY: Dover Publications, 1987; Le Corbusier, *Towards a New Architecture*, Mineola, NY: Dover Publications, 1986; M. Smith, "Repetition and Difference: Lefebvre, Le Corbusier and Modernity's (Im)moral Landscape," *Ethics, Policy & Environment* 4 (1), 2001, pp. 31–44; Z. Celik, "Le Corbusier, Orientalism, Colonialism," *Assemblage* 17, 1992, pp. 58–77.

14 For an excellent, readable account of how the orientalist vision affected the everyday life of the Turkish middle class in Instanbul, see O. Pamuk, *Istanbul: Memories and the City*, New York: Vintage, 2004.

15 See A. Whittick (ed.), *Encyclopedia of Urban Planning*, New York: McGraw-Hill, 1974, pp. 1023–4.

16 At the Pei Cobb Freed & Partners website, we may compare Pei's biography with that of the other founders and principals in the firm: Pei Cobb Freed & Partners, www.pcf-p.com, accessed June 22, 2011.

17 R.A. Caro, *The Power Broker: Robert Moses and the Fall of New York*, New York: Vintage, 1975.

18 See Paul Davidoff's classical critique of physical determinism in planning, P. Davidoff and T. Reiner, "A Choice Theory of Planning," *Journal of the American Institute of Planners*, May 28, 1962, pp. 331–8.

19 Rational–comprehensive planning in the Soviet Union and socialist bloc nations took a very different form although it shared many of the characteristics developed in the capitalist world. After the collapse of the Soviet Union in 1990 and introduction of land markets planning has come to resemble the process in Europe and North America. See Chapter Six.

20 J.M. Bryson and W.D. Roering, "Applying Private-Sector Strategic Planning in the Public Sector," *Journal of the American Planning Association* 53 (1), 1987, pp. 9–22; L. Albrechts, "Strategic (Spatial) Planning Reexamined," *Environment and Planning B: Planning and Design* 31, 2004, pp. 743–58.

21 K. Polanyi, *The Great Transformation: The Political and Economic Origins of Our Time*, Boston: Beacon Press, 1971.

22 T. Angotti, *New York for Sale*, Cambridge, MA: MIT Press, 2008; C.E. Lindblom, "The Science of 'Muddling Through'," *Public Administrative Review* 19 (2), 1959, pp. 79–88; P. Lasserre, "Planning Through Incrementalism," *Socio-Economic Planning Sciences* 8 (3), 1974, pp. 129–34.

23 This stands in contrast to the myth of the "organic city," the idea that cities grow naturally like organisms and can, if left alone, develop to their maximum potential. Lewis Mumford and Henri Pirenne both discuss the real physical differences between and within cities that grew incrementally, but they also consider how the organization of society and the state made that possible. L. Mumford, *The City in History: Its Origins, Its Transformations, and Its Prospects*, New York; Harcourt Brace, 1961; H. Pirenne, *Medieval Cities: Their Origins and the Revival of Trade*, Princeton, NJ: Princeton University Press, 1969.

24 J. Hackworth, *The Neoliberal City: Governance, Ideology, and Development in American Urbanism*, Ithaca: Cornell University Press, 2006; D. Harvey, *A Brief History of Neoliberalism*, New York: Oxford University Press USA, 2007.

25 European Commission, "Governance," http://ec.europa.eu/governance/index_en.htm, accessed June 22, 2011.

26 M. Pyatok, "The Narrow Base of the New Urbanists," *Progressive Planning* 151, 2002, pp. 1, 4–5; T. Angotti, "NU: The Same Old Anti-Urbanism," *Progressive Planning* 151, 2002, pp. 18–21; B. Resnick, "Reconstructing Cities, Restoring the Environment: New Urbanism versus Mobile/Agile Capital," in A. Anton, M. Fisk, and N. Holmstrom (eds.), *Not For Sale: In Defense of Public Goods*, Boulder, CO: Westview Press, 2000.

27 L. Benevolo, *The Origins of Modern Town Planning*, Cambridge, MA: MIT Press, 1971.

28 P. Hall, *Cities of Tomorrow: An Intellectual History of Urban Planning and Design in the Twentieth Century*, Malden, MA: Blackwell, 1988; L. Mumford, *The City in History: Its Origins, Its Transformations, and Its Prospects*.

29 J. Jacobs, *The Death and Life of Great American Cities*, New York: Random House, 1961.

30 J. Jacobs, *The Nature of Economies*, New York: Vintage, 2000; J. Jacobs, *Dark Age Ahead*, New York: Vintage, 2004, pp. 161–76.

31 LGBT stands for lesbian, gay, bisexual, and transgender.

32 L. Sandercock, "Introduction: Framing Insurgent Historiographies for Planning," in L. Sandercock (ed.), *Making the Invisible Visible: A Multicultural Planning History*, Berkeley: University of California Press, 1998.

33 L. Sandercock, *Towards Cosmopolis*, New York: John Wiley & Sons, 1998.

34 J.M. Thomas, *Redevelopment and Race: Planning a Finer City in Postwar Detroit*, Baltimore: Johns Hopkins University Press, 1997; J.M. Thomas and M. Ritzdorf, (eds.), *Urban Planning and the African American Community: In the Shadows*, Thousand Oaks: Sage Publications, 1997; J.M. Thomas and J. Darnton, "Social Diversity and Economic Development in the Metropolis," *Journal of Planning Literature* 21 (2), 2006, pp. 153–68.

35 D. Hayden, *The Power of Place: Urban Landscapes as Public History*, Cambridge, MA: MIT Press, 1995; D. Hayden, *Redesigning the American Dream: Gender, Housing, and Family Life*, New York: W.W. Norton & Company, 2002; D. Hayden, *Building Suburbia: Green Fields and Urban Growth, 1820–2000*, New York: Vintage, 2004.

36 P. Bourdieu and L. Wacquant, "On the Cunning of Imperialist Reason," *Theory, Culture and Society* 16 (1), 1999, pp. 41–58; L. Wacquant, "Deadly Symbiosis: When Ghetto and Prison Meet and Mesh," *Punishment & Society* 3 (1), 2001, pp. 95–133; L. Wacquant, *Urban Outcasts: A Comparative Sociology of Advanced Marginality*, Malden, MA: Polity Press, 2008; L. Wacquant, *Punishing the Poor: The Neoliberal Government of Social Insecurity*, Durham: Duke University Press, 2009.

37 O. Yiftachel, "Planning and Social Control: Exploring the Dark Side," *Journal of Planning Literature* 12 (4), 1998, pp. 395–406; M. Huxley and O. Yiftachel, "New Paradigm or Old Myopia? Unsettling the Communicative Turn in Planning Theory," *Journal of Planning Education and Research* 19 (4), 2000, pp. 333–42; O. Yiftachel, *Ethnocracy: Land and Identity Politics in Israel/Palestine*, Philadelphia: University of Pennsylvania Press, 2006; P. Healey, "Planning Through Debate: The Communicative Turn in Planning Theory," in

S. Campbell and S. Fainstein (eds.), *Readings in Planning Theory*, Malden, MA: Blackwell, 1996, pp. 234–57.
38 H. Lefebvre, *Critique of Everyday Life*, New York: Verso, 1992; H. Lefebvre, *The Production of Space*, Hoboken: Wiley-Blackwell, 1992; H. Lefebvre (author), E. Kofman, and E. Lebas (eds.), *Writings on Cities*, Hoboken: Wiley-Blackwell, 1996; H. Lefebvre, *The Urban Revolution*, Minneapolis: University of Minnesota Press, 2003.
39 The Right to the City Coalition, www.righttothecity.org, accessed June 17, 2011.

3 Urban and Rural Dependencies and Divides

1 See R. Patel, *Stuffed and Starved: The Hidden Battle for the World Food System*, Brooklyn, NY: Melville House, 2007, pp. 99–102; D. Koeppel, *Banana: The Fate of the Fruit that Changed the World*, New York: Plume, 2008.
2 D. Ricardo, *On the Principles of Political Economy and Taxation*, Amherst, NY: Prometheus Books, 1996.
3 P. Susman, "Spatial Equality and Socialist Transformation in Cuba," in D. Forbes and N. Thrift (eds.), *The Socialist Third World: Urban Development and Territorial Planning*, Oxford: Blackwell, 1987, pp. 250–81.
4 T. Angotti, "The Political Economy of Oil, Autos, and the Urban Environment in Venezuela," *Review of Radical Political Economics* 30 (4), 1998, pp. 98–115.
5 J. Agyeman, R.D. Bullard, and B. Evans, *Just Sustainabilities: Development in an Unequal World*, Cambridge (MA): MIT Press, 2003.
6 W.W. Rostow, *The Stages of Economic Growth: A Non-Communist Manifesto*, London: Cambridge University Press, 1960.
7 E. Banfield, *The Moral Basis of a Backward Society*, New York: Free Press, 1958; O. Lewis, "The Culture of Poverty," *Scientific American* 215, 1966, pp. 19–25. E.B. Leacock (ed.), *The Culture of Poverty: A Critique*, New York: Simon & Schuster, 1971.
8 This was an important argument in the classic, F. Engels, *The Housing Question*, Moscow: Progress Publishers, 1975.
9 M. Ravallion, *Pro-Poor Growth: A Primer*, World Bank Policy Research Working Paper 3242, March 2004; United Nations, "Millennium Development Goals," www.un.org/millenniumgoals/reports.shtml, accessed September 1, 2011.
10 Through global assembly lines, manufacturing of a product can take place in more than one country so that the most arduous and labor-intensive activities remain in countries with low wages and less rigorous social and environmental protections. See Lorraine Gray's 1986 documentary film, *The Global Assembly Line*.
11 S. Sassen (ed.), *Global Networks, Linked Cities*, New York: Routledge, 2002; E. Wallerstein, *The Capitalist World-Economy*, Cambridge: Cambridge University Press, 1979.
12 Council on Hemispheric Affairs staff, "One-way Ticket or Circular Flow: Changing of Remittances to Latin America," *Council on Hemispheric Affairs*, cohaforum.org/2011/08/04/one-way-ticket-or-circular-flow-changing-stream-of-remittances-to-latin-america, accessed September 17, 2011.
13 S. Mitchell, *Big-Box Swindle*, Boston: Beacon Press, 2006; Hunter College Center for Community Planning & Development and New York City Public Advocate Bill de Blasio, *Wal-Mart's Economic Footprint: A Literature Review*, www.hunter.cuny.edu/ccpd/community-projects, accessed August 12, 2011.
14 See U. Roberto Romano's 2010 documentary, *The Harvest*.
15 The Kyoto Protocol committed signatories to the goal of reducing greenhouse gas emissions by 5.2 percent between 1990 and 2012. 178 nations subscribed to the Kyoto agreement but the U.S., the world's largest contributor to greenhouse gases, withdrew.
16 The summit resulted in the Universal Declaration of the Rights of Mother Earth. See "The Rights of Nature," therightsofnature.org, accessed September 23, 2011.
17 D.A. Pfeiffer, "The Dirty Truth About Biofuels," http://www.oilcrash.com/articles/pf_bio.htm, accessed July 25, 2011.
18 J. Diamond, *Collapse: How Societies Choose to Fail or Succeed*, New York: Penguin, 2005.

19 J.K. Nyrere, *Ujamaa: Essays on Socialism*, London: Oxford University Press, 1968.
20 "Via Campesina," viacampesina.org/en, accessed September 17, 2011.
21 European Commission, Eurostat, 2009. This data conceals significant differences within Europe; southern, eastern and Mediterranean nations tend to have somewhat larger proportions working in agriculture.
22 F. Magdoff, J.B. Foster, and F.H. Buttel, *Hungry for Profit: The Agribusiness Threat to Farmers, Food, and the Environment*, New York: Monthly Review, 2000; E. Schlosser, *Fast Food Nation*, New York: Perennial, 2002; D.H. Boucher (ed.), *The Paradox of Plenty*, Oakland: Food First Books, 1999.
23 R. Patel, *Stuffed and Starved: The Hidden Battle for the World Food System*, Ch. 2.
24 J.B. Foster, B. Clark, and R. York, *The Ecological Rift: Capitalism's War on the Earth*, New York: Monthly Review, 2010. The forestry industry is increasingly dominated by global corporations, and many reforestation efforts promoted by the World Bank and corporate investors have resulted in extensive displacement of rural populations (see Chapter Four, India) and the destruction of biodiversity in forests. While uncontrolled and non-restorative forestry practices may diminish in time as disappearance of the world's natural forest cover threatens corporations that thrive on logging and resource extraction, and some reforestation efforts may expand, it remains to be seen whether the world's largest natural carbon sink will expand or contract.
25 N. Alexandratos, G. Bödeker, J. Bruinsma, H. de Haen, M.G. Ottaviani, and J. Schmidhuber, *World Agriculture: Towards 2015/2030*, Food and Agriculture Organization of the United Nations, 2002.
26 Jesper Stage, Jorn Stage, and G. Mcgranahan, "Is Urbanization Contributing to Higher Food Prices?" *Environment and Urbanization* 22 (1), April 2010, pp. 199–215.
27 S. Liberti, *Land Grabbing*, Roma: Novità, 2011. A recent case in which Chinese investors seek land in Argentina: P. Lopez-Gamundi and W. Hanks, "A Land-grabber's Loophole," *Council on Hemispheric Affairs*, http://www.coha.org/a-land-grabber%E2%80%99s-loophole, accessed August 12, 2011.
28 United Nations, "United Nations Millennium Development Goals Report, 2010," mdgs.un.org/unsd/mdg/SeriesDetail.aspx?srid=784&crid=, accessed August 18, 2011.
29 I. Urbana, "Regulation Lax as Gas Wells' Tainted Water Hits Rivers," *New York Times*, February 26, 2011; R.W. Howarth and A. Ingraffea, "Should Fracking Stop?" *Nature*, 477, September 25, 2011, pp. 271–3; C. Williams, *Ecology and Socialism*, Chicago: Haymarket Books, 2010.
30 J. Nash, *We Eat the Mines and Mines Eat Us: Dependency and Exploitation in Bolivian Tin Mines*, New York: Columbia University Press, 1993.
31 See "On the Commons," onthecommons.org, accessed September 17, 2011; E. Ostrom, *Governing the Commons: The Evolution of Institutions for Collective Action*, Cambridge (UK): Cambridge University Press, 1990.
32 J.B. Foster, et al., *The Ecological Rift: Capitalism's War on the Earth*, p. 352.
33 Ibid.: 63.
34 Ibid.: 61.
35 J.B. Foster, *The Ecological Revolution: Making Peace With the Planet*, New York: Monthly Review, 2009, p. 169.
36 V. Shiva, *Stolen Harvest: The Hijacking of the Global Food Supply*, Boston: South End Press, 2000; J.M. Smith, *Seeds of Deception: Exposing Industry and Government Lies About the Safety of the Genetically Engineered Foods You're Eating*, Fairfield, IA: Yes! Books, 2003.
37 On Italy's southern question, see J. Schneider (ed.), *Italy's "Southern Question": Orientalism in One Country*, Oxford: Berg, 1998, O. Venezuela. See J. Friedmann, *Regional Development Policy: Case Study of Venezuela*, Cambridge: MIT Press, 1966; T. Angotti, "Ciudad Guayana: From Growth Pole to Metropolis, Central Planning to Participation," *Journal of Planning Education & Research* 20 (3), Spring 2001, pp. 329–38.
38 W. Christaller, *Central Places in Southern Germany*, New York: Prentice-Hall, 1966; D. Rondinelli, *Secondary Cities in Developing Countries: Policies for Diffusing Urbanization*, Beverly Hills: Sage, 1983.

4 Last Chance for the Urban Village?

1 S. Sankhe, I. Vittal, R. Dobbs, A. Mohan, A. Gulati, J. Ablett, S. Gupta, A. Kim, S. Paul, A. Sanghvi, and G. Sethy, *India's Urban Awakening: Building Inclusive Cities, Sustaining Economic Growth*, McKinsey Global Institute Study, April 2010, http://www.mckinsey. com/mgi/reports/freepass_pdfs/india_urbanization/MGI_india_urbanization_full_report. pdf, accessed June 10, 2011.
2 J. Kaufman (ed.), "Planning for Community Food Systems: Special Issue," *Journal of Planning Education and Research* 23 (4), 2004.
3 These two cities are now the first and third largest cities in India. In 2010, Kolkata had an estimated population of 15.5 million, Mumbai had 20 million, and Delhi had 22 million. United Nations Human Settlements Programme (UN-HABITAT), *Cities and Climate Change: Global Report on Human Settlements 2011*, London: Earthscan, 2011.
4 Ibid.
5 Ibid.
6 Ibid. See also: V. Nath, *Urbanization, Urban Development & Metropolitan Cities in India*, New Delhi: Concept, 2007; K.C. Sivaramakrishnan, *Handbook of Urbanization in India*, New Delhi: Oxford University Press, 2005.
7 UN-HABITAT, *Cities and Climate Change: Global Report on Human Settlements 2011*.
8 V. Bajaj and S. Sengupta, "A Subcontinent Stalled," *New York Times*, May 5, 2009, pp. B1 and B7.
9 Between 1991 and 2001, growth rates in the ten largest metropolitan regions ranged from 20 to 85 percent, with the highest rates in medium-sized metros near the largest metropolitan regions. Delhi and Bengaluru also had high rates of growth, mostly at their peripheries (and at the expense of working farms), and all of the large metros had relatively low growth rates in the central cores. S. Sengupta, "India Grapples With How to Convert Its Farmland Into Factories," *New York Times*, September 17, 2008, p. A6; N. Pani, "Resource Cities Across Phases of Globalization: Evidence From Bangalore," *Habitat International* 33, 2009, pp. 114–19.
10 *India Five Year Plan*, 2007–2012. The economic plans are holdovers from an earlier period in which India formally promoted a socialist orientation, but they are also one of many instruments in which the powerful and highly diverse state bureaucracy protects its access to funding and power.
11 G. Kumar, *Local Democracy in India: Interpreting Decentralization*, New Delhi: Sage, 2006.
12 A. Pallavi, "Rooted to Earth," *Down to Earth* 36, 2009.
13 G. Bhan, "This Is No Longer the City I Once Knew: Evictions, the Urban Poor and the Right to the City in Millennial Delhi," *Environment & Urbanization* 21 (1), 2009, pp. 127–42.
14 A. Shefali, "Indian Home Buyers Struggle with Bubble," *The Wall Street Journal*, August 10, 2010.
15 M. Kripalani and A. Shameen, "Indian Land Grab: Spurred by IT Growth and a Shortage of Real Estate, Its Property Markets Are Among the Hottest in Asia," *Business Week*, September 19, 2005.
16 R. Bhuva, "Builder's Paradise: Real Estate Market Booms in Bhopal," *Business Today*, June 12, 2011.
17 V. Shiva, "The Great Land Grab: India's War on Farmers," *Al Jazeera*, June 7, 2011, available at english.aljazeera.net/indepth/opinion/2011/06/20116711756667987.html, accessed June 10, 2011.
18 J. Heitzman, *Network City: Planning the Information Society in Bangalore*, New Delhi: Oxford University Press, 2004.
19 N. Pani, "Resource Cities Across Phases of Globalization: Evidence From Bangalore."
20 T. Angotti, "Bengaluru Goes From Garden City to Nano Land," *Progressive Planning* 180 (2), 2009, pp. 9–11.
21 D. Kozhisseri, "No Apartments," *Down to Earth*, March 1–15, 2009, p. 15.
22 The latest official census data available at the time this book manuscript was completed was the 2001 census.

23 D.N. Reddy and S. Mishra (eds.), *Agrarian Crisis in India*, New Delhi: Oxford University Press, 2009, p. 4.
24 Ibid.: 5.
25 Ibid.: 7.
26 Ibid.: 47–51.
27 World Bank, *World Development Indicators*, 2008.
28 D.N. Reddy and S. Mishra (eds.), *Agrarian Crisis in India*, pp. 3–43.
29 At the extreme end of the rural–urban policy continuum was the Khmer Rouge's Kampuchea, which turned into a brutal, virulently anti-urban regime with disastrous consequences.
30 C. D'Azario, Lecture at National Institute for Advanced Studies, Alternative Law Forum, Bangalore, February 26, 2009; P. Sainath, *Everybody Loves a Good Drought: Stories from India's Poorest Districts*, New Delhi: Penguin, 1996, p. 71.
31 P. Sainath, *Everybody Loves a Good Drought: Stories from India's Poorest Districts*, p. 73.
32 This includes, for example, Himachal Pradesh (65.3%), Nagaland (64.7%), Arunachal Pradesh (57.8%) and Rajasthan (55.3%). In Bihar, Andhra Pradesh and Orissa a relatively large proportion of all those working in agriculture own no land—48%, 40% and 35% respectively. Agriculture in Bihar is particularly precarious given the large proportion of small plots. Some of India's more prosperous regions rely less on agriculture: Kerala (7%), Tamil Nadu (18.4%), and West Bengal (19.2%). In the middle of the distribution we find two states that include relatively prosperous agricultural sectors, Maharashtra (28.7%) and Karnataka (29.2%), and one of the poorest, Bihar, which has many small plots (29.3%). Thus, the relationship between dependence on agriculture and levels of poverty is not necessarily systematic or uniform.
33 D.N. Reddy and S. Mishra (eds.), *Agrarian Crisis in India*, p. 28.
34 Ibid.: 20–2.
35 S. Pal, "Managing Vulnerability of Indian Agriculture: Implications for Research and Development," in D.N. Reddy and S. Mishra (eds.), *Agrarian Crisis in India*, pp. 87–108.
36 N.R. Kleinfeld, "In India, More Wealth and More Diabetes," *The International Herald Tribune*, September 14, 2006, p. 1.
37 M. Cecchini, F. Sassi, J.A. Lauer, Y.Y. Lee, V. Guajardo-Barron, and D. Chisholm, "Tackling of Unhealthy Diets, Physical Inactivity, and Obesity: Health Effects and Cost-Effectiveness," *Lancet* 376, 2010, pp. 1775–84.
38 M.S. Swaminathan Research Foundation, *Food Insecurity Atlas of Rural India*, Chennai: TTK Healthcare Limited–Printing Division, 2001.
39 D.N. Reddy and S. Mishra (eds.), *Agrarian Crisis in India*, p. 29.
40 N.D. Kochi, *Management of Ecology, Environment and Climate Change*. Centre for Socioeconomic and Environmental Studies, Unpublished.
41 R.W. Franke and B.H. Chasin, "Kerala: Radical Reform as Development in an Indian State," in D.H. Boucher (ed.), *The Paradox of Plenty: Hunger in a Bountiful World*, Oakland, CA: Food First, 1999, pp. 278–85.
42 N.D. Kochi, *Management of Ecology, Environment and Climate Change*.
43 While Kerala is rightfully noted for some innovative and progressive social policies, especially in education and health care, rhetoric often obscures some hard realities. The decentralized participatory process has not yet become hegemonic and the major political parties do not always respect it. Historical violence against Adivasi peoples and social movements persists. M. Mukundan and M. Bray, "The Decentralisation of Education in Kerala State, India: Rhetoric and Reality," *International Review of Education* 50 (3/4), 2004, pp. 223–43; C.R. Bijoy and K.R. Raman, "Muthanga: The Real Story: Adivasi Movement to Recover Land," *Economic and Political Weekly* 38 (20), 2003, pp. 1975–82.
44 S. Visvanath, "Between Cosmology and System: The Heuristics of a Dissenting Imagination," in B. De S. Santos (ed.), *Another Knowledge is Possible: Beyond Northern EpisFemologies*, New York: Verso, 2007, pp. 182–218.
45 M. Gandhi, *Hind Swaraj or Indian Home Rule*, www.soilandhealth.org/03sov/0303critic/hind%20swaraj.pdf, 1910, accessed April 8, 2012.

46 Parallels to Gandhi's philosophy may be found in the *Ujamaa* philosophy of Julius Nyrere of Tanzania. J. Nyrere, *Ujamaa: Essays on Socialism*, Oxford: Oxford University Press, 1974.

47 M. Gandhi, *Hind Swaraj or Indian Home Rule.*, n.p.

48 Ibid., n.p.

49 M.N. Das, *The Political Philosophy of Jawaharlal Nehru*, New York: John Day Company, 1961.

50 M. Gandhi, *Hind Swaraj or Indian Home Rule*, n.p.

51 A. Pallavi, "Rooted to Earth," *Down to Earth*, March 1–15, 2009, p. 36.

52 M. Gandhi, *Hind Swaraj or Indian Home Rule*, n.p.

53 R. Patel, *Stuffed and Starved: The Hidden Battle for the World Food System*, Brooklyn, NY: Melnile House, 2007.

54 It is impossible to describe and analyze here all the social movements in India. Instead I will only suggest how they might help answer Gandhi's challenge. Clearly, most of the popular movements arise in opposition to government policies, since the state remains a powerful intermediary for private investors and an advocate of neoliberalism.

55 P. Sainath, *Everybody Loves a Good Drought: Stories from India's Poorest Districts*.

56 V. Shiva, *Ecology and the Politics of Survival: Conflicts over Natural Resources in India*, New Delhi: United Nations University Press and Sage Publications, 1991; V. Shiva, *Stolen Harvest: The Hijacking of the Global Food Supply*, Boston: South End Press, 2000; V. Shiva, *Water Wars: Privatization, Pollution, and Profit*, Cambridge, MA: South End Press, 2002.

57 S. Pande and S. Singh, *Right to Information Act 2005: A Primer*, New Delhi: National Book Trust, 2007.

58 A. Varshney, *Democracy, Development and the Countryside: Urban–Rural Struggles in India*, Cambridge: Cambridge University Press, 1998.

59 G. Bhan, "This Is No Longer the City I Once Knew: Evictions, the Urban Poor and the Right to the City in Millennial Delhi."

60 J. Harriss, "Middle-class Activism and the Politics of the Informal Working Class," *Critical Asian Studies* 38 (4), 2006, pp. 445–65.

61 S. Sengupta, "India Grapples With How to Convert Its Farmland Into Factories."

62 V. Shiva, *Stolen Harvest: The Hijacking of the Global Food Supply*.

63 S. Randeria, "Legal Pluralism, Social Movements and the Post-Colonial State in India: Fractured Sovereignty and Differential Citizenship Rights," in B. De S. Santos (ed.), *Another Knowledge is Possible: Beyond Northern Epistemologies*, London: Verso, 2007, pp. 41–74.

64 M. Sethi, "Land Reform in India: Issues and Challenges," in P. Rosset, R. Patel, and M. Courville (eds.), *Promised Land: Competing Visions of Agrarian Reform*, Oakland: Food First Books, 2006.

65 S. Randeria, "Legal Pluralism, Social Movements and the Post-Colonial State in India: Fractured Sovereignty and Differential Citizenship Rights," in B. De S. Santos (ed.), *Another Knowledge is Possible: Beyond Northern Epistemologies*, London: Verso, 2007, p. 71.

66 Ibid.: 71.

67 A. Roy, *Public Power in the Age of Empire*, New York: Seven Stories Press, 2006, pp. 281–2.

5 Orientalist Roots

1 I. Pappe, *The Ethnic Cleansing of Palestine*, London: Oneworld, 2007.

2 T. Angotti, "The Apartheid Bubble in the Desert," *Progressive Planning* 179, 2009, pp. 2–5.

3 T. Angotti, "Gaza and the Green Zone: Urban Apartheid and Occupied Territories," *Progressive Planning* 175, 2008, p. 2, 19–20.

4 G. Kessler, "U.S.-Israeli Security Ties Grow Amid Diplomatic Disputes," *Washington Post*, July 16, 2010; "U.S. Employs Israeli Tactics in Iraq: Urban Warfare Methods Adapted to Fight Insurgency," *Associated Press*, December 13, 2003.

5 O. Yiftachel, *Ethnocracy: Land and Identity Politics in Israel/Palestine*, Philadelphia: University of Pennsylvania Press, 2006; E. Weizman, *Hollow Land: Israel's Architecture of Occupation*, New York: Verso, 2007.
6 E. Weizman, *Hollow Land: Israel's Architecture of Occupation*.
7 M. Sorkin (ed.), *Against the Wall: Israel's Barrier to Peace*, New York: New Press, 2005.
8 J. Halper, *An Israeli in Palestine: Resisting Dispossession, Redeeming Israel*, London: Pluto Press, 2008.
9 Z. Bauman, *Modernity and the Holocaust*, Ithaca: Cornell University Press, 2001; H. Arendt, *Eichman in Jerusalem: A Report on the Banality of Evil*, New York: Viking Press, 1963; J. Hersh, "Inconvenient Truths about 'Real Existing' Zionism," *Monthly Review* 61 (1), 2009, pp. 19–38.
10 E. Howard, *Garden Cities of To-morrow*, London: Faber & Faber, 1946.
11 E. Weizman, *Hollow Land: Israel's Architecture of Occupation*.
12 P. Hall, *Cities of Tomorrow: An Intellectual History of Urban Planning and Design in the Twentieth Century*, Malden, MA: Blackwell, 1988.
13 I. Munshi, "Patrick Geddes: Sociologist, Environmentalist and Town Planner," *Economic and Political Weekly* 35 (6), 2000, pp. 485–91.
14 N. Hysler-Rubin, *Patrick Geddes and Town Planning: A Critical Review*, New York: Routledge, 2011.
15 I. Pappe, *The Ethnic Cleansing of Palestine*.
16 Ibid. An Israeli NGO, *Zochrot*, seeks to raise awareness of the meaning of the Nakba to Palestinians. "Zochrot," www.zochrot.org/en, accessed September 23, 2011.
17 O. Yiftachel, *Ethnocracy: Land and Identity Politics in Israel/Palestine*.
18 The British mandate in Palestine followed the pattern of state ownership of land that it inherited from the period of Ottoman rule. This assured legal control over most land in a Palestinian society that was largely rural and traditionally had little experience with private property. See R. Khalidi, *Palestinian Identity: The Construction of Modern National Consciousness*, New York: Columbia University Press, 1997. Indeed, the arrival of Jewish settlers coincided historically with the emergence of modern capitalist relations in Palestine.
19 J. Halper, *An Israeli in Palestine: Resisting Dispossession, Redeeming Israel*. Halper counts 18,147 Palestinian house demolitions by the Israeli state between 1967 and 2006.
20 Information provided by Neighbors, an Israeli–Palestinian NGO.
21 Ibid.
22 Zochrot, "Remembering Jaffa's al-Ajami Neighborhood," 2007, www.zochrot.org/index.php?id=642, accessed June 27, 2011.
23 Interview with anonymous community organizer in Jaffa, January 2009.
24 T. Margalit, "Public Assets Versus Public Interest: 50 years of High-Rise Building in Tel-Aviv," unpublished manuscript, 2009.
25 T. Angotti, *New York for Sale*, Cambridge, MA: MIT Press, 2008.
26 Y. Jabareen, "'Space of Risk': The Contribution of Planning Policies to Conflicts in Cities, Lessons from Nazareth," *Planning Theory and Practice* 7 (3), 2006, pp. 305–23.
27 Information provided by Neighbors, an Israeli–Palestinian NGO.
28 G. Falah, "Israeli 'Judaization' Policy in Galilee and Its Impact on Local Arab Urbanization," *Political Geography Quarterly* 8 (3), 1989, pp. 229–53.
29 Information provided by Neighbors.
30 Israel Ministry of Agriculture and Rural Development, http://www.moag.gov.il/agri/files/agriculture/index.html, accessed June 24, 2011.
31 D. Bartram, "Migration, Ethno-Nationalist Destinations, and Social Divisions: Non-Jewish Immigrants in Israel," *Ethnopolitics* 10 (2), 2011, pp. 23 –52; S.H. Miaari and R.M. Sauer, "The Labor Market Costs of Conflict: Closures, Foreign Workers and Palestinian Employment and Earnings," *Review of Economics of the Household* 1, 2011, pp. 129–48.
32 O. Yiftachel, *Ethnocracy: Land and Identity Politics in Israel/Palestine*. The book and picture, *Lemon Tree*, tells a poignant story of the personal suffering brought on a Palestinian farm family placed under siege by the Israeli security state. S. Tolan, *The Lemon Tree: An Arab, a Jew, and the Heart of the Middle East*, London: Bloomsbury, 2007.

33 M. Margalit, "Jerusalem Municipality's 2020 Master Plan. *Palestine-Israel Journal of Politics, Economics and Culture* 17 (1/2), 2010, pp. 141–7. Information also provided by Bimkom, January 2009.

34 Israel Central Bureau of Statistics, 2008.

35 E.P. Wolf, "The Tipping Point in Racially Changing Neighborhoods," *Journal of the American Planning Association* 29 (3), 1963, pp. 217–22.

36 E. Weizman, *Hollow Land: Israel's Architecture of Occupation.*

37 "Report: Arab Households Twice as Likely to Be In Poverty as Jewish Families," *Jerusalem Post*, March 23, 2010.

38 O. Yiftachel, *Ethnocracy: Land and Identity Politics in Israel/Palestine.*

39 Ibid.: 107.

40 E. Weizman, *Hollow Land: Israel's Architecture of Occupation.*

41 S. Skirski and Y. Hasson, *Invisible Cities: Israeli Government Policy Toward the Negev Bedouin*, Beer Sheva: Ben Gurion University, 2006; O. Yiftachel, *Ethnocracy: Land and Identity Politics in Israel/Palestine.*

42 Israel Central Bureau of Statistics, "The 2008 Integrated Census of Population and Housing," www.cbs.gov.il/reader/?MIval=cw_usr_view_Folder&ID=141, accessed September 23, 2011.

43 O. Yiftachel, *Ethnocracy: Land and Identity Politics in Israel/Palestine.*

44 S. Skirski and Y. Hasson, *Invisible Cities: Israeli Government Policy Toward the Negev Bedouin.*

45 E. Weizman, *Hollow Land: Israel's Architecture of Occupation*, pp. 205–8.

46 The Regional Council of Unrecognized Villages, "Unrecognized Bedouin Villages," http://www.rcuv.wordpress.com, accessed September 17, 2011.

47 J. Halper, *An Israeli in Palestine: Resisting Dispossession, Redeeming Israel.*

48 S. Razack, "A Hole in the Wall; A Rose at a Checkpoint: The Spatiality of Colonial Encounters in Occupied Palestine," *Journal of Critical Race Inquiry* 1 (1), 2010, pp. 90–108.

49 R. Backmann, *A Wall In Palestine*, New York: Picador, 2006; I. Braverman, "Powers of Illegality: House Demolitions and Resistance in East Jerusalem," *Law & Social Inquiry* 32 (2), 2007, pp. 33–7.

50 The small state of Israel may be evolving into one giant poly-nucleated urbanized area defined by an East–West axis from Tel Aviv to Jerusalem (and beyond Jerusalem to the border with Jordan if Israel goes through with its plans to build settlements in the occupied territories there); and from Haifa in the north through Tel Aviv to Beer Sheva in the south.

51 For more information about the peaceful resistance see: eng.bimkom.org; www.icahd.org; www.stopthewall.org; www.btselem.org, sites accessed September 23, 2011.

52 O. Yiftachel, *Ethnocracy: Land and Identity Politics in Israel/Palestine.* Another result of the regime is the segregation and encirclement of Palestinians in the isolated enclaves of the Occupied Territories.

53 J. Hersh, "Inconvenient Truths about 'Real Existing' Zionism." Hersh quotes Churchill on Zionism: "In violent contrast to international communism, it presents to the Jew a national idea of a commanding character" (p. 29).

6 Lessons from Twentieth Century Socialism

1 G. Vidal, "Gore Vidal on the 'United States of Amnesia,' 9/11, the 2000 Election and the War in Iraq," *Democracy Now*, May 13, 2003, www.democracynow.org/2003/5/13/gore_vidal_on_the_united_states, accessed September 27, 2011.

2 The terms capitalist city and socialist city are used in only a descriptive way, to identify cities under capitalism and cities under socialism. These are not ideal types with universal characteristics but can only be defined with respect to the specific historic contexts and regimes of capitalism and socialism.

3 K. Marx and F. Engels, "Manifesto of the Communist Party," in *Selected Works*, New York: International Publishers, 1977, p. 39.

4 Ibid.: 53.
5 Adapted from R. Segre, *Arquitectura y Urbanismo Modernos*, Habana: Editorial Arte y Literatura, 1988, pp. 465–6.
6 World Marxist Review Working Group, *World Marxist Review* 28 (7), 1985, p. 121.
7 M. Zeitlin, "Soviet Urbanization and Urban Planning," *Political Affairs* 64 (4), 1985, pp. 27–34.
8 J. Jacobs, *The Death and Life of Great American Cities*, New York: Random House, 1961, pp. 143–238.
9 F. Engels, *The Housing Question*, Moscow: Progress Publishers, 1975.
10 K. Marx and F. Engels, *Selected Works*, p. 403.
11 Ibid.: 97.
12 F. Fukuyama, *The End of History and the Last Man*, New York: Free Press, 1992.
13 Reuters, "Bush Hails Pursuit of 'American Dream'," July 31, 1991.
14 N. Klein, *The Shock Doctrine: The Rise of Disaster Capitalism*, New York: Metropolitan Books, 2007; J.E. Stiglitz, *Globalization and Its Discontents*, New York: W.W. Norton & Company, 2002; S. Keen, *Debunking Economics: The Naked Emperor of the Social Sciences*, New York: Zed Books, 2001; C. Humphrey, *The Unmaking of Soviet Life: Everyday Economies after Socialism*, Ithaca: Cornell University Press, 2002.
15 J.D. Sachs, "Russia's Tumultuous Decade: An Insider Remembers," *Washington Monthly*, March 2000; J. Sachs and K. Pistor, *The Rule of Law and Economic Reform in Russia*, Boulder: Westview Press, 1997.
16 A. Shleifer and D. Treisman, "A Normal Country: Russia After Communism," *Journal of Economic Perspectives* 19 (1), 2005, pp. 151–74 ; R.M. Schneiderman, "Did Privatization Increase the Russian Death Rate?" *New York Times*, January 15, 2009.
17 I. Vocatch-Boldyrev, "The Promotion and Privatization of Medical Services in the Russian Federation, Ukraine and Georgia," *International Labor Organization Interdepartmental Action Programme on Privatization, Restructuring and Economic Democracy*, Working Paper IPPRED-15, 2000.
18 P. Luica, "Russia's Privatisation Plan Adds Up Billions of Dollars in Railway Investments," *Railway PRO*, December 16, 2010.
19 A.E. Kramer, "Russia Close to Privatizing Huge Electricity Producer," *New York Times*, April 9, 2008.
20 T.F. Remington, *The Politics of Inequality in Russia*, Cambridge (UK): Cambridge University Press, 2011.
21 J. O'Loughlin and V. Kolossov, "Moscow–Post-Soviet Developments and Challenges," *Eurasian Geography and Economics* 43 (3), 2002, pp. 161–9.
22 C.A. Newland, "Transformational Challenges in Central and Eastern Europe and Schools of Public Administration," *Public Administration Review* 56 (4), 1996, pp. 382–9; N. Pichler-Milanovich, "Urban Housing Markets in Central and Eastern Europe: Convergence, Divergence or Policy 'Collapse'," *European Journal of Housing Policy* 1 (2), 2001, pp. 145–87; S.D. Iyer, "The Urban Context for Adjustments to the Planning Process in Post-Soviet Russia: Responses from Local Planners in Siberia," *International Planning Studies* 8 (3), 2003, pp. 201–23.
23 S. Guriev and A. Rachinsky, "The Role of Oligarchs in Russian Capitalism," *Journal of Economic Perspectives* 19 (1), 2005, pp. 131–50.
24 See Develop Don't Destroy Brooklyn, dddb.net and the Atlantic Yards Report, atlantic-yardsreport.blogspot.com, accessed September 18, 2011.
25 "Russia Beyond the Headlines," A Special Advertising Supplement to *The New York Times*, August 10, 2011.
26 S. Lentz, "More Gate, Less Community? Guarded Housing in Russia," in G. Glasze, C. Webster, and K. Frantz (eds.), *Private Cities: Global and Local Perspectives*, New York: Routledge, 2005.
27 A. Shleifer and D. Treisman, "A Normal Country: Russia After Communism," *Journal of Economic Perspectives* 19 (1), 2005, pp. 151–74; I. Gorst, "Russia's Car Market: Back on Track," *Financial Times*, July 5, 2011; RNCOS, *Booming Russian Automobile Sector*, March, 2011.

28 M. Petrick and M.R. Carter, "Critical Masses in the Decollectivisation of Post-Soviet Agriculture," *European Review of Agricultural Economics* 36 (2), 2009, pp. 231–52.

29 M. Sysoyeva, "Russian Rainfall Boosts Black Earth Farming's Crops, CEO Says," *Bloomberg*, June 27, 2011.

30 S.K. Wegren, "The Development of Agrarian Capitalism in Post-Soviet Russia," *Journal of Agrarian Change* 11 (2), 2011, pp. 138–63.

31 D.J. O'Brien and S.K. Wegren (eds.), *Rural Reform in Post-Soviet Russia*, Washington, DC: Woodrow Wilson Center Press, 2002; C.S. Leonard, "Rational Resistance to Land Privatization: The Response of Rural Producers to Agrarian Reforms in Pre- and Post-Soviet Russia," *Post-Soviet Geography and Economics* 41 (8), 2000, pp. 605–20.

32 Between 2000 and 2010, China urbanized at a rate of 3.39 percent, reflecting a somewhat reduced rate of growth as the nation becomes more urbanized.

33 T. Zhang, "Urban Development Patterns in China: New, Renewed, and Ignored Urban Spaces," in Y. Song and C. Ding (eds.), *Urbanization in China: Critical Issues in an Era of Rapid Growth*, Cambridge, MA: Lincoln Institute of Land Policy, 2007, p. 4.

34 C. Ding, "Policy and Praxis of Land Acquisition in China," in Y. Song and C. Ding (eds.), *Urbanization in China: Critical Issues in an Era of Rapid Growth*, p. 77.

35 J. Friedmann, *China's Urban Transition*, Minneapolis: University of Minnesota Press, 2005.

36 W. Hinton, *Fanshen: A Documentary of Revolution in a Chinese Village*, Berkeley: University of California Press, 1966; R. MacFarguhar, *The Origins of the Cultural Revolution, Volume 2: The Great Leap Forward, 1958–1960*, New York: Columbia University Press, 1983.

37 M.J. Meisner, *Mao Zedong: A Political and Intellectual Portrait*, Cambridge, MA: Polity Press, 2007. A much more extreme form of this anti-urbanism took hold in the Pol Pot regime in Cambodia. There it was one element in a messianic vision of a pure peasantry whose power was threatened by cities and urban culture. The regime forcefully evacuated cities, destroyed cultural sites and murdered or forced into bondage urban intellectuals and technocrats. K. Frieson, "The Political Nature of Democratic Kampuchea," *Pacific Affairs* 61 (3), 1988, pp. 405–27; M. Shaw, "New Wars of the City: Relationships of 'Urbicide' and 'Genocide'," in S. Graham (ed.), *Cities, War and Terrorism: Towards an Urban Geopolitics*, Malden: Blackwell, 2004, pp. 141–53.

38 J. Friedmann, *China's Urban Transition*.

39 Ibid.

40 Ibid.

41 D.G. Johnson, "Economic Reforms in the People's Republic of China," *Economic Development and Cultural Change* 36 (3), 1988, pp. 225–45.

42 There are now over 60,000 city planners working at various levels of government in China, and city planning is taught in academies throughout the country. Shanghai is home to the "Palace of Urban Planning," which contains a scale model of the entire city comparable to the "Panorama" Robert Moses built in 1964 to demonstrate the scope of his New York City megaprojects. The "Palace" reflects the country's powerful myths about urban growth. It says very little about actual planning, let alone equity or community involvement. It is part of the urban growth machine.

43 P. Gaubatz, "Globalization and the Development of New Central Business Districts in Beijing, Shanghai and Guangzhou," in L.J.C. Ma and F. Wu (eds.), *Restructuring the Chinese City: Changing Society, Economy and Space*, New York: Routledge, 2005, pp. 87–108.

44 J. McDonald, "China Leading High-Rise Boom," *Associated Press*, December 19, 2010.

45 D. Leonhardt, "In China, Cultivating the Urge to Splurge," *New York Times*, November 24, 2010.

46 United Nations Human Settlements Programme (UN-HABITAT), *Cities and Climate Change: Global Report on Human Settlements 2011*, London: Earthscan, 2011.

47 D. Barboza, "Building Boom in China Stirs Fears of Debt Overload," *New York Times*, July 6, 2011.

48 G. Hay, "China Hires Atkins to Plan 48 Cities the Size of London," *Building*, December 2, 2005.

49 C. He and L. Yang, "Urban Development and Climate Change in China's Pearl River Delta," *Land Lines* 23 (3), 2011, pp. 2–8.

50 L. Erickson, "Land from the Tiller: The Push for Rural Land Privatization in China," *China Left Review* 1, 2008.

51 F. Lawrence, "Global Food Crisis, China Land Deal Causes Unease in Argentina," *The Guardian*, June 1, 2011.

52 T. Zhang, "Urban Development Patterns in China: New, Renewed, and Ignored Urban Spaces."

53 M. Hart-Landsberg and P. Burkett, "China and Socialism: Conclusion," *Monthly Review* 56 (3), 2004, pp. 109–15; K.E. Brodsgaard and Z. Yongnian, *The Chinese Communist Party in Reform*, New York: Routledge, 2006; J. Huang, *Factionalism in the Chinese Communist Party*, Cambridge: Cambridge University Press, 2000.

54 J. Friedmann, *China's Urban Transition*.

55 E. Lichtenberg and C. Ding, "Assessing Farmland Protection Policy," in Y. Song and C. Ding (eds.), *Urbanization in China: Critical Issues in an Era of Rapid Growth*, pp. 101–115.

56 Y. Song, Y. Zenou, and C. Ding, "The Role of China's Urbanizing Villages in Housing Rural Migrants," in Y. Song and C. Ding (eds.), *Urbanization in China: Critical Issues in an Era of Rapid Growth*, pp. 145–68.

57 Y. Song, Y. Zenou, and C. Ding, "The Role of China's Urbanizing Villages in Housing Rural Migrants."

58 E. Lichtenberg and C. Ding, "Assessing Farmland Protection Policy."

59 Despite the enormous decrease in farmland, China has not actually experienced a major decline in food supply. This is evidence of China's increased reliance on industrial agriculture and large-scale international imports, as well as a testament to the power of the centralized state to respond quickly to massive internal changes. T. Zhang, "Urban Development Patterns in China: New, Renewed, and Ignored Urban Spaces."

60 W. Wu, "Urban Infrastructure and Financing in China," in Y. Song and C. Ding (eds.), *Urbanization in China: Critical Issues in an Era of Rapid Growth*, pp. 251–69.

61 T. Plafker, "Shanghai Puts on a Green Face," *New York Times*, April 29, 2010.

62 Ibid.

63 J. Wu, H. Huang, R.B. Primack, and Z. Shen, "The Three Gorges Dam: An Ecological Perspective," *Frontiers in Ecology and the Environment* 2, 2004, pp. 241–8.

64 R. Stone, "Three Gorges Dam: Into the Unknown," *Science* 321 (5889), August 1, 2008, pp. 628–32.

65 J. Friedmann, *China's Urban Transition*.

66 R. Stone, "Three Gorges Dam: Into the Unknown,".

67 Jia Zhangke's 2006 film *Still Life* was shot on location in Fengjie, as the town was being dismantled and prepared for flooding. Markings painted high on buildings show the future water levels and warn residents that the impending floods are inevitable.

68 L. Heming, P. Waley, and P. Rees, "Reservoir Resettlement in China: Past Experience and the Three Gorges Dam," *The Geographical Journal* 167 (3), 2001, pp. 195–212.

69 J. Friedmann, *China's Urban Transition*.

70 W. Wu, "Urban Infrastructure and Financing in China."

71 M. Robins, "China's New Industrial Revolution," *BBC News*, August 1, 2010.

72 K. Bradsher, "High-Speed Rail Poised to Alter China," *New York Times*, June 22, 2011.

73 W. Wu, "Urban Infrastructure and Financing in China."

74 L.T. Chang, *Factory Girls: From Village to City in a Changing China*, New York: Spiegel & Grau, 2008.

75 T. Zhang, "Urban Development Patterns in China: New, Renewed, and Ignored Urban Spaces."

76 J. Friedmann, *China's Urban Transition*; G. Hooks, "The Policy Response to Factory Closings: A Comparison of the United States, Sweden and France," *Annals of the American Academy of Political and Social Science* 475, 1984, pp. 110–24; D. Yang, *Beyond Beijing: Liberalization and the Regions in China*, London: Routledge, 1997.

77 "Labour Ministry Announces End to 'Iron Rice Bowl' Policy of Jobs for Life," *Xinhua News Agency*, April 18, 1996; J. Kahn and J. Yardley, "Amid China's Boom, No Helping Hand for Young Qingming," *New York Times*, August 1, 2004.

78 J. Muldavin, "China's Poor Left Behind: SARS in the Hinterland," *International Herald Tribune*, May 3, 2003.

79 J. Muldavin, "Beyond the Harbin Chemical Spill," *International Herald Tribune*, December 1, 2005.

80 C. Ding, "Policy and Praxis of Land Acquisition in China," in Y. Song and C. Ding (eds.), *Urbanization in China: Critical Issues in an Era of Rapid Growth*, pp. 81–2.

81 Migrant workers are underpaid, often below local minimum wage standards. Work hours can be grueling and breaks limited. Workers are exposed to health risks, including hazardous chemicals and unsafe working conditions. Sexual exploitation is common; many migrant workers are young women, despite national child labor laws. Workers sleep in overcrowded dorms or on factory premises. Migrant workers are often indentured servants, their wages withheld until they stay past a certain period of time. Though the formal sector is integrated into the state's union system, and some independent unions are being formed, very few migrant workers have any form of union representation. L.T. Chang, *Factory Girls: From Village to City in a Changing China*; J. Friedmann, *China's Urban Transition*.

82 J. Friedmann, *China's Urban Transition*; T. Zhang, "Urban Development Patterns in China: New, Renewed, and Ignored Urban Spaces."

83 A.M. Broudehoux, "Delirious Beijing: Euphoria and Despair in the Olympic Metropolis," in M. Davis and D.B. Monk (eds.), *Evil Paradises: Dreamworlds of Neoliberalism*, New York: The New Press, 2007, pp. 87–102; S. Sosefielde, "Illusions of Transitions: Russia's Muscovite Future," *Eastern Economic Journal* 31 (2), 2005, pp. 285–99.

84 S. LaFraniere and M. Wines, "Protest Over Chemical Plant Shows Growing Pressure on China From Citizens," *New York Times*, August 15, 2011.

85 F. Weir, "Russia Protests: Thousands Rally in 'Day of Wrath' Against Putin," *The Christian Science Monitor*, March 21, 2010.

7 The Free-Market Metropolis and Enclave Urbanism

1 As with the chapters on India, Israel/Palestine and Latin America, this case study is highly synthesized and necessarily omits many important details. Our purpose is not a definitive analysis of metropolitan development and planning in the U.S. but an illustration of the historic roots and meanings of the leading ideas and practices feeding urban orientalism.

2 *Merriam-Webster's Desk Dictionary*, Springfield, MA: Merriam-Webster, 1995.

3 L. Mumford, *The City in History: Its Origins, Its Transformations, and Its Prospects*, New York: Harcourt, Brace and World, 1961.

4 The plantation economy in the south had many characteristics, including human bondage, that were also present in European feudalism. However, slaveholders were more akin to entrepreneurs and had close ties with the emerging capitalist economy and institutions, including banks and global traders.

5 H. Zinn, *A People's History of the United States*, New York: Harper & Row, 1980; N. Chomsky, "Knowledge and Power: Intellectuals and the Welfare-Warfare State," in P. Long (ed.), *The New Left*, Boston: Porter Sargent, 1970, pp. 172–99.

6 R. Wright, *Stolen Continents: The "New World" Through Indian Eyes*, Boston: Houghton Mifflin, 1992, as quoted in J. Conant, *The Poetics of Resistance: The Revolutionary Public Relations of the Zapatista Insurgency*, Oakland: AK Press, 2010.

7 G. Sorel, *Reflections on Violence*, Cambridge: Cambridge University Press, 1999, pp. 28–30.

8 Kelo v. City of New London, US Supreme Court, 545 U.S. 469 (2005).

9 E. Foner, *The Story of American Freedom*, New York: W.W. Norton & Company, 1999; A. Sen, *Development as Freedom*, New York: First Anchor Books, 1999.

10 For an analysis of collective consumption see M. Castells, *The City and the Grassroots: A Cross-Cultural Theory of Urban Social Movements*, Berkeley: University of California Press, 1985.

11 T. Veblen, *The Theory of the Leisure Class*, New York: Modern Library, 1961.

12 V. Packard, *The Waste Makers*, New York: D. McKay, 1960.

13 H. Molotch, "The City as a Growth Machine: Toward a Political Economy of Place," *The American Journal of Sociology* 82 (2), 1976, pp. 309–32.

14 M.P. Smith and J.R. Feagin (eds.), *The Bubbling Cauldron: Race, Ethnicity and the Urban Crisis*, Minneapolis: University of Minnesota Press, 1995; D.S. Massey and N.A. Denton, *American Apartheid: Segregation and the Making of the Underclass*, Cambridge: Harvard University Press, 1993; W.W. Goldsmith and E.J. Blakely (eds.), *Separate Societies: Poverty and Inequality in U.S. Cities*, Philadelphia: Temple University Press, 1992; D. Hayden, *Redesigning the American Dream: The Future of Housing, Work, and Family Life*, New York: W.W. Norton & Company, 1984; L.K. Weisman, *Discrimination by Design*, Urbana, IL: University of Illinois Press, 1992.

15 J.H. Kunstler, *The Geography of Nowhere: The Rise and Decline of America's Man-Made Landscape*, New York: Touchstone, 1993; P. Newman and J. Kenworthy, *Sustainability and Cities: Overcoming Automobile Dependence*, Washington, DC: Island Press, 1999.

16 R. Bruegmann, *Sprawl: A Compact History*, Chicago: University of Chicago Press, 2005; J.L. Nasar and J.S. Evans-Crowley, "McMansions: The Extent and Regulation of Super-Sized Houses," *Journal of Urban Design* 12 (3), 2007, pp. 339–58.

17 R.E. Lang and P.A. Simmons, "'Boomburbs': The Emergence of Large, Fast-Growing Suburban Cities," in B. Katz and R.E. Lang (eds.), *Redefining Urban and Suburban America: Evidence from Census 2000*, Washington, DC: The Brookings Institution, 2003.

18 J.M. Thomas and M. Ritzdorf (eds.), *Urban Planning and African American Community*, Thousand Oaks: Sage, 1997.

19 R. Starr, *Urban Choices: The City and its Critics*, New York: Penguin, 1969.

20 G.L. Boggs, *The Next American Revolution: Sustainable Activism in the Twenty-First Century*, Berkeley: University of California Press, 2011; T.J. Sugrue, *The Origins of the Urban Crisis: Race and Inequality in Postwar Detroit*, Princeton, NJ: Princeton University Press, 2005; A. Chakalis, D. Keating, N. Krumholz, and A.M.Wieland, "A Century of Planning in Cleveland," *Journal of Planning History* 1 (1), 2002, pp. 79–93; D. Stradling and R. Stradling, "Perceptions of the Burning River: Deindustrialization and Cleveland's Cuyahoga River," *Environmental History* 13 (3), 2008, pp. 515–35; L. Wacquant, *Urban Outcasts: A Comparative Sociology of Advanced Marginality*, Malden, MA: Polity Press, 2008.

21 S. Low, *Behind the Gates: Life, Security, and the Pursuit of Happiness in Fortress America*, New York: Routledge, 2004; J. Garreau, *Edge City: Life on the New Frontier*, New York: Doubleday, 1991.

22 M. Kohn, *Brave New Neighborhoods: The Privatization of Public Space*, New York: Routledge, 2004; J. Hackworth, *The Neoliberal City: Governance, Ideology, and Development in American Urbanism*, Ithaca: Cornell University Press, 2006; M. Sorkin (ed.), *Variations on a Theme Park: The New American City and the End of Public Space*, New York: Hill and Wang, 1992.

23 D. Immergluck, *Foreclosed: High-Risk Lending, Deregulation, and the Undermining of America's Mortgage Market*, Ithaca: Cornell University Press, 2009; A. Katz, *Our Lot: How Real Estate Came to Own Us*, New York: Bloomsbury, 2009.

24 See Develop Don't Destroy Brooklyn, dddb.net and the Atlantic Yards Report, atlantic-yardsreport.blogspot.com, accessed September 18, 2011; T. Angotti, *New York for Sale*, Cambridge, MA: MIT Press, 2008, pp. 215–22.

25 Simon Property Group website, www.simon.com, accessed July 19, 2011.

26 Hines Real Estate Investments website, www.hinesrei.com, accessed July 19, 2011.

27 ProLogis website, www.prologis.com, accessed July 19, 2011.

28 P. Marcuse and R. van Kampen (eds.), *Globalizing Cities: A New Spatial Order?* Oxford: Blackwell, 2000, p. 3.

29 C. Hartman, *Between Eminence & Notoriety: Four Decades of Radical Urban Planning*, New Brunswick: Rutgers Center for Urban Policy Research, 2002, Part One: Displacement

and Urban Renewal, pp. 59–209. L. Lees, T. Slater, and E. Wyly, *Gentrification*, New York: Routledge, 2008.

30 For a comparison of New York, Chicago and Los Angeles see J. Abu-Lughod, *New York Chicago Los Angeles: America's Global Cities*, Minneapolis: University of Minnesota Press, 1999.

31 J. Brash, *Bloomberg's New York: Class and Governance in the Luxury City*, Athens: University of Georgia Press, 2011.

32 T. Angotti, *New York for Sale*; R. Weber, "Extracting Value from the City: Neoliberalism and Urban Redevelopment," in N. Brenner and N. Theodore (eds.), *Spaces of Neoliberalism: Urban Restructuring in North America and Western Europe*, Malden, MA: Blackwell Publishers, 2002, pp. 172–93; J.R. Short, *Alabaster Cities: Urban U.S. Since 1950*, Syracuse: Syracuse University Press, 2006.

33 D.R. Judd and S.S. Fainstein (eds.), *The Tourist City*, New Haven: Yale University Press, 1999.

34 The other top tourist destinations in the U.S. are Disneyland and Disneyworld which, though imbedded in metropolitan regions are separate entertainment enclaves. V. Murray, "America's Top Tourist Attractions," *Forbes*, May 20, 2010.

35 T. Mitchell, *Big Box Swindle: The True Cost of Mega-Retailers and the Fight for America's Independent Businesses*, Boston: Beacon Press, 2006.

36 A. Bull, "Deserted Shopping Mall Bleak Symbol of Fed Bailout," *Reuters*, October 21, 2009.

37 One U.S.-based corporation, Clear Channel, now owns and controls programming on 850 radio stations in 150 cities. The same company also owns over 700,000 outdoor advertising spaces in 45 countries, and controls a large share of live music concert sales and promotions in the U.S. and elsewhere. See Clear Channel website, www.clearchannel.com, accessed July 1, 2011.

38 R. Florida, *The Rise of the Creative Class: And How It's Transforming Work, Leisure, Community and Everyday Life*, New York: Basic Books, 2003; J. Peck, "Struggling with the Creative Class," *International Journal of Urban and Regional Research* 29 (4), 2005, pp. 740–70.

39 D.L. Elliott, *A Better Way to Zone: Ten Principles to Create More Livable Cities*, Washington, DC: Island Press, 2008; W.A. Fischel, "An Economic History of Zoning and a Cure for its Exclusionary Effects," *Urban Studies* 4 (2), pp. 317–40.

40 J.M. Pogodziniski, "The Effects of Fiscal and Exclusionary Zoning on Household Location: A Critical Review," *Journal of Housing Research* 2 (2), 1991, pp. 145–60.

41 Ibid.; W.A. Fischel, *The Economics of Zoning Laws: A Property Rights Approach to American Land Use Controls*, Baltimore: Johns Hopkins University Press, 1985; E.S. Mills and W.E. Oates (eds.), *Fiscal Zoning and Land Use Controls*, Lanham, MD: Lexington Books, 1975.

42 J.C. Teaford, *The Metropolitan Revolution: The Rise of Post-Urban America*, New York: Columbia University Press, 2006.

43 P. Jargowsky, "Sprawl, Concentration of Poverty and Urban Inequality," in G.D. Squires (ed.), *Urban Sprawl: Causes, Consequences and Policy Responses*, Washington, DC: The Urban Institute Press, 2002, pp. 39–72.

44 M. Orfield, *Metropolitics: A Regional Agenda for Community and Stability*, Washington, DC: Brookings Institution Press, 1997; D. Rusk, *Inside Game/Outside Game: Winning Strategies for Saving Urban America*, Washington, DC: Brookings Institution Press, 2001.

45 B. Katz, "Metro Policy: A New Partnership for a Metropolitan Nation," Summit for American Prosperity, Washington, DC, June 2008; B. Katz (ed.), *Reflections on Regionalism*, Washington, DC: Brookings Institution Press, 2000.

46 B. Katz (ed.), *Reflections on Regionalism*; D. Rusk, *Cities Without Suburbs*, Washington, DC: Woodrow Wilson Center Press, 1995.

47 American Planning Association, "Policy Guide on Smart Growth," ratified April 15, 2002, www.planning.org/policy/guides/adopted/smartgrowth.htm, accessed July 1, 2011.

48 M. Jenks, E. Burton, and K. Williams (eds.), *The Compact City: A Sustainable Urban Form*, London: Spon Press, 2000.

49 NAIOP: Commercial Real Estate Development Association, *Smart Growth/Growth Management: Initiatives in the States*, 2008, www.naiop.org/governmentaffairs/growth/initiatives.pdf, accessed July 15, 2011.

50 E.H. Ziegler, "Urban Sprawl, Growth Management and Sustainable Development in the United States: Thoughts on the Sentimental Quest for a New Middle Landscape," *Virginia Law Review* 11, 2003, pp. 26–65; J.R. Meredith, "Sprawl and the New Urbanist Solution," *Virginia Law Review* 89 (2), 2003, pp. 447–503.

51 J.R. Logan and H.L. Molotch, *Urban Fortunes: The Political Economy of Place*, Berkeley: University of California Press, 1987.

52 T. Angotti, "The Seventh Generation: How Smart Growth Can Save Growth," *Progressive Planning* 138, 1999, pp. 1,6; F. Roble, "Who Benefits from Smart Growth," *Progressive Planning* 138, 1999, pp. 1,7,10; G. Fujioka, "Transit-Oriented Development and Communities of Color: A Field Report," *Progressive Planning* 186, 2011, pp. 12–15; A. Winstanley, D.C. Thorns, and H.C. Perkins, "Nostalgia, Community and New Housing Developments: A Critique of New Urbanism Incorporating a New Zealand Perspective," *Urban Policy and Research* 21 (2), 2003, pp. 175–89.

53 TOD planning occurred in Seattle (Washington), Portland (Oregon), San Francisco, and later Los Angeles.

54 G. Fujioka, "Transit-Oriented Development and Communities of Color: A Field Report."

55 B. Paul, "How 'Transit-Oriented Development' Will Put More New Yorkers in Cars," *Gotham Gazette*, April 2010, www.gothamgazette.com/article/transportation/20100421/16/3247, accessed July 4, 2011.

56 Congress for a New Urbanism, *Charter of the New Urbanism,* 2001, www.cnu.org/charter, accessed July 1, 2011.

57 N. Smith, "New Globalism, New Urbanism: Gentrification as Global Urban Strategy," *Antipode* 34 (3), 2002, pp. 434–57.

58 D. Harvey, "The New Urbanism and the Communitarian Trap," *Harvard Design Magazine*, Winter/Spring 1997, pp. 68–9.

59 E. Talen, *New Urbanism and American Planning: The Conflict of Cultures*, New York: Routledge, 2005; M. Pyatok, "Martha Stewart vs. Studs Terkel?" *Places* 13, Winter 2000 pp. 40–3; M. Southworth, "New Urbanism and the American Metropolis," *Built Environment* 29, 2003, pp. 210–26.

60 A.J. Cherlin, "Demographic Trends in the United States: A Review of Research in the 2000s," *Journal of Marriage and Family* 2010, 72 (3), pp. 403–19.

61 United States v. City of Yonkers, filed 1980, settled 2007.

62 E.J. Blakely and M.G. Snyder, *Fortress America: Gated Communities in the United States*, Washington, DC: Brookings Institution Press, 1997; S. Low, *Behind the Gates: Life, Security, and the Pursuit of Happiness in Fortress America*, New York: Routledge, 2004.

63 K.E. Portney, *Taking Sustainable Cities Seriously*, Cambridge: MIT Press, 2003; D. Finn and L. McCormick, "Urban Climate Change Plans: How Holistic?" *Local Environment* 16 (4), 2011, pp. 397–416; S.M. Wheeler, "Planning for Metropolitan Sustainability," *Journal of Planning Education and Research* 20 (2), 2000; P. Selman, "Local Agenda 21: Substance or Spin?" *Journal of Environmental Planning and Management* 41 (5), 1998, pp. 533–53; T. Angotti, "Is New York's Sustainability Plan Sustainable?" Sustainability Watch Working Paper, www.hunter.cuny.edu/ccpd/sustainability-watch, accessed August 8, 2011.

8 Latin America

1 Portions of this chapter are from a paper, "Apartheid in Postcolonial Latin American Cities: Enclave Urbanism and the Newly Fractured Metropolis," presented at the Congress of the Latin American Studies Association, Rio de Janeiro, June 13, 2009.

2 United Nations Human Settlements Programme (UN-HABITAT), *Cities and Climate Change: Global Report on Human Settlements 2011*, London: Earthscan, 2011, p. 3.

3 "A Second Look at Latin American Social Movements," Theme issue of *Latin American Perspectives* 176 (38: 1), January 2011.

4 G. Grandin, *Empire's Workshop: Latin America and the Roots of U.S. Imperialism*, New York: Henry Holt, 2006; E. Galeano, *Open Veins of Latin America: Five Centuries of the Pillage of a Continent*, New York: Monthly Review Press, 1973.

5 T. Angotti, "Latin American Urbanization and Planning: Inequality and Unsustainability in North and South," *Latin American Perspectives* 91 (23:4), 1996, pp. 12–34.

6 D. Hayden, *Redesigning the American Dream: The Future of Housing, Work, and Family Life*, New York: W.W. Norton, 1984.

7 E. Blakely, "Gated Communities for a Frayed and Afraid World," *Housing Policy Debate* 18 (3), 2007, pp. 475–80; E.J. Blakely and M.G. Snyder, *Fortress America: Gated Communities in the United States*, Washington, DC: Brookings Institution Press, 1997; S. Low, *Behind the Gates: Life, Security, and the Pursuit of Happiness in Fortress America*, New York: Routledge, 2004.

8 A. Cockburn, "The Parable of the Shopping Mall," *The Nation*, March 9, 2009, p. 9; P. Coleman, *Shopping Environments: Evolution, Planning and Design*, Burlington, MA: Architectural Press, 2006.

9 T. Angotti, *New York for Sale*, Cambridge, MA: MIT Press, 2008; S. Fainstein, *The City Builders: Property Development in New York and London, 1980–2000*, Lawrence: University of Kansas Press, 2001.

10 E. Ben-Joseph, "Land Use and Design Innovations in Private Communities," *Land Lines* 15 (4), 2004.

11 P.R. Kuri, "La Ciudad de Mexico: Globalización, Entorno Urbano y Megaproyectos Comerciales," in *Ciudades Latinoamericanas: Modernización y Pobreza*, Mexico: Insituto de Investigaciones Sociales, UNAM, 1998, pp. 65–77.

12 D. Sax, "If you build it...," *Canadian Business* 78 (8), 2005, pp. 23–24.

13 E. Vesselinov, M. Cazessus, and W. Falk, "Gated Communities and Spatial Inequality," *Journal of Urban Affairs* 29 (2), 2007, pp. 109–27. For the original concept of the urban growth machine in North America, see J.R. Logan and H. Molotch, *Urban Fortunes: The Political Economy of Place*, Berkeley: University of California Press, 1987.

14 M. Coy, "Gated Communities and Urban Fragmentation in Latin American Megacities: The Brazilian Experience," *Geo Journal* 66 (1–2), 2006, pp. 121–32; M. Coy and M. Pholer, "Gated Communities in Latin American Megacities: Case Studies in Brazil and Argentina," *Environment and Planning B: Planning and Design* 29 (3), 2002, pp. 355–70.

15 T. Caldeira, *City of Walls: Crime, Segregation, and Citizenship in São Paulo*, Berkeley: University of California Press, 2000.

16 Favela is the term referring to relatively poor neighborhoods in Brazil.

17 J. Costa Vargas, "The Politics of Race and Urban Space in Rio de Janeiro: When a Favela Dared to Become a Gated Condominium," *Latin American Perspectives* 33, 2006, p. 49.

18 L.C. de Q. Ribeiro and E.E. Telles, "Rio de Janeiro: Emerging Dualization in a Historically Unequal City," in P. Marcuse and R. van Kampen (eds.), *Globalizing Cities: A New Spatial Order?* Malden, MA: Oxford, 2000, pp. 78–94. For a comparison of Rio de Janeiro and New York City, see N.D.S. Oliviera, "Favelas and Ghettos: Race and Class in Rio de Janeiro and New York City," *Latin American Perspectives* 91 (23:4), 1987, pp. 71–89.

19 S. Roitman, "Who Segregates Who? The Analysis of a Gated Community in Mendoza, Argentina," *Housing Studies* 20 (2), 2005, pp. 303–21.

20 C. Irazábal, *City Making and Urban Governance in the Americas: Curitiba and Portland*, Aldershot: Ashgate, 2005.

21 Ibid.

22 M. Mycoo, "The Retreat of the Upper and Middle Classes to Gated Communities in the Poststructural Adjustment Era: The Case of Trinidad," *Environment & Planning A* 38 (1), 2006, pp. 131–48.

23 K.P. Gallagher and L. Zarsky, *The Enclave Economy: Foreign Investment and Sustainable Development in Mexico's Silicon Valley*, Cambridge, MA: MIT Press, 2007.

24 R. Centner, "Conflictive Sustainability Landscapes: The Neoliberal Quagmire of Urban Environmental Planning in Buenos Aires," *Local Environment* 14 (2), 2009, pp. 171–92; M. Castells and P. Hall, *Technopoles of the World: The Making of 21st Century Industrial*

Complexes, London: Routledge, 1994; S. Graham and S. Marvin, *Telecommunications and the City: Electronic Spaces, Urban Places*, London: Routledge, 1996.

25 Squarestone Brasil, "Golden Square," www.squarestone.com.br/projects/golden-square.php, accessed August 19, 2011.

26 W. Xiaotian and C. Jia, "RMB Fund Planned to Aid Latin America," *China Daily*, April 29, 2011.

27 R. Salcedo and A. Torres, "Gated Communities in Santiago: Wall or Frontier?" *International Journal of Urban and Regional Research* 28 (1), 2004, pp. 27–44; A. Borsdorf, R. Hidalgo, and R. Sanchez, "A New Model of Urban Development in Latin America: The Gated Communities and Fenced Cities in the Metropolitan Areas of Santiago de Chile and Valparaiso," *Cities* 24 (5), 2007, pp. 365–78.

28 D. Sax, "If you build it…"

29 J. Stillerman, "Private, Parochial, and Public Realms in Santiago, Chile's Retail Sector," *City & Community* 5 (3), 2006, pp. 293–317.

30 N.L. De Duren, "Planning à la Carte: The Location Patterns of Gated Communities around Buenos Aires in a Decentralized Planning Context," *International Journal of Urban and Regional Research* 30 (2), June, 2006, pp. 308–27; N.L. De Duren, "Urban Planning and State Reform," *Journal of Planning Education and Research* 28 (3), Spring, 2009, pp. 310–22.

31 T. Caldeira, "Fortified Enclaves: The New Urban Segregation," in S. Low (ed.), *Theorizing the City: The New Urban Anthropology Reader*, Piscataway, NJ: Rutgers University Press, 1999, pp. 83–110.

32 E. Galeano, *Upside Down: A Primer for the Looking-Glass World*, New York: Picador, 2000, pp. 11–12.

33 This is not to suggest that urban segregation did not characterize pre-Colombian settlements in America. Spatial fragmentation has been a part of all human settlements in which private property and class divisions play a significant role. However, colonialism fundamentally altered the structure and composition of cities in Latin America, and began the long march toward the modern metropolis. See T. Angotti, "Latin American Urbanization and Planning: Inequality and Unsustainability in North and South"; J. Hardoy, "Two Thousand Years of Latin American Urbanization," in *Urbanization in Latin America*, J. Hardoy (ed.), Garden City, NY: Anchor, 1975, pp. 3–55.

34 A.D. King, *Urbanism, Colonialism, and the World Economy: Cultural and Spatial Foundations of the World Urban System*, London: Routledge, 1990.

35 See, for example, the *Plan Rotival* for Caracas. M. Vallmitjana, et al., *El Plan Rotival: La Caracas Que No Fue*, Caracas: Ediciones Instituto de Urbanismo, Universidad Central de Venezuela, 1991.

36 J. Perlman, *The Myth of Marginality*, Berkeley: University of California Press, 1976; J. Perlman, *Favela: Four Decades of Living on the Edge in Rio de Janeiro*, New York: Oxford University Press USA, 2011.

37 J.F.C. Turner and R. Fichter (eds.), *Freedom to Build*, New York: Macmillan, 1972.

38 H. de Soto, *The Mystery of Capital: Why Capitalism Triumphs in the West and Fails Everywhere Else*, New York: Basic Books, 2003. Some local planners have also imported notions of "participatory planning" advocated in the North to help legitimize orientalist alternatives in the "slums." However, participation has been a constant of indigenous planning and there are a growing number of alternatives that have emerged from urban social movements and been adopted by progressive local governments. These include, for example, the Brazilian experience of participatory budgeting and participatory experiences started in Cuba and Venezuela. See M. Harnecker, *Alcaldía de Caroní/Gobernar: Tarea de Todos*, Havana: Centro de Recuperación y Difusión de la Memoria Histórica del Movimiento Popular Latinoamericano, 1994; C.B. Weyh and D.R. Streck, "Participatory Budgeting in Southern Brazil: A Collective and Democratic Experience," *Concepts and Transformation* 8 (1), 2003, pp. 25–42; E. Hernández-Medina, "Social Inclusion through Participation: The Case of the Participatory Budget in São Paulo," *International Journal of Urban and Regional Research* 34 (3), September 2010, pp. 512–32.

39 The World Bank, "Data: Latin America and Caribbean," http://data.worldbank.org/region/ LAC, accessed August 18, 2011.
40 B.Z. Kaup, "A Neoliberal Nationalization? The Constraints on Natural-Gas-Led Development in Bolivia," *Latin American Perspectives* 37 (3), 2010, pp. 123–38.
41 The reversal of privatization left numerous problems that have not been easy to solve. D. Leonard, "Water is Life: De-Privatization and the Search for Alternatives in Cochabamba, Bolivia," *Progressive Planning* 169, 2006, pp. 10–14. For an authoritative collection of articles, see B. Kohl and R. Bresnahan, (Issue eds.), "Bolivia Under Morales: Consolidating Power, Initiating Decolonization," Theme issue of *Latin American Perspectives* 172 (37:3), May 2010, pp. 5–17.
42 See B. Kohl and R. Bresnahan, (Issue eds.), "Bolivia Under Morales: Consolidating Power, Initiating Decolonization."
43 B.H. Kohl and L.C. Farthing, *Impasse in Bolivia: Neoliberal Hegemony & Popular Resistance*, London: Zed, 2006, pp. 168–9.
44 R. Albro, "Confounding Cultural Citizenship and Constitutional Reform in Bolivia," *Latin American Perspectives* 37 (3), 2010, pp. 71–90.
45 *The Rights of Nature: The Case for a Universal Declaration of the Rights of Mother Earth*, San Francisco: Global Exchange, 2011.
46 Ibid.: 10.
47 Ibid.: 11.
48 For an excellent analysis of the process in Venezuela, where urban social movements have played a significant role in support of the government of Hugo Chávez, see S. Ellner, "Hugo Chávez's First Decade in Office," *Latin American Perspectives* 170 (37:1), 2010, pp. 77–96.
49 M.T. Vázquez Castillo, *Land Privatization in Mexico: Urbanization, Formation of Regions, and Globalization in Ejidos*, New York: Routledge, 2004.
50 Friends of the MST website, www.mstbrazil.org, accessed September 15, 2011.
51 Friends of the MST, "MST's Proposal for a 'People's Agrarian Reform'," 2009, www.mstbrazil.org/resource/msts-proposal-peoples-agrarian-reform, accessed August 19, 2011.
52 Via Campesina website, viacampesina.org/en, accessed September 15, 2011.
53 E. Boorstein, *The Economic Transformation of Cuba*, New York: Monthly Review, 1968.
54 J.E. Sweig, *Cuba: What Everyone Needs To Know*, New York: Oxford University Press, 2009; "Cuba: Interpreting a Half Century of Revolution and Resistance," *Latin American Perspectives* 164 and 165 (36:1/2), 2009. For a lively popular version of the Cuban Revolution, see Rius, *Cuba For Beginners*, Atlanta: Pathfinder Press, 2001.
55 J.L. Scarpaci, R. Segre, and M. Coyula, *Havana: Two Faces of the Antillean Metropolis*, Chapel Hill: University of North Carolina Press, 2002.
56 Presentation by Miguel Coyula, Grupo Para el Desarrollo Integral de la Capital, January 10, 2011.
57 Presentation by Fernando Funes Aguilar on January 18, 2011, Havana.
58 Presentation at Instituto Nacional de Investigación Fundamental en Agricultura Tropical (INIFAT), January 11, 2011, Havana.
59 An authoritative text on urban agriculture in Cuba is Fernando Funes, et al., *Sustainable Agriculture and Resistance: Transforming Food Production in Cuba*, Oakland: Food First Books, 2002.
60 Presentation by Miguel Salcines López, UBPC Organopónico Vivero Alamar, January 11, 2011.
61 M.C. Cruz, R. Sánchez Median, and C. Cabrera (eds.), *Permacultura Criolla*, Habana: Fundación Antonio Núñez Jiménez de la Naturaleza y el Hombre, 2006.
62 M.A. Altieri and F.R. Funes-Monzote, "The Paradox of Cuban Agriculture," *Monthly Review* 63 (8), January 2012, p. 30.
63 Cuba is getting oil from Venezuela at favorable prices. The question remains whether this relationship will only feed reliance on imported goods bought with the savings on energy, similar to the years of dependency on Soviet oil.

9 New Century, New Ways of Planning

1   P.R. Ehrlich, *The Population Bomb*, New York: Ballantine Books, 1968.
2   D.H. Meadows, D.L. Meadows, J. Randers, and W.W. Behrens III, *The Limits to Growth: A Report for the Club of Rome's Project on the Predicament of Mankind*, New York: Signet, 1972.
3   T. Beatley, *Green Urbanism: Learning from European Cities*, Washington, DC: Island Press, 2000.
4   The twentieth century also proved the severe limitations of electoral democracy. The legitimacy of political parties and political figures is at an all-time low in the U.S. and Europe, especially due to the vast influence of money. Politicians have become a commodity and voting a contest for financial backing. See G. Palast, *The Best Democracy Money Can Buy*, New York: Plume, 2003.

Selected Bibliography

T. Angotti, *Metropolis 2000: Planning, Poverty and Politics*, New York: Routledge, 1993.

T. Angotti, *New York for Sale*, Cambridge, MA: MIT Press, 2008.

L. Benevolo, *The Origins of Modern Town Planning*, Cambridge, MA: MIT Press, 1971.

E.J. Blakely and M.G. Snyder, *Fortress America: Gated Communities in the United States*, Washington, DC: Brookings Institution Press, 1997.

H. Blumenfeld, *The Modern Metropolis*, Cambridge, MA: MIT Press, 1971.

T. Caldeira, *City of Walls: Crime, Segregation, and Citizenship in São Paulo*, Berkeley: University of California Press, 2000.

M. Castells, *The Urban Question: A Marxist Approach*, Cambridge, MA: MIT Press, 1979.

M. Davis, *Planet of Slums*, New York: Verso, 2007.

J. Diamond, *Collapse: How Societies Choose to Fail or Succeed*, New York: Penguin, 2005.

F. Engels, *The Housing Question*, Moscow: Progress Publishers, 1975.

J.B. Foster, B. Clark, and R. York, *The Ecological Rift: Capitalism's War on the Earth*, New York: Monthly Review, 2010.

J. Friedmann, *China's Urban Transition*, Minneapolis: University of Minnesota Press, 2005.

F. Funes, L. García, M. Bourque, N. Pérez, and P. Rosset, *Sustainable Agriculture and Resistance: Transforming Food Production in Cuba*, Oakland: Food First Books, 2002.

E. Galeano, *Open Veins of Latin America: Five Centuries of the Pillage of a Continent*, New York: Monthly Review Press, 1973.

E. Galeano, *Upside Down: A Primer for the Looking-Glass World*, New York: Picador, 2000.

M. Gandhi, *Hind Swaraj or Indian Home Rule*, www.soilandhealth.org/03sov/0303critic/hind%20swaraj.pdf, 1910, accessed April 8, 2012.

E. Glaeser, *Triumph of the City*, New York: Penguin, 2011.

G. Grandin, *Empire's Workshop: Latin America and the Roots of U.S. Imperialism*, New York: Henry Holt, 2006.

J. Hackworth, *The Neoliberal City: Governance, Ideology, and Development in American Urbanism*, Ithaca: Cornell University Press, 2006.

P. Hall, *Cities of Tomorrow: An Intellectual History of Urban Planning Design in the Twentieth Century*, Malden, MA: Blackwell, 1988.

J. Halper, *An Israeli in Palestine: Resisting Dispossession, Redeeming Israel*, London: Pluto Press, 2008.

J.E. Hardoy, *Urban Planning in Pre-Columbian America*, New York: George Braziller, 1968.

D. Harvey, *A Brief History of Neoliberalism*, New York: Oxford University Press USA, 2007.

D. Hayden, *The Power of Place: Urban Landscapes as Public History*, Cambridge, MA: MIT Press, 1995.

D. Hayden, *Redesigning the American Dream: Gender, Housing, and Family Life*, New York: W.W. Norton & Company, 2002.

D. Hayden, *Building Suburbia: Green Fields and Urban Growth, 1820–2000*, New York: Vintage, 2004.

E. Howard, *Garden Cities of To-morrow*, London: Faber & Faber, 1946.

K. Jackson, *Crabgrass Frontier: The Suburbanization of the United States*, New York: Oxford University Press USA, 1987.

J. Jacobs, *The Death and Life of Great American Cities*, New York: Random House, 1961.

J. Jacobs, *The Nature of Economies*, New York: Vintage, 2000.

J. Jacobs, *Dark Age Ahead*, New York: Vintage, 2004.

D.R. Judd and S.S. Fainstein (eds.), *The Tourist City*, New Haven: Yale University Press, 1999.

B. Katz (ed.), *Reflections on Regionalism*, Washington, DC: Brookings Institution Press, 2000.

A.D. King, *Urbanism, Colonialism, and the World Economy: Cultural and Spatial Foundations of the World Urban System*, London: Routledge, 1990.

A.D. King, *Colonial Urban Development: Culture, Social Power and Environment*, New York: Routledge, 2007.

N. Klein, *The Shock Doctrine: The Rise of Disaster Capitalism*, New York: Metropolitan Books, 2007.

D. Kleinman, *Human Adaptation and Population Growth: A Non-Malthusian Perspective*, Lanham, MD: Rowman & Littlefield, 1980.

L. Lees, T. Slater, and E. Wyly, *Gentrification*, New York: Routledge, 2008.

H. Lefebvre, *Critique of Everyday Life*, New York: Verso, 1992.

S. Low, *Behind the Gates: Life, Security, and the Pursuit of Happiness in Fortress America*, New York: Routledge, 2004.

P. Marcuse and R. van Kampen (eds.), *Globalizing Cities: A New Spatial Order?* Oxford: Blackwell, 2000.

K. Marx and F. Engels, *Selected Works*, New York: International Publishers, 1977.

H. Molotch, "The City as a Growth Machine: Toward a Political Economy of Place," *The American Journal of Sociology* 82 (2), 1976, pp. 309–32.

L. Mumford, *The City in History: Its Origins, Its Transformations, and Its Prospects*, New York: Harcourt, Brace and World, 1961.

J.K. Nyrere, *Ujamaa: Essays on Socialism*, Oxford: Oxford University Press, 1968.

M. Orfield, *Metropolitics: A Regional Agenda for Community and Stability*, Washington, DC: Brookings Institution Press, 1997.

I. Pappe, *The Ethnic Cleansing of Palestine*, London: Oneworld, 2007.

R. Patel, *Stuffed and Starved: The Hidden Battle for the World Food System*, Brooklyn, NY: Melville House, 2007.

J. Perlman, *The Myth of Marginality*, Berkeley: University of California Press, 1976.

D.N. Reddy and S. Mishra (eds.), *Agrarian Crisis in India*, New Delhi: Oxford University Press, 2009.

A. Roy, *Public Power in the Age of Empire*, New York: Seven Stories Press, 2006.

D. Rusk, *Cities Without Suburbs*, Washington, DC: Woodrow Wilson Center Press, 1995.

E. Said, *Orientalism*, New York: Vintage, 1979.

P. Sainath, *Everybody Loves a Good Drought: Stories from India's Poorest Districts*, New Delhi: Penguin, 1996.

L. Sandercock, *Towards Cosmopolis*, New York: John Wiley & Sons, 1998.

L. Sandercock (ed.), *Making the Invisible Visible: A Multicultural Planning History*, Berkeley: University of California Press, 1998.

B. De S. Santos (ed.), *Another Knowledge is Possible: Beyond Northern Epistemologies*, London: Verso, 2007.

S. Sassen, *Globalization and its Discontents*, New York: New Press, 1999.

S. Sassen (ed.), *Global Networks, Linked Cities*, New York: Routledge, 2002.

A. Sen, *Development as Freedom*, New York: First Anchor Books, 1999.

V. Shiva, *Ecology and the Politics of Survival: Conflicts over Natural Resources in India*, New Delhi: United Nations University Press and Sage Publications, 1991.

V. Shiva, *Stolen Harvest: The Hijacking of the Global Food Supply*, Boston: South End Press, 2000.

V. Shiva, *Water Wars: Privatization, Pollution, and Profit*, Cambridge, MA: South End Press, 2002.

Y. Song and C. Ding (eds.), *Urbanization in China: Critical Issues in an Era of Rapid Growth*, Cambridge, MA: Lincoln Institute of Land Policy, 2007.

J.E. Stiglitz, *Globalization and Its Discontents*, New York: W.W. Norton & Company, 2002.

United Nations Human Settlements Programme (UN-HABITAT), *The Challenge of Slums*, New York: UN-HABITAT, 2003.

United Nations Human Settlements Programme (UN-HABITAT), *State of the World's Cities 2010/2011*, New York: UN-HABITAT, 2010.

United Nations Human Settlements Programme (UN-HABITAT), *Cities and Climate Change: Global Report on Human Settlements 2011*, London: Earthscan, 2011.

L. Wacquant, *Urban Outcasts: A Comparative Sociology of Advanced Marginality*, Malden, MA: Polity Press, 2008.

L. Wacquant, *Punishing the Poor: The Neoliberal Government of Social Insecurity*, Durham: Duke University Press, 2009.

E. Weizman, *Hollow Land: Israel's Architecture of Occupation*, New York: Verso, 2007.

O. Yiftachel, *Ethnocracy: Land and Identity Politics in Israel/Palestine*, Philadelphia: University of Pennsylvania Press, 2006.

H. Zinn, *A People's History of the United States*, New York: Harper & Row, 1980.

Index

Abu Dhabi 75, 76
Aeromall, 134
Africa: and colonialism 79, 132; commodification of land in 51; dependent nations
  of, 25; energy consumption in 14; and
  orientalist myths 41;and popular uprisings
  48; representations of 125; urbanization
  of 4, 9, 29
African Americans: and central cities, 7–8;
  displacement of 15, 122; migration to
  cities by 16; as "Others" 38; post-Katrina
  17; and suburbs 11; see also "Others";
  racism; segregation
agriculture: and arable land 66, 150;
  collectivization of 93, 96, 98, 102, 104,
  111; and genetically modified organisms
  (GMOs) 53, 69, 73, 146; Green Revolution 51, 53, 71, 72; industrialized 42, 48–9,
  53, 63, 66, 158; industrialized in Brazil
  145, 146; industrialized in China 108, 109,
  178n59; industrialized in Cuba 150–51;
  industrialized in India 59, 67, 69;
  industrialized in Israel 86; industrialized in
  Russia 102–3; monopoly control of 12, 53,
  147, 148; Palestinian 77, 86; peasant
  farming 95, 143–44, 145, 146, 147, 151;
  peri-urban, 48, 66, 68, 102, 108, 146;
  reliance on industrialized 22, 109, 178n59;
  and soil depletion 52, 150; and seed
  industry 50, 53, 59, 67, 73, 86; small-scale
  local 50, 69; urban 61, 142, 146–48 149,
  150–51; and Via Campesina 49, 146; see
  also Cuba; food security; labor; rural areas
Aguilar, Fernando Funes 150
Alamar Organic Farm 149–50
Alianza Bolivariana para los Pueblos de
  Nuestra América (ALBA) 144, 145, 151
All-India People's Science Network 73
American Dream 116, 134: as housing choice
  21, 37, 117, 118, 126; preservation of 120,
  131; rebranding of 120, 129–30; see also
  housing; planning

American Institute of Planners, 127
American Planning Association 127–28
Ankara, Turkey 32
apartheid: Israel 77–8, 80, 86–8, 91–2, 93;
  South Africa 54; spatial 122; see also
  segregation
Arequipa, Peru 54
Argentina 106, 132, 134–35, 142
Asia: and colonialism 79, 132;
  commodification of land in 51; dependent
  nations of 25; energy consumption in 14;
  and orientalist myths 41; and popular
  uprisings 48; representations of 125; and
  urban traditions 29; urbanization of 4, 9;
  see also China
Atatürk, Kemal 32
Athens, Greece 29
Atlanta, Georgia 125
Atlantic Yards, New York City, New York
  102, 122
Aztecs 29–30

Balfour Declaration 79
Balfour, Arthur James 17, 79
Banfield, Edward 5
Bangalore, India see Bengaluru, India
Batista, Fulgencio 147
Bauhaus 139
Beatley, Timothy 160
Beer Sheva, Israel 90–1, 92
Beijing, China 3, 10, 107; Central Business
  District 106; and infrastructure
  funding 109; and internal migrants 110;
  and regional authority 108; see also China
Benevolo, Leonardo 37
Bengaluru (Bangalore), India 62–3; growth
  of 65; and mass transit 65; social
  movements in 72
Ben-Gurion University, 91
Bethlehem, 76–7, 91
Bhopal, India 64
Bihar, India 68

Bimkom 155
Black Earth Farming 102
Bloomberg, Michael 5, 124
Blumenfeld, Hans 6–7
Bolivia 39, 48, 142–45; and mining 51; water privatization in 39
Boston, Massachusetts 8, 15, 124
Brazil 39, 59, 106, 151; agriculture in 66; gated communities in 134–35; social movements in 140–42, 145–46, 155, 161, 162; urbanization of 62; U.S. support for 132
Brazilian Workers Party 140
Buenos Aires, Argentina 10, 133; and European planning 139; and mixed-use development, 136; and social movements 140
Burnham, Daniel 32
Bush, George H.W. 100

Calcutta, India *see* Kolkata
Canada 11, 51, 134
capital: accumulation 32, 39; and the American Dream 117–18; central city disinvestment 119, 120; and commodification 10, 11; concentration of 4, 5, 139; expansion of global 18, 34, 65, 106, 108, 112; and external costs 20, 21, 45, 105; and the FIRE sector 32, 34, 113, 119, 121, 123–24; global and commodification of land, 45; mobility of 13, 24, 43, 136; relationship with labor 6, 10, 21, 24, 41, 43, 46, 115, 135–36; revolutions against 94–5; social 96, 98, 99; *see also* capitalism
capitalism: alternatives to 21, 39, 94, 96, 151, 162; and comparative advantage 42, 52, 147, 148, 157; and commodification 4, 12, 19, 23, 44–5; crisis of 20, 40; dependent 44, 54, 133; and financial centers, 7, 8; and free-market ideology 113; global 3, 8, 37, 41–2, 59, 69, 103, 105, 115, 142; globalization 39, 46, 133, 134, 161; Great Transformation 4, 35; Keynesian 36, 73; monopoly 14, 18; and Paris Commune 1871; and perception of others 4; post-Mao 104; in post-Soviet Russia 103; really existing 21; state 93, 96; taboo against criticism 20–1; and urban orientalism 17, 135, 155; *see also* socialism
Caracas, Venezuela 134, 139, 140
Castro, Fidel 147
Central Business District (CBD) 32, 123–25; in China 106; in Latin America 135; in Moscow 102; proliferation of 133, 134
The Challenge of Slums (UN-HABITAT) 15
Chang, Leslie 110

Channai, India 62–3
Charlotte Gardens, New York, New York 120
Chennai, India 62, 65
Chicago World's Fair (1893) 32
Chiang, Kai-shek 104
Chicago, Illinois 8, 15, 130; 1909 Master Plan 32, 35
Chicago School of Urban Sociology, 11
China: alternatives to capitalist city 93, 112; as center of global capital, 21; City Planning Act 105; and climate change 23, 25, 48, 106; Cultural Revolution 104, 105; and industrialized agriculture 50, 106, 108; and infrastructure development 108–10; and "others" 107, 110–11; pace of urbanization 33, 94, 103, 108; and private property 67, 108; revolution of 1949 94, 104; and social movements 112; and state planning 106; turn toward capitalism 95; and urban planning 103–5; urban population of 62
Chinese Communist Party 104, 108
Chongqing, China 108
Christaller, Walter 54
Churchill, Winston 93
Clash of Civilizations (Huntington) 27
Cleveland, Ohio 7, 119–20
climate change 3, 4, 8, 16, 18–19, 23; in China 106; corrective measures 47–8, 74, 160; and environmental catastrophe 156; greenhouse gases 4, 8, 19, 20, 22, 48; historical occurrence of 48; and industrial agriculture 22, 50; and orientalist planning 39–40, 155; and really existing capitalism 21, 22, 50, 156; and rights of the earth 144; and sea level rise, 4, 18, 48, 106; skepticism about 130; and Smart Growth 127; and social movements 142, 144, 145; and Soviet city planning 103; and urbanization 47
Cochabamba, Bolivia 48, 142, 143, 144, 145, 158
Cold War 21, 35–6, 94
Collapse (Diamond) 4
colonialism 29–30, 41, 42, 51, 75; and Chinese occupation 105; and international trade 42; and Latin American independence 132; neo- 52; post- 16, 25, 59; waning of 26, 156; *see also* Great Britain
Columbus, Ohio 125
Communist Manifesto (Marx and Engels) 95
consumption 16, 17, 21, 22, 32, 51, 117; and American Dream 117, 130; conspicuous 20, 24, 117, 130, 159; and diseconomies of scale 19; diversity of 7; and green fixes

19; over- 10, 11, 14, 20; rates of 158–59, 160; and Soviet Union 99; sustainable 69; and unrestrained free market 60; *see also* energy; planning

Copenhagen, Denmark 23, 48, 144

crime: and gated communities 134; and Latin American urbanism 136–37; as myth 12–13; and prison system 38; and slums 15, 140

Critique of the Gotha Program (Marx) 52

Cruz, Caridad 150

Cuba: and comparative advantage 147, 148; resilience 148, 150, 151; revolution of 1959 143, 147; and urban agriculture 142, 146–51, 155; and U.S. intervention 132, 133

Curitiba, Brazil 135

Dallas, Texas 12

Davis, Mike 15–16

de Soto, Hernando, 140

Death and Life of Great American Cities (Jacobs) 37

Delhi, India 59, 61, 62, 69; slum clearance in 64; and social movements 72

Deng, Xiaoping 104, 105, 108, 111

Designcorp, 134

Detroit, Michigan 7, 119, 120

Diamond, Jared 4

Dickens, Charles 14

discrimination: and farm laborers 37; in Israel 38, 80–1; in Latin America 139; and spatial apartheid 122; and Wal-Mart 36; *see also* apartheid; "Others"; segregation

Disneyworld 125, 129

displacement 15, 17, 18, 59; and Chinese redevelopment 107–8; and City Beautiful 31; and enclave urbanism 114; and gentrification 119, 122, 127; and Juda- ization 78, 81, 82–3; and infrastructure projects 109; low-income in India 63, 64; and market-driven development 122; Palestinians 77, 80–5; and private capital 115; resistance to 72, 92, 140, 138; and state-directed planning, 95; *see also* migration; slums

Dubai 75–6

economy: auto dependent 23, 24, 110, 125; and centralized planning 96; and comparative advantage 42, 52, 147, 157; diversity of 7; and "economy rentals" 46; FIRE sector 121; Great Leap Forward 104; and inequality: 15, 100–1, 107–8, 128; indigenous 61, 67, 70; informal 15, 17, 45, 66; inward-focused 103; oil

dependent 43; Open Economic Areas 108; Palestinian 86; quantitative expansion 98; remittance 46; service sector of 134; and social movements 146; Soviet economic model 99; Special Economic Zones 108; *see also:* capital; capitalism; consumption;; labor; neoliberalism; socialism

education: access to 43, 47, 87, 156, 157; enclaves 65; as local responsibility 126; universal 95, 111, 115, 146

Ehrlich, Paul 12, 156

employment *see* labor

enclave urbanism 113–31, 107–8, 113–31, 155, 160; and the environment 22–5; fragmentation of 145; and inequality 95, 101–3, 133–37; in Palestine 76–8; reform of 141–42; strengthening of 10; *see also* displacement; planning; segregation

energy 5, 8; and alternatives 48, 106, 127, 157; and building technology 19–20, 75, 158; consumption 14, 20, 23–4, 76, 130, 142, 148; large-scale projects 59; rural electrification program 95; shortages 156; Three Gorges Dam 109; and underground resources 51; *see also* climate change; consumption

Engels, Friedrich 99, 100, 112

Enlightenment 18, 33, 52

environment 6, 10, 20, 105, 148; Chinese urbanization and 106; deforestation 145–46; desertification 50; fracking 51; and green technology 19, 23, 25; and industrial by-products 111;; inequality 43; in India 59, 65, 69; and population density 12; and post-Soviet pollution 102; rights of the earth 144; and social movements 141–46; *see also* climate change; planning; sustainability

environmental justice 23, 43, 48, 141–46, 156

ethnic cleansing: ethnocracy 38, 89; exploitation of 79; migration of labor 47; of Palestine 80, 81; policy of 84–5; and self-determination 143–44

The Ethnic Cleansing of Palestine (Pappe) 80

European Union 21, 36, 92, 115

Farthing, Linda 143

Finance, Insurance and Real Estate (FIRE) 32, 34, 113, 119, 123–24

Florida, Richard 125

food security 11, 18, 51, 59; in Brazil 146, 162; carbon-intensive system 19; in China 106; in Cuba 148, 150–51; global crisis of, 22, 41–2, 43, 48; in India 68–70, 72, 73; in Israel 86; and planning 61; and processed foods 50; *see also* agriculture

Forbes Magazine 5
Forest City Ratner 121
Foster, John Bellamy 51–52
Friedmann, John 37–38
Fukuyama, Francis 100
Fundación Antonio Nuñez 150

Galeano, Eduardo 136
Galilee 81–2, 84–6
Gandhi, Mahatma 69, 70, 71–2, 74, 155
Garden Cities *see* planning, Garden Cities
Garnier, Tony 96
Geddes, Patrick 74, 78, 79–80, 83; and
    China 104; and enclave urbanism 114;
    and regionalist ideal 127
General Growth Properties 136
gentrification *see* displacement
Glaeser, Edward 5, 22
Grandin, Greg 132
Great Britain 52, 69, 70; British Land Acqui-
    sition Act of 1894 64; in China 103; and
    colonialism 50, 60, 61, 74, 67, 79, 89;
    and orientalism 16–17, 114; in Palestine
    75, 78–80, 89, 93
Green Urbanism (Beatley) 160
Gropius, Walter 31, 32
Guangzhou, China 104, 106, 110
Gurgaon, India 28

Haifa, Israel 79, 81, 84, 92
Haiti 17, 46, 132, 142
Hall, Peter 37
Harvey, David 128–29
Hausmann, Georges-Eugene 15, 114, 139
Havana, Cuba 43, 147–49; *see also*
    agriculture, urban; Cuba
Hayden, Dolores 38
health 12, 19, 24, 25, 50, 54; access to care
    47, 156; as local responsibility 126; public
    23, 67, 68, 71, 127, 130; universal 43, 95,
    101, 111, 115
Hersh, Jacques 93
Himachel Pradesh, India 68
Hind Swaraj (Gandhi) 70
Hines Real Estate Investments 121
*Hollow Land: Israel's Architecture of
    Occupation* (Weizman) 77
Holston, James 38
Honduras 42, 132
Hong Kong 8, 103–4
housing 5, 38, 117, 118; access to 39, 53, 82,
    84, 89, 129; and American Dream house
    21, 23, 24, 37, 116, 117, 118, 120, 126,
    129, 130, 131, 134; in China, 102, 106;
    competition for 47; and Hurricane
    Katrina 15; inclusionary 128; and

redlining 119; Soviet 97, 98, 99; *see also*
    displacement; ethnic cleansing; enclave
    urbanism; segregation
The Housing Question (Engels) 99
Howard, Ebenezer 114
Huntington, Samuel 27
Hurricane Katrina 17

immigrants 13, 15, 89; living conditions of
    47; and remittance economy 46; *see also*
    labor; migration
Incas 29–30
India: 2005 Right to Information Act 72;
    and agriculture 50, 66; and dependent
    urbanization 55, 59–74; and enclave
    urbanism 114; as post-colonial nation 59;
    and transnationalized system 46; urban
    population of 62
Indian Institute of Science 65
infrastructure 86, 110, 116–17; and
    auto-dependent cities 24, 102, 118, 125,
    130; automobiles and alternative fuels
    48; and China's high-speed rail 109, 110;
    control in Occupied Territories 89–90,
    92; energy efficient modes 20; highway
    infrastructure in India 65; and intermodal
    transit networks 24; mass transit
    options 126; Moscow's subway system 96;
    National Trunk Highway System 110; and
    planned communities 139; and private
    development 101, 109; rural electrification
    program 95; U.S. interstate highway system
    35, 119; *see also* energy
International Congress of Modern
    Architecture (CIAM) 31
International Development, U.S. Agency for
    (USAID) 101–2
International Monetary Fund (IMF) 39, 63,
    100, 144
Ir Amim 155
Iraq 76, 77
Iriquois Confederacy 157
Israel: establishment of, 80–1; and geopoliti-
    cal strategy 82; and orientalist planning
    75; Security Barrier 77–8, 91–2; and
    vertical occupation 77, 90, 91–2; *see also*
    apartheid; Palestine
Israeli Committee Against House
    Demolitions (ICAHD) 92, 155
Israeli Defense Forces 84
Israel Land Authority (ILA) 82, 85
Italy 54

Jacobs, Jane 37, 38; integrated diversity 98;
    and The New Urbanism (TNU) 128, 129;
    and urban street life 123

Jaffa, Israel 82–3, 85
Japan 12, 25, 62, 104, 109, 121
Jawaharlal Nehru National Urban Renewal
    Mission (JNNURM) 64, 65
Jericho, 91
Jerusalem: diversity of 86–8; master plan 86,
    89; merger with Tel Aviv 92; and military
    checkpoints 76–7; and symbolic relics 85;
    see also Israel; Palestine
Jharkhand, India 68
Jiaozhou Bay Bridge 109

Katz, Bruce 128
Kerala, India 68, 69
King, Mel 15
Kohl, Benjamin 143
Kolkata (Calcutta), India 59, 60–1, 69

La Paz, Bolivia 142
labor: agricultural 47, 50, 63, 66, 67, 86,
    150; commodification of 41; cooperative
    144; cross-border flow and zoning, 136;
    exploitation of 11, 75, 99, 106, 109, 142;
    highly educated 65, 69; international
    division of 11, 25; migrant 86, 111;
    mobility of 13, 24, 43, 115; and MST in
    Brazil 145, 146; organized 21, 36, 115,
    116, 146; post-Soviet reserves 101; power
    in the United States 115; regulation of
    market 106; relationship to capital 6, 7,
    10, 14, 21, 41, 46, 54, 96, 135; and
    remittance economy 46; reproduction of
    19, 41, 49; reserves 8, 11, 13, 45–7, 53,
    95, 111, 147; rural-to-city migration 6, 67,
    97, 145; and segregated work
    environments 81; and social movements
    112; and socialism 43; as source of wealth
    52; transnationalization of 46–7; volunteer
    96; see also migration
Lagos, Nigeria 42
land 10, 52, 73, 117, 150; alternative sce-
    narios 49; appropriation of Palestinian 91;
    clearing of urban 15, 46, 59, 64; as com-
    modity 4, 11, 12, 23, 24, 41, 44–5, 49, 50,
    52, 121, 145; constitutional guarantees
    143–44; control of 73, 77, 81–3; "empty"
    79, 81; exploitation of 11, 109; Home-
    stead Act of 1862 117; Israeli regulation
    of 84; and post-colonial acquisition 50–1;
    privatization of in India 64; privatization
    of state 82, 84; and productive capacity
    71; and public space 102, 123, 134; as
    shared space 159; and speculative invest-
    ment, 95; state ownership 51, 106; stew-
    ardship of 28; suburban occupation of 8,
    12–13, 23; tenure in India 64; urban 15,

17, 23, 32, 39, 49; see also planning, and
    land use; natural resources; rural areas
land use: change 146; control 158; local
    control 125–26; policy 63, 87, 116;
    regulations 84; sharp divisions 60; see also
    planning; natural resources; rural areas
Las Vegas, Nevada 119, 124
Latin America: 4, 62, 132–51; and Chinese
    investment 136; and colonialism 9, 132;
    and dependent nations, 25; energy
    consumption in 14; and level of
    urbanization 132, 139; and orientalist
    myths 41; and remittance economy 46;
    representations of 125; and urban
    traditions 29; see also individual countries
Le Corbusier 32, 139
Lefebvre, Henri 39
LGBT communities 38
Lima, Peru 28, 29, 42, 54, 140
London, England 15
Los Angeles, California 12, 124, 130

Mackaye, Benton 127
Madhya Pradesh, India 68
Manchester, England 15
Mao, Zedong 94, 95, 104
Marcuse, Peter 122
Margalit, Talia 83
Marx, Karl 52, 99, 100, 112
Mayas 29–30
McLean, William H. 89
Meadows, Donnella H. 156
Mexico 11, 39, 145
Mexico City, Mexico 11, 43, 134, 139, 140
migration: and capital 13, 14; in China 104,
    108, 110–11; and collectivization 98; and
    homelessness 107, 109; in India 59, 63,
    67; in Latin America 139, 145;
    limitation of 13, 43, 47, 98, 104; and
    living conditions 59, 60; and NAFTA 11,
    145; to Palestine 79; and resource
    extraction 55; rural to urban 6, 11, 13, 55,
    63, 67, 110–11; state sanctioned 95; and
    war 13; see also labor
Miliutin, Nikolai A. 96
Morales, Evo 143, 144
Moscow, Russia 96; post-Soviet 101–2; see
    also Russia; Soviet Union
Moses, Robert 33
Movement Toward Socialism (MAS,
    Bolivia) 144
Movimento Sem Terra (MST) 142, 145, 146,
    155, 161, 162
Mumbai, India 59, 62, 64
Mumford, Lewis 11, 12,
    37, 127

myth 26, 36, 43–4; the American Dream
116–18; central city/suburban divide 7;
environmental quality 130; of free housing
89; free market utopia 21; isolated local
communities 160; Israeli settlers 86; local
land development 116, 126; Malthusian
156; race 87; the socialist city 112;
underdevelopment 4, 41; and urban
density 5, 12–13, 141; urban marginality
140; *see also* planning

National Front (France) 47
National March for Employment Justice and
Agrarian Reform 146
natural resources: 11, 17, 20, 33, 48, 161;
and Amazon Basin 146; appropriation of
state-owned 101; and Bolivia 142, 143,
144; and dependent nations 25; and
economies of scale 47; extraction of 21–2,
63, 139, 166n45; public control of 143;
and public land reserves 51; shortage of
156; social movements 144–45;
underground 51, 88; water ownership
146; water rights in Argentina 106; *see
also* consumption; energy; environment;
land; rural areas; sustainability
Nazareth, Israel 84, 85, 86
Negev 90–1
Nehru, Jawaharlal 64,
70–1
neoliberalism: and dependent urbanization
63–4; and displacement 140; as economic
foundation 13, 21, 36; and ethnic
cleansing 82; in India 59–60, 63, 64, 65–6,
67; and inequalities 134; Payments in
Lieu of Taxes (PILOT) 124; and prison
system 38; and rural areas 145; and shock
therapy 39; and short-term development
34; and social movements 71; Tax
Increment Financing (TIF) 124; in the
United States 71, 120; and urban policy
65, 120; *see also* capital; capitalism
New Delhi, India 28
New Orleans, Louisiana 17
New South China Mall 106
New York City, New York 8, 11, 12, 124;
and climate change 130; and
comprehensive planning 35; Regional
Plan Association 124; and slums 15; and
subway system 110; as tourist destination
124; and Transit Oriented Development
(TOD) 128; and Wal-Mart 125
New York Times 28
North American Free Trade Agreement
(NAFTA) 11, 134, 145
Northern League of Italy 47
Nyrere, Julius 49

Orfield, Myron 126
Orientalism (Said), 75
The Origins of Modern Town Planning
(Benevolo) 37
Orlov, Michel 102
Osaka, Japan 12
"Others" 27–34, 37–40, 87, 94, 137; immi-
grants as 130; and myth 41; objectification
of 114; *see also* migration; Palestinians

Palestine: control of infrastructure 92; and
enclave urbanism 76, 114; and orientalist
planning 75
Palestinian Authority 78, 88, 91
Palestinians: invisibility of 75, 80, 92; popu-
lation in Israel 81, 84; and poverty 89; *see
also* ethnic cleansing; Israel
Pappe, Ilan 80
Paris, France 12, 15, 65, 95, 114, 161
Parque D. Pedro Shopping, 134
Patel, Raj 50, 71
Pei, I.M. 32–33
Pei Cobb Freed & Partners 33
People's Science Movement (KSSP), 72–73
Perlman, Janice 140
Peru 52
Phoenix, Arizona 119
Planet of Slums (Davis) 15
Planners for Planning Rights (Bimkom) 92
planning 3–4, 7, 11; centralized 36, 43, 95,
96, 97, 98, 106; City Beautiful 30–31, 32,
33, 96, 139, 159; communicative 38; and
disurbanists 95–6, 160; dualism 17, 26–7,
39, 134, 137, 140, 159; failure of, 16, 22,
141; Garden Cities 30, 33, 79, 96, 160;
and green technology 23; incrementalist
and pragmatist approach, 35; and land
use 25, 35, 86–7, 101–2, 105; limits to
156–57; master plans, 33–4, 36, 96, 98;
modernism and physical determinism
31–2, 33, 139; orientalist 7, 16–18, 26–40,
53–5, 59–74, 75, 78, 134, 139–141, 155;
for the "Others" 16, 26–40; rational-
comprehensive 33, 34–5, 37, 96, 100,
105, 139, 156; and reductionist reason-
ing 33; and slums 14–15; and Smart
Growth 127–28; strategic 34–5, 36; The
New Urbanism (TNU) 128, 129; *see also*
American Dream; climate change; enclave
urbanism; environment; land; land use;
neoliberalism; rural areas; ; socialism;
urban/rural divide
population: breakdown in Israel 81, 84, 85,
87; density 3, 8, 9, 118–19; growth 11–13,
156; neo-Malthusian predictions on 50,
156; and urban dispersal 43, 47
The Population Bomb (Enrlich) 12

Port Au Prince, Haiti 17
poverty 12, 23, 112; in Israel 81, 89; Latin
    American 141; rural 67, 103; and slums
    14–15, 140; *see also* labor; migration
Prokhorov, Mikhail 102
ProLogis 121
Punjab, India 68

racism 5, 38; and enclave urbanism 113–14;
    institutional, 7, 116, 119; and Jim Crow
    118; and nonphysical boundaries 115; and
    population density 13; and space 118, 127,
    135; and the American Dream 118, 119,
    129–30; and "tipping point" 87; Wal-
    Mart 46; and urban renewal 38, 122; *see
    also* immigrants; segregation; slums
Ramallah, 91, 92
Randeria, Shalini: 73
Reagan, Ronald 36
real estate industry 15; and agricultural
    production, 48–9; and Bengaluru, India
    65; and development 120–21; global 20,
    34, 145; and greenwashing 130–31, 158;
    India's urban market 64; and Latin
    America 132; malls 10, 106, 125, 134,
    136; and Palestinian vulnerability 82; Real
    Estate Investment Trusts (REITs) 121; and
    U.S. governance 125; *see also* displacement;
    FIRE; planning; slums; transportation
Regional Council of Unrecognized Villages
    in the Negev, 90–1, 155
Ricardo, David 42, 52
Right to the City 6, 39, 45, 92–3, 141, 144,
    159, 162
Right to the Land 145
Rio de Janeiro, Brazil 10, 17, 145
Rome, Italy 3, 11, 12, 29, 94
Rostow, Walt 44
Roy, Arundhati 74
rural areas: abandonment of 3; collective
    rural settlements 93; commodification
    of 4; communization in China 104, 105;
    dependency 49; depopulation 54; elec-
    trification program 95; importance in
    Bolivia 142; Indian land reform legislation
    67; Israeli confiscation of 86; mining 51;
    population of 47; subordination to capital
    54; and urban domination 109; *see also*
    agriculture; displacement; infrastructure;
    land; migration; urban/rural divide
Rusk, David 126
Russia 25, 59, 100–3, 112; and Jewish emi-
    gration to Israel 38, 84, 89, 93

Sachs, Jeffrey 100
Said, Edward 16–17, 26, 27, 75

San Francisco, California 77, 124
Sandercock, Leonie 37–38
Santa Cruz, Bolivia 142
São Paulo, Brazil 62, 136
Saudi Arabia 75
segregation 3, 54; by class 22, 35, 38, 44,
    87, 89, 98, 113–14, 117, 122, 126, 137;
    economic 133, 134; and Israeli planning
    87; and Jim Crow 118; Latin American
    135; migrant workers 75; and nonphysical
    boundaries 115; and physical separation
    130; post-slavery 139; rationalization of
    140; and Security Barrier 77–8; social 112,
    133, 134; of traffic 88
Semionov, Vladimir 97
Sen, Amartya 116
Shanghai, China: Central Business District
    106; and global trade 103–4; and
    infrastructure funding 109; and internal
    migrants 110; and regional authority 108
Sharon, Ariel 77, 84
Shenzhen, China 106, 108
Shiva, Vandana 72, 73, 155
Shopping Aricanduva, 134
Simon Property Group 121
Skidmore, Owens & Merrill 32
slavery: 7, 118, 138–39
slums 4, 38; and anti-urban ideology 14–15;
    displacement in India 64, 65; and orien-
    talist myths 41; as planning myth 156;
    replacement of 139–40; sensationalization
    of 26; and urban orientalism 27;
    usefulness of 46; *see also* displacement
Smart Growth 5, 127–28, 129; *see also*
    sustainability
Smith, Neil 128–29
Social Darwinism 13, 33, 35
social justice 23, 38; as element of freedom
    116; and food sovereignty 150; and in-
    digenous rights 143; movements for 142;
    new approaches on 141; and structural
    inequalities 39, 41; and urban
    planning 155
social movements 16, 155; and alternatives
    141; in China 112; civil rights 116; Day
    of Wrath 112; and enclave urbanism 134;
    against GMOs 73; India 69, 72; and indig-
    enous populations 144; in Israel 92–3; and
    Latin America 116, 132; possibilities for
    39; *see also* individual issue
socialism 94–112; collapse of 20, 36; erosion
    of 105; and housing costs 99; levels of
    urbanization 43; and participatory democ-
    racy 100, 112, 151; power in the United
    States 115; predominance of 93; really
    existing 94; and rural-urban integration

109; safety net 100; for the twenty-first century 112
Sorel, Georges 116
Soria y Mata, Arturo, 96
South Africa 21, 38, 51, 54
South Bronx, New York City, New York 119–20
Soviet Union 93, 94–103; Bolshevik Revolution (1917) 35, 94, 95; and Cuba 148–49; New Economic Policy (NEP) 95; see also Moscow; Russia
Spain 52, 132; Laws of the Indies 29, 137
Squarestone 136
St. Louis, Missouri 13
Stalin, Joseph 96
Stein, Clarence 127
Storrs, Ronald 89
Stuffed and Starved (Patel) 50
Sunbelt 8
sustainability 4, 10, 11, 14, 18, 19; Dubai 75–6; in India 67, 68, 69, 73; and migrant labor 111; and mixed-use development 136; and policymakers 151; and Smart Growth, 5, 127–28, 129; and social movements 141, 144; and technology 70; and transportation costs 129; see also climate change; consumption; environment; planning

Tel Aviv, Israel: 79, 83–4, 92
Thatcher, Margaret 36, 64, 94, 161
Thomas, June Manning 38
Three Gorges Dam 109
Tianjin, China: 108
Tiberias, Israel 85
Togliatti, Palmiro 97
Togliattigrad, Soviet Union 97
Tokyo, Japan 12, 62
tourism 22; and Central Business Districts 124, 136; development for 69; preservation for 71, 80, 85, 89, 107
transit-oriented development 19, 128
transportation 14, 19–20, 24–25, 39, 46, 54, 60, 69, 86, 105,127, 129, 150, 158; automobile 19, 48, 65, 102, 116–18, 139
Triumph of the City (Glaeser) 5
Tsfat, Israel 85
Turner Construction 32
Turner, John 140

Ujamaa (Nyerere) 49
Unified Energy Systems, 101
United Nations:Biosphere Reserve 51; Cancún (2010) 48; Center for Human Settlements (UN-HABITAT) 5, 15; The Challenge of Slums 5; Cities Without Slums 5; Copenhagen (2009) 48; and dualism 27; Kyoto Protocol (1997) 48; Millennium Goals 46; and urbanization in China 103
United States: agricultural labor 50; and homeownership as policy 120; and legalized slavery 118; and level of urbanization, 43; and mass transit 24; and master plans 35; military intervention by 132–33; as model for development 25, 113, 133, 134; policy toward Israel 92, 93; and population density 118–19; and public health 71; and right to organize 116; role in global economy 113; Universal Declaration of the Rights of Mother Earth 144, 145, 158
Upside Down (Galeano) 136
urban development: alternative strategies 59, 114, 127–28; and environmental improvements 130; inefficient 14–15, 23–25; in-fill 129–30; infrastructure 63–4; and master plans 33–34, 36; mixed-use 136; models 20–21, 23, 52, 98, 116, 119, 159; post-colonial 41–45, 59–60; and role of state 36, 125–26; and rural life 71; segregated 133; and social movements 72, 141–46; suburban 30; Transit Oriented Urban development (TOD) 19, 128; unequal 44, 122; uneven 44; unsustainable 10, 11; see also enclave urbanism; neoliberalism; the "Other"; planning; rural areas
urban fallacy 3–10; balanced regions 54–5; and economic dependency 42; growth poles 54; immigrant poverty 15; population size 112; role of climate change 18
urban/rural divide 8, 20, 22, 99–100, 105, 155, 159; see also rural areas
urbanization 3, 9, 11, 18, 78; in China 103–11; and compact cities 128; dependent 22, 41–5, 54–5, 59–74, 114, 134, 142; and districts 113–14; disurbanists 95–6, 160; and dualisms 112; India 59–74; and Latin America 132; limitation on 96; and optimal city size 160; post-World War II 97–8; as priority 105; rate of 15, 45, 47; really existing 19; and social movements 39; and spatial formation 127; state-driven 108; see also global warming; neoliberalism; planning; Smart Growth
Union of Soviet Socialist Republics (USSR) see Soviet Union

Van Kampen, Peter 122
Venezuela 43, 54, 142, 144, 151
Via Campesina 49, 146

Vidal, Gore 94
Vietnam 28, 67

Wacquant, Loïc 38
Wal-Mart 46, 124–25, 134
Washington, DC 7, 119–20, 124
Weizmann, Chaim 79
Weizman, Eyal 77, 88, 89, 90
welfare state 21, 93, 106, 115, 144; absence
    of 126; attack on 120
West Bank 76–77, 81, 82, 83, 84, 91
West Bengal, India 72
women: and the American Dream 118; and
    labor 45, 46, 66; migrant 110, 111; and
    public space 35; and social movements 72,
    162; and urban history 37–8
World Bank 15; 1991 structural adjustment
    program for India 64; pro-poor strategy
    of 46; and resource extraction 54–5; and
    rural infrastructure 60, 63; and urban
    spending 63
World Health Organization (WHO) 68

World People's Conference on Climate Change
    and the Rights of Mother Earth (2010) 144
World Social Forum 39
World Trade Organization (WTO) 105
World War II 18, 25, 97; post- 54, 80, 94,
    117, 124, 126, 150
World Zionist Organization 79
Wright, Ronald 116
Wuhan, China 106

Yiftachel, Oren 38, 89
Yonkers, New York 130

Zapatistas 161
Zeckendorf, Howard 32
Zeitlin, Morris 97
Zhou, Enlai 104
zoning: and duty-free manufacturing 136;
    exclusionary 119, 126; fiscal 126; and
    growth points 108; and land use planning
    35, 84, 127; and suburban sprawl 12;
    tourist 108